Elections, Voting, Technology

Series Editor
Kathleen Hale
Political Science
Auburn University
Auburn, AL, USA

This series examines the relationships between people, electoral processes and technologies, and democracy. Elections are a fundamental aspect of a free and democratic society and, at their core, they involve a citizenry making selections for who will represent them. This series examines the ways in which citizens select their candidates—the voting technologies used, the rules of the game that govern the process—and considers how changes in processes and technologies affect the voter and the democratic process.

More information about this series at
http://www.palgrave.com/gp/series/14965

J. S. Maloy

Smarter Ballots

Electoral Realism and Reform

J. S. Maloy
University of Louisiana
Lafayette, USA

Elections, Voting, Technology
ISBN 978-3-030-13030-5   ISBN 978-3-030-13031-2   (eBook)
https://doi.org/10.1007/978-3-030-13031-2

Library of Congress Control Number: 2019932937

This Palgrave Macmillan imprint is published by the registered company Springer Nature
Switzerland AG
The registered company address is: Gewerbestrasse 11, 6330 Cham, Switzerland

SERIES EDITOR'S FOREWORD

The mechanics of modern voting are relatively recent. America's current era of election reform is rooted in the years following the 2000 presidential election and the US Supreme Court decision in *Bush v. Gore*. The electronic voting systems and voter registration databases that now support voters in the nation's 8000 election jurisdictions were ushered in through the Help America Vote Act in 2002. At first glance, these reforms reprise the themes of access and participation that have defined the nation's election system since its inception, and much has been made of the importance of recent reforms in improving the voting experience.

Participation has been encouraged through experiments that allow for different methods of registration and increase the number of days for voters to come to the polls or to cast ballots by mail. Automatic voter registration, online voter registration, early voting, vote-by-mail, and no-excuse absentee voting are now commonplace terms in the field. New attention has been paid to broadened opportunities and assistance for particular groups, such as voters with disabilities and non-native English speakers. Eligibility requirements have been extended in some places to those with criminal convictions and noncitizens. Not all of these practices have been embraced across the country, and, within the parameters of the current electoral rules, effects have been to both increase voter participation and discourage it. Increasingly, these practices are the subject of academic study as reforms have created new pressures for local and state election officials.

And yet, in spite of these changes, American political participation remains a paradox. Despite thousands of legislative proposals and interpretations through hundreds of judicial decisions over the last few decades, much remains the same. Decision rules (e.g., first-past-the-post) and an intractable electoral architecture tied to geography (e.g., the redistricting system) combine to offer voters few competitive choices between political parties that, not surprisingly, continue to reinforce rules that limit the number of viable political parties.

Smarter Ballots: Electoral Realism and Reform takes an important step in expanding our field of vision about what is possible from the vantage point of public participation. Its focus on Ranked-Choice Voting demonstrates the efficacy of new decision rules in election design. Although Ranked-Choice Voting rules differ from jurisdiction to jurisdiction, the approach is intended to more clearly reflect voter preferences than is possible through current ballot structures. Expression of voter preferences through robust voting is a canon of healthy democracies, signaling citizen engagement and trust in political institutions. America's comparatively (very) low turnout has long been the subject of much study and speculation. Ranked-Choice Voting, once a true outlier among decision rules, has emerged in municipal elections and in one state. It remains to be seen whether this and other new election practices can emerge more broadly against the first-past-the-post approach that dominates American election rules.

The modern era of American election reform has focused on administrative practices and operating strategies; although these reforms have been achieved *through* the political process, they do not fundamentally *alter* that process. Through the scholarship in this volume, we learn more about the possibilities and effects of changing the rules behind the ballot, and how new rules can be utilized to engage the public more broadly. The entrenched nature of political interests suggests that policy change in election decision rules will come slowly. And yet, the current heightened state of public awareness about American election practices—security, integrity, allegations of voter fraud and voter suppression—may provide the opportunity for just such consideration.

Auburn, USA

Kathleen Hale
Series Editor, Professor and
Director, Graduate Program in
Election Administration
Auburn University

PREFACE

My professional research career so far has consistently pursued a basic question: How much "people power" (*demokratia*, in ancient Greek) is operative in the actual political systems of our times? A lot or a little? Too much, not enough, or just right? My first two books explored conceptual histories that exposed partialities or flaws in key assumptions and standards that people in North American and European societies are instructed to use when judging such a question. Now this book, more analytical and empirical than historical, has taken an unexpected turn—while still traveling the same road.

When examining the history of thinking about democratic institutions in the 2008 book, I found that regular elections were invented not as vehicles of people power but as anti- or counter-democratic substitutes for other, more effective, non-electoral institutions. When examining the interface of democratic institutional thought with the history of political realism in the 2013 book, I again felt compelled to notice the elitist tendencies of elections and the populist tendencies of non-electoral alternatives. But in these projects I was taking for granted a rather simplistic view of elections, not taking care to consider some of their most crucial features, or the possibilities of institutional variation on those features. When I proposed in 2008 that a Constituency Jury system be instituted to audit and sanction representatives between one election and the next, I had only a narrow idea of what sorts of *ballots* would be used, and in what sorts of *contests*, to elect representatives in the first place. In short,

I was merely being as naive about elections as most people who act as citizens or officers in actual democracies, and not much worse (as I later found out) than many professional scholars of politics.

Once I realized how powerful some of these dimensions of electoral variation can be, especially ballot structure and contest structure, I had to re-evaluate the realistic range of answers to my fundamental questions: How much people power do we have, do we want, can we get? Having explored plenty of theoretical reasons for elections' inadequacy, it seemed only fair that I take seriously the possibility of varying their institutional forms to make them less inadequate. That's why this book is about election reform.

OUTLINE OF THE BOOK

Chapter 1 frames the problem of election reform in democratic theory by suggesting that the turmoil of established democracies in the post-2008 era is part of a larger and longer story about democratic deficits within basic institutions, including elections. Some of the fundamental concepts that are employed throughout the book are introduced as tools for understanding and evaluating reform responses to democratic deficits. These include electoral realism, electoral structure, naturalism vs. constructivism in elections research, and the triad of voter empowerment. Above all, the distinction between ballot structure and contest structure will prove crucial to grasping why conventional approaches to studying the design and reform of electoral systems are inadequate.

Chapter 2 explains how, since the end of the Cold War, academic research has advocated increasing levels of skepticism about the empowerment of voters through the electoral accountability of governments. This recommendation is visible from three different angles on the scholarly literature: a review of empirical studies covering topics such as economic performance and governmental corruption; a reconsideration of the thought of V. O. Key, often misread as having vindicated the idea of electoral accountability; and a survey of research on a wide variety of conditions and institutions that hinder accountability, yielding a "top ten" list of reasons to embrace electoral skepticism.

Chapter 3 delves into topics that have been less well covered by academic research, especially the symbiotic pathology of vote-splitting and "lesser evil" choices. These two features of elections sustain a host of electoral misincentives, associated with "wasted" votes and "spoiler" candidates, which combine to impose a dilemma of disempowerment on voters. A ballot with too few options risks the lesser-evil problem, in which voters are coerced into a false choice, but a ballot with too many options risks the vote-splitting problem, in which an unpopular winner prevails when voters divide their support for several alternatives. This dilemma breathes life into electoral dysfunction and spoils efforts to reform contest structure by addressing issues of ballot access, number of seats, and stages of voting.

The prioritizing of ballot structure over contest structure to seek a way out of the dilemma of disempowerment is explored in Chapter 4. Here readers are plunged into a deep, dark pool of theory—but with air-tight goggles and a powerful flashlight. A good conceptual framework is an indispensable guide to reform options, the most promising of which use distributive instead of exclusive input rules for the expression of variable levels of support across multiple candidates per contest: Multi-mark ballots are smarter ballots. The lessons of theory reveal that the dilemma of disempowerment's apparent strangle-hold on voters is an artifact of the input structure of one-mark ballots (1MB).

Chapter 5 further explores the multi-mark reform options by consulting the lessons of experience. Ranking and grading ballots emerge as the two general alternatives with the greatest practical potential, and a fair amount of observational and experimental evidence has been collected about them. Contrary to the presumptions of recent voting theory, the superiority of grading over ranking ballots cannot (yet) be supported by the available evidence, and both kinds of multi-mark alternative should be considered equally viable.

Chapter 6 reports some original retrospective election simulation (RES) analyses of contests related to the 2016 American presidential elections. Most notably, the 2016 Republican Party primaries in the USA are simulated to show that the hypothetical use of Ranked-Choice Voting (RCV) rather than the actual 1MB input rules could have resulted in dramatically different outcomes in several states that helped to select Donald Trump as the party's nominee—provided that certain assumptions about hard-to-measure voter preferences are used rather than others. The general theory suggested by previous election simulations in other countries, that 1MB voting constructs a unique electoral advantage for polarizing parties and candidates which crumbles when multi-mark ballots are used, is supported by this analysis.

Every conceivable voting system has its defects, but some of these may be resolved through creative design, and Chapter 7 canvasses some possibilities. Further (and better) academic experiments are needed to spur innovation, and the best hope for fixing broken ballots and making them serve the cause of democracy lies in local experiments with creative combinations of contest structure and ballot structure. In political systems where the range of viable ballot options is habitually quite limited, such combinations are likely to pair a contest structure featuring a "jungle" primary with either ranking or grading ballot structures. Two original templates for smarter ballots in single-winner contests are proposed, as well as innovative proposals for designing multi-option referendums.

The Appendix offers supplementary material to Chapters 2 and 4 by covering a variety of theoretical and methodological issues in comparative electoral studies and voting theory. Here the research-design and measurement choices for large-N empirical studies of electoral accountability are discussed, and the book's new conceptual scheme or taxonomy of ballot structures is more fully elaborated.

Lafayette, LA, USA   J. S. Maloy

Acknowledgments

I have undertaken the research and writing for this book while holding the Judge Kaliste Saloom Jr. Endowed Chair in Political Science at the University of Louisiana, Lafayette. The resources provided by the Chair have made it possible for me to make steady progress on this and other research projects alongside my teaching and service commitments at the university. It is therefore a pleasure to acknowledge the late Judge, the Saloom family, the University of Louisiana Board of Supervisors, and my many supportive colleagues in the Department of Political Science and the College of Liberal Arts.

Also at UL Lafayette, my research assistants have shown tremendous versatility. Anna Akhmetova, Caitlin Ard, Jacob Authement, Alisha Large, Christine Savoie, and Mia Tolliver have contributed to this project in a myriad of ways. A public lecture that I gave on campus about "lesser evil" elections provoked a well-timed (October 2016) and interesting discussion, thanks in no small part to the advice and encouragement of colleagues like Pearson Cross, Bryan-Paul Frost, Jordan Kellman, Christie Maloyed, Chad Parker, Jamie Rush, Rick Swanson, and Ryan Teten.

In the summer of 2017, I was able to meet with knowledgeable people who are involved in administering, studying, and reforming elections in a few of the places that use multi-mark (such as ranking) ballots. In Maine, I got valuable information and perspective from Kyle Bailey, Matthew Dunlap, Kathy Jones, Ann Luther, David Sammarco, Scott Thistle, and Jill Ward. In Ireland, David Farrell, Michael Gallagher, and Michael Marsh were generous with their time and insight.

In Scotland, I was warmly received by Alistair Clark, Thomas Lundberg, and Anthony McGann; and special mention must go to Chris Highcock and David Miller, chief election administrators for (respectively) the cities of Edinburgh and Glasgow. Others whom I could not meet in person but who furnished me with critical information from a distance include Marco Biagi, Kenneth Palmer, Jonathan Tonge, Graham Walker, Nicholas Whyte, and Dick Woodbury.

Though my analysis of V. O. Key's views on electoral accountability occupies only one portion of one chapter of this book, my investigations into the intellectual history of his final, posthumously published work led me into incur many professional debts. The staff of the Harvard University Archives, where the V. O. Key papers are housed, were tremendously helpful. I am also grateful to several colleagues who shared their personal and professional recollections of Key himself or his influence on contemporaries, including Joseph Cooper, Sheldon Goldman, Morris Fiorina, Harvey Mansfield, and David Mayhew.

Various members of the academic community in the USA have helped with other research tips, large and small: Shaun Bowler, Barry Burden, Kellen Gracey, David Kimball, John McCormick, Jason McDaniel, Francis Neely, Timothy Peterson, and Shane Singh.

It is very satisfying to compile the record of collaborative effort in one place. All who are mentioned above took some pains to help me without being sure in advance that I would produce anything worth a damn. Their meager repayment is the opportunity to judge whether I did.

Finally, I would like to thank others who probably do not care a great deal about the results, one way or the other. Great help with all the illustrations in this book was provided by Francisco Farrera. Yolanda Landry and Dan Phillips were amiably indispensable from their perches in the Inter-Library Loan Office of the Dupré Library at UL Lafayette. (Dan's portfolio of contribution to the local community includes hosting a weekly radio show on KRVS-FM called "Funkify Your Life.") The Lafayette Public Library is an essential civic institution; if only it didn't serve quite so many of my fellow citizens, I would have spent more working hours there myself. Some of my Lafayette neighbors who are business-owners inadvertently provided congenial spaces for research and writing. Those downtown businesses include Black Cafe, Carpe Diem, and Cloves Indian Cafe.

PRAISE FOR *SMARTER BALLOTS*

"With the capacity of elections and referendums to resolve political issues increasingly questioned, *Smarter Ballots* asks whether this is the case and, if so, whether there is anything that can be done about it. It interrogates these issues through a sophisticated blend of political theory and empirical research and makes a powerful case for electoral reform that enables voters to express their preferences through ballot opportunities that do not confine them to mere approval or disapproval of the options but, rather, enable them to rank or grade these. This timely and accessible book is an important contribution to the literature on electoral system design and is very relevant to current political discussions about how to increase electoral accountability and policy responsiveness."

—Michael Gallagher, *Professor of Comparative Politics, Trinity College, Dublin, Ireland*

"Election outcomes are not unmediated reflections of public opinion. The ballots that voters are able to cast, and the rules for counting the ballots, are just as important as voters' preferences. Social choice theorists have pressed this point against populists who uncritically hold up election outcomes as if they were revelations of the 'will of the people.' But populists are not the only ones who, neglecting the importance of electoral structure, make unwarranted inferences from election outcomes. Maloy shows that democracy's detractors would also do well to keep electoral structure in mind: bad electoral rules can make voters out to look more foolish than they actually are. Instead of wishing for smarter voters, we should try to design smarter ballots which allow voters to express a greater range of judgments than simply which option they consider best. Anyone interested in the prospects of empowering voters through electoral reform will benefit from reading this book."

—Sean Ingham, *Assistant Professor of Political Science,*
University of California, San Diego, USA

"An impressive study of the democratic dilemmas that electoral systems impose, often restricting individual expression and reducing systemic accountability. Maloy provides a critical assessment of why giving voters the possibility of ranking parties or candidates may solve this dilemma. The reader is guided through possible reform options with a compelling conceptual framework and rigorous evaluation of observational evidence, as well as original election simulations. The lessons we learn by reading this book apply equally well to the conduct of referendums, with innovative proposals for designing multi-option referendums. Political researchers and reformers will want to add this book to their reading list."

—Carolina Plescia, *Assistant Professor of Government,*
University of Vienna, Austria

CONTENTS

ABBREVIATIONS

1MB   One-mark ballot
2RS   Two-round system
GPA   Grade-point average
PR   Proportional representation
RCV   Ranked-choice voting
RES   Retrospective election simulation
SSP   Single-seat plurality
STV   Single transferable vote

LIST OF FIGURES

CHAPTER 1

Introduction:
Electoral Dysfunction and Political Realism

Democracy's time of troubles in the early twenty-first century can be summed up as a tale of two years, 2008 and 2016. The first of these years witnessed the global financial crisis, triggering the Great Recession. The second date delivered an extraordinary electoral cycle across multiple democracies around the world, most notably (but not only) the "Brexit" referendum in the UK and the Trump election in the USA. Put together, these two moments made what was supposed to be democracy's time of triumph look like an era of dysfunction and danger.

What makes democracy special, in theory, is its unique ability to deliver political power to ordinary citizens rather than family dynasties, institutional elites, or moneyed tycoons. Elections are crucial to this mission because they are supposed to make governing authorities accountable to voters rather than oligarchs, to outsiders rather than insiders. The ability of outsider candidates and causes to gain ground through elections is therefore a strength of democracy, not a weakness. Yet electoral processes and outcomes alike have been increasingly derided and discredited in recent years. When a majority of British voters chose to exit (hence "Brexit") the European Union, and the USA's Electoral College selected Donald Trump as president, these were merely the most celebrated cases. In 2016 and ensuing years, democracies around the globe—from Australia to Italy, from Colombia to France and Spain—have experienced snap elections with inconclusive outcomes, referendum results that destabilized or brought down sitting governments, and "lesser of two evils" contests that yielded pre-emptively delegitimized

© The Author(s) 2019
J. S. Maloy, *Smarter Ballots*, Elections, Voting, Technology,
https://doi.org/10.1007/978-3-030-13031-2_1

winners. Are elections now undermining democracies' unique theoretical strengths, instead of sustaining them?

This book explains why the answer may be a disturbing "yes"—but also shows how election reform might yet convert that answer to "no." The design of electoral institutions, especially ballot structure, has played a role in democracy's recent troubles and will continue to do so in democracy's future recovery, decline, or stagnation.

Though conventional wisdom says that competitive elections provide tools of democratic accountability for ordinary citizens to keep governments in check, the story emerging from academic research is quite different: Political elites have given us electoral processes, whether deliberately or not, which project the image of accountability without providing the substance. By synthesizing and extending scholarly findings about how elections work in different contexts, this book attempts to bridge the gap between two fields of research: voting theory and comparative electoral studies. Too often they work in mutual isolation, thereby diminishing the public voice of political science as a source of insight about real democracy. My goal is to integrate the virtues and insights of both. Somewhere between the reformers in voting theory, on the one hand, and the realists in empirical research, on the other, we may be able to locate a pathway to realistic reform.

Once academic findings come together in this way, it appears that the central problem with our electoral institutions is that they too often devalue the vote, in the process opening up deficits of accountability. The most direct solution to the problem is to redesign those same institutions so that they revalue the vote. Toward that end, the insights and proposals found in this book are applicable across a wide range of democratic regimes and electoral systems. My argument is that better elections require smarter ballots, not smarter voters. If ballots can be redesigned to elevate the value of the vote, voters might raise their game in response. Elections would then be a platform for "people power"—the conceptual root of "democracy," and still the main source of its appeal—rather than a disorienting merry-go-round of dysfunctional elites.

Democratic Deficits

In reaction to the electoral upheavals of 2016, a growth industry has emerged in Western academia and civil society with publications on "democratic erosion," "de-democratization," "deconsolidation," and "democratic back-sliding." These attempts to diagnose decline or to forecast regime change have gained a sizeable audience because the success of outsider candidates and parties is viewed by some as a clear and present danger, even (or especially) in the older democracies. Populists of the left and of the right have entered the upper echelons of major political parties, garnered large blocs of votes with brand-new parties, or even taken the reins of government itself in places like Brazil, Italy, Germany, Greece, Mexico, Spain, the UK, and the USA. The outsiders lack the customary reverence for established institutions, and political elites are scrambling for their plan of counter-attack.[1]

It is easy amid such excitement to lose sight of relevant realities that academic researchers have already been looking into for decades. Any discussion of the troubles of the post-2008 or -2016 eras must take account of a larger and longer story about democratic deficits.

The term "democratic deficit" initially began circulating prior to the end of the Cold War, among intellectuals and policy-makers in Europe who were concerned about the future course of the European Union (EU). Their worry was that increasing the centralized powers of the EU (based in Brussels) might create problems of legitimacy in the minds of citizens of member states, who normally would look to their national capitals (e.g., London or Paris) as sites of democratic accountability. This line of thought gained more traction in the 1990s and has become a staple of both academic and journalistic commentary on the EU in our century.[2]

The concept of democratic deficits has also been extended beyond the confines of the EU or of any other trans-national organization that detracts from national sovereignty. Now we speak about democratic deficits within sovereign countries, as the gap between a government and its people. Two specific types of extension have occurred in the use of this concept. First, democratic deficits are sometimes identified in the operations of unelected, expert-led bodies that now play crucial roles in domestic policy-making, such as central banks, regulatory agencies, and constitutional courts. Where interest rates or utility rates are set, or where a duly enacted law is subsequently edited or deleted from the

---

[1] For the view that "democracies become dictatorships when one set of actors attempts to disassemble democratic institutions and another set of actors fails to marshal an appropriate defense": Bermeo (2019, 229); see also Levitsky and Ziblatt (2018).

[2] Majone (1998, 12–15).

statute books, these matters affect the lives of citizens who have no electoral connection to the decision-makers. As Yascha Mounk has written, "the withdrawal of important topics from domestic political contestation is one major reason why political systems throughout Western Europe and North America have become less democratic."[3]

It is likely that the increased use of national referendums in European countries has been an effort to close this representational gap by electoral means. Brexit was following a twenty-year trend of putting the nature of a country's EU ties on a direct ballot. Between 2000 and 2005 alone, no fewer than seven member states held referendums on constitutional relations with the EU or the euro currency zone.[4]

Has more and more voting now proven its ineffectiveness as a way to close the gap? The second extension that has occurred with the concept of democratic deficits is potentially more telling and disturbing, when even elected authorities find room for maneuver to act in unresponsive and unaccountable ways. Citizens' frustration with the loss of control in their lives has not been confined to the activities of unelected bankers, regulators, and judges; elected politicians are even less trusted worldwide than members of media or business. One of the first overt uses of the concept of democratic deficits in an actual political campaign occurred in Canada in 2003, when Paul Martin was the leader of the Liberal Party. Martin identified declining voter turnout and disgust with political parties as symptoms of a yawning gap within Canadian democracy, and the Liberals rode his message to victory in the general election that year. Yet the same symptoms were subsequently documented across all the European democracies by Peter Mair, the late political scientist whose posthumous book eloquently elaborated the story of decline. The book's title employs slightly different language for gaps and empty spaces: *Ruling the Void*. Similar trends exist in the USA, where the phrase "democratic deficit" has also been used.[5]

[3]Mounk (2018, 101–5, quotation at 105).

[4]Beramendi et al. (2008, 12, 43–44).

[5]For indicators of global distrust: Edelman (2017). On Canada: Carty (2010, 227–29). On Europe: Mair (2013, 26–28, 31–33); see also Chwalisz (2015, 15). On deficits in the USA: Levinson (2007). On partisan decomposition (i.e., weakening ties to voters) in the USA: Wattenberg (1998, ix–x, 58–63).

Brexit and Trumpism, seen from the perspective of democratic deficits, were on the cards for some time. The economic and cultural pressures of globalization have well and truly overwhelmed the capacity of established political institutions to deal with them. Now is the time for a fresh look at institutional and structural issues, especially with the set of democratic institutions that are supposed to secure the connection between citizens and governments: periodic competitive elections.

What Is Electoral Realism?

Academic researchers are in a good position to explain how and why elections have become implicated in the larger syndrome of democratic deficits. The reason is that scholarly knowledge, at its best, offers a dose of realism as an antidote to various forms of idealism to which citizens are routinely mistreated. Recent trends in the social sciences suggest that realism is in the ascendant, not only in political theory but also among empirical scholars and quantitative analysts.[6]

The basic thrust of realism in any pursuit, academic or civic, is to ensure that our adherence to ideals not be allowed to distort our grasp of realities. But electoral realism is a particularly tall order because elections, more than most democratic institutions, tend to be regarded with more veneration than observation. Voting, according to electoral idealism, lets democratic citizens speak in a collective voice. Election returns help to direct governmental policy and personnel by presenting a definitive articulation of the public will. Parties and office-holders are thereby made accountable to the citizens whom they serve, by dint of being prone to voters' rewards or punishments.

Would the upheavals of 2008 and 2016 have transpired in the way they did if this vision of elections were plausible? The persistence of democratic deficits, and of popular backlashes against them, suggests otherwise. But the realist's contribution must be about more than just astute observation, whether at the micro- or macro-level. Realism, then, involves a distinctive methodology of interpreting observations, not just gathering them. As a framework for interpreting evidence, electoral realism is bound to be flawed and incomplete if we do not replace *naturalist* assumptions with *constructivist* ones.

---

[6]For realism in political theory: Shapiro (2005), Geuss (2008), Maloy (2013), and Sleat (2013). For realism in empirical political research: Mead (2010), Sil and Katzenstein (2010), Schrodt (2014), and Achen and Bartels (2016).

Many researchers (not to mention university students) are familiar with the contrast between naturalism and constructivism thanks to the classic encounter between Thomas Hobbes and Jean-Jacques Rousseau in the history of political thought. Hobbes' provocative theory of human nature included the proposition that "a perpetual and restless desire of power after power" animates men and renders social conflict inevitable in the absence of a strong state. Hobbes based his ideas on a reading of the empirical record of human history, as well as on common-sense observations about social life: Would everyone be using locks and keys, for instance, if human nature were co-operative and trustworthy? Rousseau's critique of Hobbes focussed not on the observations themselves but on the method of reasoning from those observations. The crucial move, as he saw it, was to import into a theory about nature "the need to satisfy a multitude of passions which are the product of society." Rousseau interpreted the evidence differently, denying that real humans' "need, avarice, oppression, desires, and pride" were innate. Instead, he called them the products of social forces that transform natural inclinations before they can express themselves in observable actions.[7]

Replace "natural inclinations" with "voters' judgments," and "social forces" with "electoral institutions," and we can see how Rousseau's commentary on Hobbes offers a template for electoral realism. The lense of constructivism is needed to deepen the vision of electoral realism because, compared to naturalism, it calls attention more to institutional structures than to people's natures.

For this approach, there is no such thing as a true and natural state of public opinion. Elections' function is to construct public opinion at a particular point in time—electoral judgments are therefore assembled, not discovered, by electoral institutions. Campaigns are dedicated to shaping and shifting voters' underlying attitudes and ultimate choices in ways preferred by the shapers and shifters, the very elites who seek a mandate to govern. Working with the thoughts and feelings of real people, turning their raw materials into electoral outcomes, is an act of transformation more than translation. Yet there are formal rules that set parameters for all that goes on in elections, offering opportunities for and imposing constraints on citizens which do not exist in the same form from one electoral system to the next. Those rules compose the structure

[7]The relevant texts are Hobbes' *Leviathan* (1651) and Rousseau's "Origins of Inequality" (1754): Hobbes (1996, 70, 88, 89) and Rousseau (1987, 33–34, 38, 53).

of elections, the fundamental properties that help to construct electoral outcomes. Institutional structures must be regarded as active social forces, or at least as comparably significant to such forces, even when they appear passive or inert, observationally.

Many academic researchers would readily acknowledge the general appeal of constructivism. The epithets "naive" and "barefoot" empiricism are reserved for the contrary approach, and they are not meant as compliments. Whether or not Rousseau was correct in attributing a naturalist approach to Hobbes in particular, it was and is fair play to target an intuitive and prevalent mode of thinking about human affairs. Naturalist assumptions have tremendous staying power in elections research, and electoral realists need to keep the constructivist alternative handy to keep naturalism at bay.

Electoral naturalism, to be clear, is not the same thing as electoral idealism. A naturalist may well be (as Hobbes appeared to be) a resolute foe of idealism, using empirical observations to undermine conventional assumptions. Indeed, naturalism can take a dim view of some of the ideals in which democratic citizens (professional scholars not excluded) are habitually instructed. "There is no alchemy in the ballot box," wrote W. G. Sumner in 1876; "it transmutes no base metal into gold." Put more coarsely, in terms increasingly heard since 2016: "garbage in, garbage out." Elections are a conveyor belt, on this view, taking voter ignorance and packaging it in the form of governments. For many observers after 2016, the package stinks; for those who are naturalists, allocating blame for the stench is as simple as finding its source. No one thinks to inspect the conveyor belt itself unless constructivism holds sway.[8]

Whereas many observers appear to believe that voter irrationality decided key elections in 2016, V. O. Key wrote 50 years earlier that "voters are not fools." What he appears to have meant in that pithy and oft-quoted phrase (see Chapter 2) is that voters are only made to look foolish by the larger structures of power that political elites surround them with. Constructivism, then, suggests that foolish voters may be made as well as born; electoral constructivism adds that electoral institutions may be prospering in the fool-making business. Institutional structures therefore demand our attention.[9]

[8] Quotation at Sumner (1934, 2:205).
[9] Quotation at Key (1966, 7).

THE CONCEPT OF ELECTORAL STRUCTURE

I use *electoral structure* as an umbrella term for the variety of institutions that set the basic rules of the game for voting. Such rules are structures in two senses: they tend to be durable over time, and they structure or frame voters' participation in ways that can determine outcomes differently with different rules in place.

An easy way to imagine the impact of electoral structure is to take the first and most famous component: suffrage. Consider an American "swing state" like North Carolina. In the first hypothetical scenario, imagine that the state legislature could change the voting rules to eliminate all black residents from the registration rolls. In the second scenario, imagine that blacks are reinstated but all residents of towns with fewer than 200,000 inhabitants are now eliminated. Based on some well-known facts about American demography, statewide elections under these two scenarios could be predicted to give lop-sided victories to the Republican Party in the first case and the Democratic Party in the second. This is one kind of difference that electoral structure can make. But suffrage rules are just one of at least eight key facets of electoral structure (see Fig. 1.1).

This book gives a lot attention to two sets of related components, contest structure and ballot structure. What makes one electoral contest distinct from another is that a discrete set of voters creates a set of inputs which is put through a counting or aggregation process to produce a discrete set of outputs. The outputs of one contest then lead directly

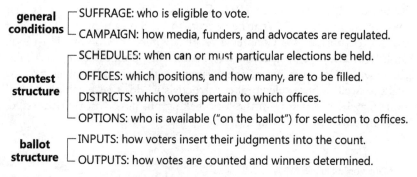

general conditions
- SUFFRAGE: who is eligible to vote.
- CAMPAIGN: how media, funders, and advocates are regulated.

contest structure
- SCHEDULES: when can or must particular elections be held.
- OFFICES: which positions, and how many, are to be filled.
- DISTRICTS: which voters pertain to which offices.
- OPTIONS: who is available ("on the ballot") for selection to offices.

ballot structure
- INPUTS: how voters insert their judgments into the count.
- OUTPUTS: how votes are counted and winners determined.

Fig. 1.1   Elements of electoral structure

to some corresponding political outcome, such as the authorization of a particular office-holder. The foundation of contest structure concerns which offices are to be filled by the outcome of the contest: the "how many winners" question. Contest structure also includes the set of voters that can participate in a particular election; the scheduling of the contest over time; and the ballot options among which voters have to choose (especially, are there three or more, or only two?).

Contest structure is analytically distinct from ballot structure, but the latter must fit into the former. Ballot structure is about input rules and output rules; the latter in turn have two components, counting rules and winning rules. Ballot structure is distinct from contest structure because more than one type of input–output combination can apply to any given contest. Yet the nature of the contest, especially whether it is a single- or multi-winner affair, does constrain to some extent the range of possible or desirable ballot structures.

Political research generally pays much more attention to contest structure than to ballot structure, since the former is integral to the difference between "majoritarian" and "proportional" democracies—the two classic categories of electoral system. The conventional labels for these two systems are rather misleading. Political scientists routinely call some countries "proportional" whose legislatures often show significant discrepancies between the distribution of voter support and the distribution of actual party control of legislative seats. The situation is even more embarrassing, conceptually, for so-called majoritarian systems. Majority rule simply is not a requirement to elect any member of the legislature in most of these systems, including the UK's and USA's, and many elected representatives in fact gain power with only a plurality (a minority of all voters, but a larger minority than any other single candidate's minority). What is supposed to make them majoritarian, for academics, is that the legislature as a whole is so disproportionally seated that one party can easily get a majority in the legislature with only a plurality of voters' support across the nation. Yet even this more limited, parliament-only kind of majoritarianism sometimes fails to materialize, as in Australia and the UK in the 2010s.[10]

---

[10]For the classic distinction between two families of electoral systems: Powell (2000). For the observation that a party in a "majoritarian" (single-seat) system can theoretically control the legislature with 25% of all votes, whereas the most proportional systems cannot construct a legislative majority with fewer than 50% of all votes: Przeworski (2018, 25).

What makes one electoral system different from another, in the way scholars routinely classify these things, is less the majoritarianism or proportionality of outcomes than something else. The difference is really made by the feature of contest structure that I call "offices" (a.k.a. "district magnitude" in the academic literature). This is the number of offices that are populated, or seats filled, by a single electoral contest: in broader terms, the number of winners per contest. It is much less misleading to speak of "single-seat" systems instead of "majoritarian" ones, and it is a little less misleading to speak of "multi-seat" systems instead of "proportional" ones.

This book is not about contest structure as much as its neglected partner, ballot structure. Talk about election reform tends to revolve around contest structure and the dynamics of single- vs. multi-seat systems, with relative neglect of the reform possibilities associated with ballot structure, with the input and output rules deployed inside a given contest structure. For the sake of a sustained focus on ballot structure, most of this book will take one kind of contest structure as a background condition: single-winner elections, including contests to select a single president, governor, or mayor, as well as a referendum to adopt a particular legal change. These are crucial elections in all democracies, to some degree or other, though in many countries the most important elections are multi-seat legislative contests. At times, I will directly engage interesting questions of institutionalized power and of ballot structure as they arise in multi-winner elections (e.g., in Chapters 3 and 7). Some lessons and insights appear to translate cleanly from one contest structure to the other, but not all. I have to admit at the outset that this book is intended to be more definitive for single-winner elections but more suggestive for multi-winner elections.

What is certain is that the general concept of electoral structure matters. The upheavals of 2016 can easily be misunderstood if the elements of electoral structure are ignored. American presidential elections, for example, are widely and justly appraised as relying on an unusual contest structure. To fill a single seat, fifty-one separate contests are held in fifty-one different districts (i.e., the fifty states plus the capital district) with fifty-one different procedures for candidates' ballot access. Because of malapportionment in the assignment of Electoral College votes from the outcomes of these fifty-one contests, the election of Trump in 2016 was secured by an Electoral College majority despite the fact that he received only 46.1% of all votes cast, considerably less than Hillary Clinton's

48.2%. It seems, then, that contest structure (as much as voters' nationalism, rationalism, irrationalism, etc.) enabled this wondrous feat of minority rule. But this book will make the case for ballot structure as an equally powerful component of electoral systems. In 2016, basic characteristics of the way voters were required to mark their ballots tended to hand-cuff them, leading to choices that they themselves considered poor ones (see Chapter 3). Voters are not fools, but they are often made to look foolish.

This type of constructivist interpretation becomes even more compelling when we consider the USA's nominating primaries of 2016 (in Chapter 6), the multiple state-by-state contests which helped to set the ballot options for the general election. Voting theorists and comparative elections scholars already understand that certain ballot types hand systematic advantages to polarizing parties and candidates—those whose fiercely loyal support within smaller blocs of the electorate stands against widespread hostility across larger blocs. But this book will argue that the problem goes even deeper. The distinctive and rigid input rules of voting with one-mark ballots (1MB) are responsible for a basic "dilemma of disempowerment" which cramps the expression of electoral judgments and blunts the force of voting as a tool of democratic accountability. This dilemma traps voters in a vise-like grip, between the *disgust* of electing bad governments and the *fear* that "wasted" votes and "spoiler" candidates will cause the election of worse governments. Somewhat against the grain, I will argue that the dilemma of disempowerment is largely an artifact of 1MB voting, not the number of seats filled per contest, and that certain ballot-structure effects therefore cannot be purged by well-designed contest structures.

DEMOCRATIC REALISM AND REALISTIC REFORM

Shifting the focus from contest structure to ballot structure reveals that most systems of democratic elections, whether single-seat or proportional, are prone to democratic deficits in the electoral arena because of their shared reliance on one-mark ballots. The input rules employed in the national elections of most established democracies have not changed a great deal since the middle twentieth century. Reliance on 1MB voting made sense and worked well in contexts where relatively stable cultural, ideological, and class identities anchored the voting behavior of strong partisans. Since the 1970s, however, a gradual but steadily upward trend of what political scientists call "electoral volatility" and "partisan decomposition" has changed the social and political environments of many democracies. Whether because of "post-material values" or resurgent nationalist impulses, voters are not as monotheistic in their partisan affiliations as they once were. With weaker and more mutable bonds to parties, fewer voters are intoning that "there is no god but God" when entering the voting booth to make their political confessions. As a result, year by year, the 1MB paradigm for ballot structure is deteriorating as an instrument of democracy.[11]

But what exactly are electoral institutions supposed to do for democracy? What would make an agenda of election reform—one revolving around ballot inputs and outputs, for instance—more or less "democratic"? Realism also has something to say here, entering the terrain of democratic theory.

Political realism views democracy, like any political regime, more in terms of the distribution of power than the incidence of justice. Distributing power is a large part of what elections "really" (read, primarily) do, and their effects on the dispensing of justice are secondary and indirect by comparison. A realist might care a lot about the justice of elections, but the point is that no coherent demands for justice could be placed on elections without first deciding what would constitute a just distribution of governmental or state *power* as a result of elections. Power is primary and substantive; justice is secondary.

Empirical scholars largely buy the realist paradigm for understanding elections; scholars in voting theory, less so. The realist's primary orientation toward questions of power fits uneasily with a field of scholarship which usually proceeds with conceptions of justice first and foremost.

Voting theorists tend to judge electoral institutions by the fairness or correctness of their electoral results, not by their properties as structures of power. Institutional structures are big-picture, long-term things with many ramifications for how power accumulates, circulates, and operates in a society. A democratic realist would not want to hear a voting theorist recommending a particular set of rules without some account of how they would, once institutionalized, sustain a democratic distribution of power in the larger political system. For most voting theorists,

---

[11] On electoral volatility and partisan decomposition: Mair (2013, 70–71, 78, 83).

this is simply not the kind of thing that elections do; they are just "decision rules." Accordingly, those rules should be judged simply by whether they produce good decisions, where "good" is usually defined by some property of justice or fidelity to the true underlying preferences of the voters who participate. This kind of voting theorist would not necessarily be a peddler of conventional pieties and ideals about elections—far from it—but rather a naturalist who believes that particular decisions should be more rather than less faithful to what the members of the electorate really want. This kind of naturalist would have no truck with the constructivist assumption that voters' judgments are the inessential artifacts of variable institutions.

If elections are about power before justice, a democratic realist—one who bothers to think about reform for some underlying purpose, not for reform's own sake—needs an account of what pro- and anti-democratic power structures are supposed to look like. Boiling this question down to its essence, democratic elections are generally supposed to shift institutionalized power more toward ordinary citizens than privileged elites. This formulation may seem too fluid to be useful, at first, but it beats some of the alternatives.

For instance, democratic realism finds it difficult to take the principle of majority rule as seriously as voting theorists; for some of the latter group, it is the very definition of justice. Majority rule is an ideal worth clinging to in many contexts. In the public institutions of mass democracy, the anti-majoritarian machinations of privileged elites make it look nigh irresistible. With such enemies at large, after all, how many democrats feel safe leaving the house without the weapon of majoritarianism close to hand?

The problem with using majority rule as a normative standard is that, in the real world of public elections, it generally either goes too far or not far enough. It obviously goes too far if abstention is counted as a form of political expression, rendering the requirement of majority approval virtually unattainable for most decisions in most places. Non-voters are sometimes written off as constructive non-citizens, not worth the counting, but some proportion of them know exactly what they are doing by abstaining. Moreover, various forms of partial abstention happen among active voters, in the voting booth: blanks on the ballot for this or that contest, whether through "don't know, don't care" motives or simple inadvertence. In these senses, majority rule is rather more demanding and elusive than we imagine. But it also does not go far enough in some cases, even where a vote appears to have a clear and decisive fifty-percent-plus-one winner. A two-option ballot frequently conceals multiple and substantial divisions within each camp of voters, as the Brexit referendum of 2016 illustrated. In such cases, no majority can be found if relevant differences are not elicited by the voting process, and the majority constructed by the ballot therefore resembles a decision less than it does a cheap slogan. A realist would not hold anything unique about the Brexit campaign responsible for such cheapening, which is a routine risk of many two-option referendums—a common contest structure that is specifically intended to promote majoritarianism—in many political systems. All in all, majority rule does not fit the realist's budget: Either the asking price is too high and we can't afford it, or the real value of the thing is too low for the effort of reaching into our pocket.[12]

In terms of mathematical thresholds, then, realists are prepared to be content with solid pluralities because majorities worth the name will rarely appear. But settling for solid pluralities over unlikely majorities does not mean quitting the campaign against minority rule. Now the fluid terms "ordinary citizens" and "privileged elites" come back into play. Democratic election reform—realistic reform—should aim for stable structures that systematically empower pluralities (and majorities, where feasible) over minorities. Generally, there should be little institutional room for maneuver which would enable the elites who sit atop powerful social institutions to achieve political victories without joining broader-based coalitions. As part of that goal, and more to the point, elites atop the governmental institutions that are most directly affected by elections should be consistently subject to pressure, through institutionalized sanctions, from non-privileged sectors of society. Traditionally that pressure is supposed to happen through electoral accountability.

Part of the reason for reform, too, is that political monotheism is what 1MB voting is good for. One-mark ballots do not work for voters who choose to name their political and partisan gods with a lowercase "g"; in fact, they are actively disempowered by 1MB rules, as I hope to explain in some detail below. Even if some societies still have a healthy majority of the monotheistic type of voter, the crucial analytic fact that many of the multi-mark alternatives considered in this book are incapable of stifling such voters, and unlikely to change their behavior fundamentally, means that smarter ballots can be considered a reform option anywhere.

---

[12] For a recent attempt to redefine "popular control" in terms of "multiple majorities," using the "social choice" approach of much of voting theory in the last 50 years: Ingham (2019).

BLAME STRUCTURES, NOT VOTERS

Various public reactions to the upheavals of 2016 showed that some aspects of naturalism remain powerful impediments to a realistic understanding of elections. For those who were heartened by the outcome of the Brexit referendum or the Trump victory, the electoral process was vindicated as the reassertion of popular will against corrupt elites. For a second group, frightened by one or both outcomes, the ancient horror of democracy's dark side was revived: Bad things are bound to happen, they insisted, when citizens' vicious impulses are given free rein at the ballot box. A third reaction condemned the results but shifted the blame to the intolerable economic hardships recently visited on many voters, not the public's inherently malicious or irrational nature.

These three groups, seen through the lens of political realism, might be dubbed the "triumphal outsiders," the "horrified liberals," and the "defensive democrats." Notice that, despite their differences, they all share something fundamental: the assumption that the existing electoral machinery gives us a legitimate representation of the will of the people. The triumphal outsider is most obviously reliant on this idea, but neither the horrified liberal's nor the defensive democrat's reaction can do without it. Naturalism tends to trace the credit or blame for electoral results directly back to their source; electoral constructivism tends to blame structures, not voters.

Special attention to the flaws in the thinking of the losers of 2016 is called for. The errors of pro-Brexit and pro-Trump thinking are also important, but those of anti-Brexit and anti-Trump thinking have more power to distort or derail future efforts at election reform. Wherever the political pendulum swings back, the losers of 2016 may find themselves with the power to set (or sabotage) new rules.

The horrified liberal's story about 2016 recalls the motto of "garbage in, garbage out." The most educated members of society soundly rejected Brexit and Trump at the ballot box, a fact that this line of thought takes as evidence that progress cannot be assured by taking a poll and following the majority. Harkening to the anti-democratic philosophers of ancient Greece, the horrified liberals warn us that demagogues will always be on hand to steer an ignorant herd into the pathways of self-destruction. The practical up-shot of this elitist revival is that popular participation in major political decisions should be restrained, whether through reduced reliance on referendums, tighter control over how candidates get ballot access, or more restrictive suffrage qualifications.[13]

This basically anti-democratic response ignores research suggesting that competitive elections typically do not channel public opinion into policy or empower voters over politicians. Yet that scholarship is directly relevant to the question of where the garbage is originating.

The defensive democrats have a very different story, emphasizing economic structures and conditions. Since the 1970s, the narrative goes, Western economies have undergone steady and at times painful transitions associated with globalization. With a new system of deregulated trade and investment across borders, older democracies' manufacturing jobs have trickled out to countries with lower labor costs and have been replaced with a mixture of high-skill jobs in the information-based economy and low-skill jobs in the service sector—plums for the educated elite, crumbs for everyone else. The problem in 2016, then, was not with voters themselves but with the intolerable pressures that were heaped on them by economic policies. On this view, the desperate conditions that were exploited so effectively by Brexiteers and Trumpsters can be abolished by political choices. Make the economy work for more than just cosmopolitan liberals and corporate barons, and voters will follow.[14]

The problem is that the defensive democrat's reaction to 2016 remains fully compatible with the assumption that ballots translate voters' will into election returns. It is still stuck in a kind of electoral naturalism, albeit one with a sunnier assessment of voter competence than the heirs of Sumner hold. With respect to electoral institutions, on this view, why try to fix what isn't broken when the problems lie elsewhere?

If elections were like calculators or weighing scales, electoral naturalism might be defensible. After all, a calculator is not to be faulted for the size of a tax bill, and a scale is not to be credited for a loss of weight. Sometimes academics provide well-credentialed intellectual resources for this kind of thinking about voting. There has been a long-running debate in American political science between those who claim that voters behave irrationally and those who reply that, on the contrary, voters

---

[13]On post-2016 "undemocratic liberalism" and its attraction to decision-making by unaccountable experts: Berman (2017). For explicit voting restrictions: Brennan (2016). For taking candidate-entry decisions out of voters' hands and restoring them to major-party elites: Levitsky and Ziblatt (2018).

[14]Piketty (2016), Starmer (2017), and Galston (2018, 7–8).

use their political tools and opportunities in rational ways. A political realist, assisted by electoral constructivism, is able to locate a point on which both sides can agree: When voters' activities are heavily structured by irrational institutions, they are often made to look like fools. The key interpretive insight, if it can be called that, is denial of the assumption that electoral institutions are like conveyor belts, calculators, or weighing scales. They are instead powerful engines of construction. It is at least plausible, therefore, that different electoral structures would make voters look like different political animals. Mounk has channeled this constructivist logic in suggestive terms: Given that "many supposed democracies now resemble competitive oligarchies," we should wonder whether "voters may be disengaged partly because they believe that the system would not be very responsive even if they did pay attention." Conceiving of electoral structure as a different, altogether more powerful kind of contrivance than a conveyor belt, electoral constructivism takes "construct" as an antonym of "translate," "channel," and "reflect."[15]

We need electoral constructivism to get us closer to understanding the reality of democratic deficits. If something is wrong circumstantially with the procedures of any given election, it may not matter if the voters are right. If something is wrong institutionally over a long period of time, chronic democratic deficits may cause grievances to build up until ordinary citizens lash out at the entire system. Realistic reform would therefore call for better-designed structures to empower voters, installing a pressure-release valve which should make the explosions of 2016 less likely or less destructive in future.

WHAT IS VOTER EMPOWERMENT?

The concept of voter empowerment which I employ in this book to guide and substantiate the realist agenda for election reform has three components. First, voters must be able to select the best available candidates and parties to hold future offices of authority. Second, voters must be able to hold candidates and parties accountable for past conduct while in office. Third, and essential to the preceding two requirements, voters must have versatile tools for inserting their judgments into electoral contests.

[15] Quotation at Mounk (2018, 107). For the futility of debates about voter rationality: Lenz (2018).

1. Power of **SELECTION** of future office-holders,
   requiring ADEQUATE ALTERNATIVES on ballots.

2. Power of **ACCOUNTABILITY** for past office-holding,
   requiring EFFECTIVE SANCTIONS through electoral outcomes.

3. Power of **JUDGMENT** over ballot options,
   requiring EXPRESSIVE POTENTIAL through electoral inputs.

Fig. 1.2   Triad of voter empowerment

These components of voter empowerment are simple and intuitive—and vague. They must be operationalized as criteria for assessing different aspects of real elections (see Fig. 1.2). First, the power of selection requires *adequate alternatives* from which to choose. Second, the power of accountability requires outcomes that count as *effective sanctions* (i.e., rewards or punishments). Third, both selection and sanction require a ballot structure that has *expressive potential* to incorporate voters' judgments.

A renewed focus on voter empowerment may be useful in a time beset by anxieties about democratic erosion. But it sits uneasily with anti-populist trends of thought which picture the politics of the post-2016 era as a binary combat of white hats against black hats, the heroic saviors of democracy against its villainous assailants. From the perspective of undemocratic liberalism, elections already empower voters too much, and going further is out of the question. By tacitly accepting naturalist assumptions and neglecting the structuring effects of electoral institutions, this view may be paving the way for a post-electoral future that, according to Mair, would mean "NGOs + judges = democracy."[16]

Before deciding that we want less voting in our democracies, the perspective of electoral realism suggests putting more democracy in our voting. What would that look like? The argument of this book is that the

---

[16]Quotation at Mair (2013, 11); "NGO" stands for "non-governmental organization," a designation covering lobbyists and activists.

rule of only one vote per voter per contest is the problem. This 1MB structure is the common denominator in multiple cases of voter disempowerment discussed below, including some multi-seat, proportional systems. Such electoral systems have shown considerable potency, when working in tandem with other structures of "institutionalized popular inclusion," to promote representative policy-making in certain respects. But reforms to contest structure alone (e.g., from single-seat to multi-seat contests) would likely be inadequate to narrow the democratic deficits of our times.[17]

The general solution is therefore multi-mark ballots with distributive input rules, making room for registering more than one judgment per voter per contest. Input and output rules determine how blunt or sharp, how dull or smart, are the tools that voters have to apply democratic pressure. In this respect, voters have not been served well by 1MB voting. If they had access to smarter ballots, elections might make fools of them less often.

In light of the crucial but overlooked distinction between one-mark and multi-mark ballots, even a perfectly enlightened citizenry would struggle to achieve democratic accountability with 1MB. The flip-side of this claim is that even an imperfect mass of voters can manage the feat better with multi-mark alternatives. By the end of this book, I hope to establish the first proposition and to provoke reflection about whether the second—which has barely been formulated, much less proved, before now—is worth putting to the test.

References

Achen, C., & L.M. Bartels. 2016. *Democracy for Realists*. Princeton: Princeton University Press.

Beramendi, V., A. Ellis, B. Kaufman, M. Kornblith, L. LeDuc, P. McGuire, T. Schiller, & P. Svensson. 2008. *Direct Democracy: The International IDEA Handbook*. Stockholm: Institute for Democracy and Election Assistance.

Berman, S. 2017. "The Pipe Dream of Undemocratic Liberalism." *Journal of Democracy* 28: 29–38.

Bermeo, N. 2019. "Can American Democracy Still Be Saved?" *Annals of the American Academy of Political and Social Science* 681: 228–33.

---

[17] On the role of PR as one aspect of "institutionalized popular inclusion" in reducing military conflict and protecting human rights: Joshi et al. (2015 [for conflict]; 2019 [for rights]).

Brennan, J. 2016. *Against Democracy*. Princeton: Princeton University Press.
Carty, R.K. 2010. "Canadian Democracy: An Assessment and an Agenda." *Auditing Canadian Democracy*, ed. W. Cross. Vancouver: University of British Columbia Press.
Chwalisz, C. 2015. *The Populist Signal: Why Politics and Democracy Need to Change*. Lanham, MD: Rowman & Littlefield.
Edelman. 2017. "Global Implosion of Trust." January 15 (Accessed on January 16, 2017 at www.edelman.com/news/2017-edelman-trust-barometer-reveals-global-implosion).
Galston, W.A. 2018. "The Populist Challenge to Liberal Democracy." *Journal of Democracy* 29: 5–19.
Geuss, R. 2008. *Philosophy and Real Politics*. Princeton: Princeton University Press.
Hobbes, T. 1996 (1651). *Leviathan*, ed. R. Tuck. Cambridge, UK: Cambridge University Press.
Ingham, S. 2019. *Rule by Multiple Majorities: A New Theory of Popular Control*. New York: Cambridge University Press.
Joshi, D.K., J.S. Maloy, & T.M. Peterson. 2015. "Popular vs. Elite Democratic Structures and International Peace." *Journal of Peace Research* 52: 463–77.
Joshi, D.K., J.S. Maloy, & T.M. Peterson. 2019. "Popular vs. Elite Democracies and Human Rights: Inclusion Makes a Difference." *International Studies Quarterly* 63: 111–26.
Key, V.O. 1966. *The Responsible Electorate: Rationality in Presidential Voting, 1936–60*, ed. M.C. Cummings. Cambridge, MA: Harvard University Press.
Lenz, G.S. 2018. "Time for a Change." *Critical Review* 30: 87–106.
Levinson, S. 2007. "How the United States Constitution Contributes to the Democratic Deficit in America." *Drake Law Review* 55: 859.
Levitsky, S., & D. Ziblatt. 2018. *How Democracies Die*. New York: Crown.
Mair, P. 2013. *Ruling the Void: The Hollowing of Western Democracy*. London: Verso.
Majone, G. 1998. "Europe's 'Democratic Deficit': The Question of Standards." *European Law Journal* 4: 5–28.
Maloy, J.S. 2013. *Democratic Statecraft: Political Realism and Popular Power*. New York: Cambridge University Press.
Mead, L.M. 2010. "Scholasticism in Political Science." *Perspectives on Politics* 8: 453–64.
Mounk, Y. 2018. "The Undemocratic Dilemma." *Journal of Democracy* 29: 98–112.
Piketty, T. 2016. "We Must Rethink Globalization, or Trumpism Will Prevail." *Guardian* (London), November 16 (Accessed on January 15, 2017 at www.theguardian.com/commentisfree/2016/nov/16/globalization-trump-inequality-thomas-piketty).

Powell, G.B. 2000. *Elections as Instruments of Democracy: Majoritarian and Proportional Visions*. New Haven: Yale University Press.

Przeworski, A. 2018. *Why Bother with Elections?* Cambridge, UK: Polity.

Rousseau, J.-J. 1987. *The Basic Political Writings*, trans. D.A. Cress. Indianapolis: Hackett.

Schrodt, P.A. 2014. "Seven Deadly Sins of Contemporary Quantitative Political Analysis." *Journal of Peace Research* 51: 287–300.

Shapiro, I. 2005. *The Flight from Reality in the Human Sciences*. Princeton: Princeton University Press.

Sil, R., & P.J. Katzenstein. 2010. *Beyond Paradigms: Analytic Eclecticism in the Study of World Politics*. Basingstoke, UK: Palgrave Macmillan.

Sleat, M. 2013. *Liberal Realism: A Realist Theory of Liberal Politics*. Manchester, UK: Manchester University Press.

Starmer, K. 2017. "Labour Can Tackle the Challenges of Brexit in a Way Theresa May Simply Cannot." *Guardian* (London), January 3 (Accessed on January 9, 2017 at www.theguardian.com/commentisfree/2017/jan/03/labour-challenges-brexit-theresa-may-ivan-rogers-values).

Sumner, W.G. 1934. *Essays of William Graham Sumner*, ed. A.G. Keller. 2 vols. New Haven: Yale University Press.

Wattenberg, M.P. 1998. *The Decline of American Political Parties, 1952–96*. 2nd edn. Cambridge, MA: Harvard University Press.

CHAPTER 2

What Research Reveals: Deficits of Electoral Accountability

The American presidential election of 2004 unfolded in a way that illustrates some of the ambiguities inherent in securing accountability through elections. George W. Bush had soared in popularity after the terrorist attacks of 2001 and the ensuing invasion of Afghanistan, but he had declined more slowly and surely in public esteem after the 2003 invasion of Iraq. Apart from easy renomination by the Republican Party, the summer of '04 was a turbulent one for Bush: failure to find the fabled WMD ("weapons of mass destruction") in Iraq, scandals over intelligence-gathering in connection with the war, exposure of domestic surveillance programs of dubious legality. With anyone but Karl Rove managing his re-election campaign, Bush might have been vacating the White House in 2005. Instead, he took John Kerry's congratulatory phone-call on election night.

According to an illustrious tradition of thought in the USA, election day is a supreme moment of accountability when the governed pass judgment on the governors. Writing in favor of the newly proposed Constitution of 1787, Alexander Hamilton and James Madison collaborated on the famous *Federalist* papers. There they praised "frequent elections" for creating "an immediate dependence on and an intimate sympathy with the people." They further suggested that elections would "maintain a proper responsibility to the people," since elected officers would be "compelled to anticipate the moment when their power is to cease ... unless a faithful discharge of their trust shall have entitled them to a renewal of it." Much later, similar notions about accountability

© The Author(s) 2019
J. S. Maloy, *Smarter Ballots*, Elections, Voting, Technology,
https://doi.org/10.1007/978-3-030-13031-2_2

were enshrined in modern political science as "the electoral connection," established by "retrospective voting" that delivers rewards and punishments as merited by governments' past performance. It is now so intuitive and obvious to many political scientists that it can seem perplexing that statesmen like Hamilton and Madison bothered to write it down.[1]

Pres. Bush was well prepared to deploy this conception of electoral accountability. Early in 2005, when asked whether his administration would hold anyone in the American government accountable for faulty intelligence and poor planning in the Iraq war, his answer was negative. As the president put it, "we had an accountability moment, and that's called the 2004 elections." Bush's father had lost a re-election bid in 1992 (ironically, after the first and relatively trouble-free Iraq war) in a rare three-way race in American presidential history. Some observers believed that the independent candidate, Ross Perot, had spoiled the Republican incumbent's chances in that year by luring away some conservatives' votes. Others considered Bush the elder's defeat, despite the three-way race, a just verdict by a majority of voters on a failed presidency. In any case, the son in '04 avoided the father's fate in '92 by winning the reward of re-election.[2]

Hamilton, Madison, and Bush the younger may be strange bedfellows in the pantheon of American political thought, but there is also room for doubts about electoral accountability. V. O. Key would probably not have bought Bush's "accountability moment" in 2004. Though long dead by that time, the Harvard professor had helpfully devised a metaphor for understanding democratic elections in the 1960s, describing "the voice of the people" as an echo from campaign messages put into the chamber by political elites—implying a rather different understanding of voting, but one that a strategist like Rove might appreciate. In recent years, academic political science has rediscovered some of Key's skepticism about elections. More and more election scholars have come to understand what many voters also feel: The vote is a thin twig on which to hang citizens' hopes of democratic empowerment.

---

[1] Quotations at Hamilton et al. (2005, 286, 311). For "the electoral connection": Mayhew (1974). For "retrospective voting": Fiorina (1981).

[2] Quotation at VandeHei and Fletcher (2005). For the judgment of public-opinion scholars that not enough of Perot's voters would have supported Bush to secure his re-election, even if Perot had not been on the ballot: Norpoth (2001, 425n).

How (Not) to Measure Accountability

The first challenge for research on political accountability applies to the social sciences in general: What exactly is the thing we are studying, and how do we know it when we see it? Like power, justice, or fear, accountability is a property of human relationships, which in turn are complex and multi-faceted phenomena. The nub of this methodological problem is that the most interesting things about human relationships are not directly observable. We cannot simply observe a child with a bloody nose and say, "that is evidence of power" or "justice" or "fear"; we need more, and sometimes a lot more.

Learning about accountability does require observing things in the political world, but it is not always clear what to look for. What would count as an accountability-relevant observation? Some political researchers consider the answer to be obvious, at least for *electoral* accountability: votes. When we measure official election returns, with attention to votes cast for particular parties and candidates, we are measuring "vote-share." When we record what individuals tell us about how they voted, or how they plan to vote, we are measuring "vote-choice."

Though superficially plausible, these are the wrong answers for measuring electoral accountability. To understand why simply observing votes is inadequate, we need a clean and precise conceptual framework that specifies what kinds of accountability relationship are important enough to merit systematic study.

The big divide among social scientists on this question is between two concepts of accountability, one based on communicating and the other on sanctioning. "Accountable" originally meant "answerable," describing a relation of communication, as in telling stories or calculating numbers. In law and politics, however, people are only fully "accountable" when they face consequences after certain stories are related and certain numbers added up. Sanctions, which could involve either reward or punishment, are the power behind the accounting. If accountability is supposed to involve relations of power, then electoral accountability must have a lot to do with electoral sanctions.[3]

The first rule of measuring accountability, therefore, is that votes have to be connected in some intelligible manner to relationships of sanction, whether of reward or of punishment. Measurements of vote-share and

[3] On two concepts of accountability: Bovens (2005) and Mansbridge (2014).

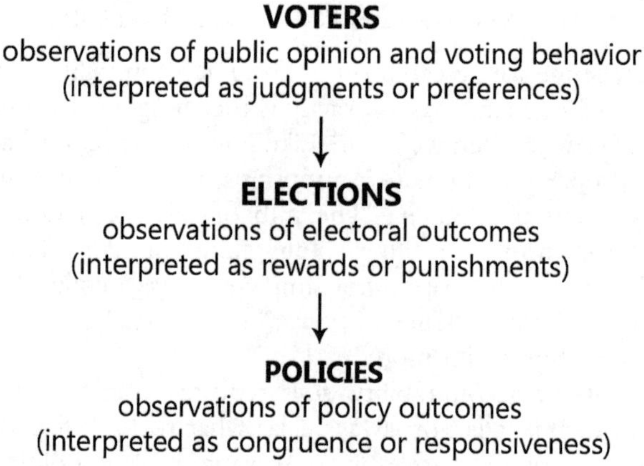

VOTERS
observations of public opinion and voting behavior
(interpreted as judgments or preferences)

↓

ELECTIONS
observations of electoral outcomes
(interpreted as rewards or punishments)

↓

POLICIES
observations of policy outcomes
(interpreted as congruence or responsiveness)

Fig. 2.1   Causal chain of electoral accountability (*Source* Maloy [2014])

vote-choice do not say enough about accountability unless and until we can specify what votes have to do with sanctions. Here too the simple answer is the electoral result: Victory or defeat is how votes lead to consequences for politicians. For example, in European elections held in the aftermath of the global financial crisis of 2008, 14 out of 22 (64%) resulted in a loss of power for the incumbent government. This kind of result is supposed to be what hurts. But several of these elections saw the incumbents decline in vote-share while remaining in office. Losing votes without losing power happens with some regularity, and politicians understand this fact; researchers should as well.[4]

The second rule of measuring accountability corresponds to a second link in the causal chain: Follow the linkage between electoral outcomes and policy outcomes. The appropriate conceptual framework for research on electoral accountability includes both a voter-election linkage and an election-policy linkage (see Fig. 2.1).[5]

[4]On post-2008 elections: LeDuc and Pammett (2013). This study analyzes 27 elections between 2008 and 2011, 24 of which were the first to occur after the crisis; I excluded two of these from my count where the incumbent was a "caretaker" government unconnected to pre-2008 policies.

[5]This conceptual scheme and the accompanying Fig. 2.1 are adapted from Maloy (2014, 14–15).

Each of the two links in the chain of electoral accountability requires particular kinds of observations. For the first link, we have to observe not only voting behavior but also election results; for the second, not only election results but also policy-making behavior.

If evidence about voters and policy-makers is considered, the effective role of election outcomes in linking the two remains to be proven. If data on voters and elections are considered, we will not necessarily learn about accountability unless policies are too. If evidence on election results and policy is considered, the effective role of voters in exercising their supposed power is still missing.

Empirical measures and analyses must be guided by good concepts. Our basic concepts now tell us that evidence on voters and voting is necessary but not sufficient to tell us about electoral accountability; we also need to measure electoral outcomes and to be able to interpret them as rewards or punishments. Some political scientists have therefore used data on victories and defeats, the loss of power and the retention of power, re-election and deselection, to measure effective electoral sanctions. Such variables are typically called "survival in office" or "hazard rate"—the probability that any given government will lose power. Other scholars have added variables on politicians' policy-making behavior to cover the second link in the chain.

As we now survey the findings and results of empirical analyses of data surrounding democratic elections around the world, knowing how to measure electoral accountability, and how not to, is essential to interpreting the evidence. Equipped with the right tools for understanding, readers will notice a clear trend.

CORRUPTION, PROSPERITY, AND RESPONSIVENESS

There are two general types of political issue which researchers have examined in their efforts to assess electoral accountability with empirical evidence: valence issues and positional issues. Valence issues are ones in which most people tend to share the same goals; positional ones see different people taking different positions with respect to what the goals should be. On valence issues, with broad agreement on what counts as a good and bad outcome, voters normally focus on politicians' competence at achieving the widely desired results. On positional issues, with a wider range of disagreement among the public, voters normally focus on politicians' ideology and how it aligns with one side or the other of a debate.[6]

Corruption and prosperity are two classic valence issues: nearly everyone dislikes corruption and likes prosperity. Voters being virtually unanimous, the task of the researcher in measuring accountability should be at its easiest. When people believe that the government is responsible for high corruption or low prosperity, obviously elections should result in throwing the rascals out.

The general consensus is that democracies experience significantly less corruption than non-democracies, and it was long assumed that electoral accountability was the mechanism responsible for this fact. However, as analysts started looking more closely at the middle of the chain of accountability, at election results themselves, serious doubts emerged. As Catherine De Vries and Hector Solaz have explained, "the empirical evidence on the electoral punishment of corruption is mixed," and "most research to date suggests that voters often do not hold politicians accountable for corruption." What happens instead is that, while some voters definitely intend to punish corruption at the ballot box, either corrupt politicians are able to win elections through emphasizing other issues (like group loyalties and identities), or else corrupt politicians are replaced by new electoral winners who end up doing little different from their predecessors. The initial conventional wisdom about elections and corruption has been overturned through more careful research.[7]

Economic prosperity is, if anything, an even riper valence issue for studying electoral accountability than corruption is. What better way to understand voters' success or failure at rewarding and punishing politicians, therefore, than to ply the vast waters in the academic ocean of "economic voting" studies?

Alas, elected officers cannot necessarily be expected to pay the price for economic disaster on a regular basis—not even in the European or North American heartlands of modern capitalism. As we have already noticed, several European governments actually gained more votes after 2008, while several others that lost votes managed to stay in office.

---

[6]Wattenberg (1991, 92–93).

[7]Quotations at De Vries and Solaz (2017, 392, 393). On the gap between voters' intentions and effective outcomes: Crisp et al. (2014). On the many conditions required for successfully punishing corruption through voting: De Vries and Solaz (2017, 398–403).

Academic research on accountability for economic outcomes has been plagued by mixed results. But the key to the mixed results lies in the different measurement strategies described above. Pro-accountability studies tend to measure approval ratings, vote-choice, and vote-share to demonstrate that voters intend to punish politicians for poor economic conditions, whereas those studies that directly measure the loss of elections (not just the loss of votes) tend to be skeptical about the effectiveness of electoral accountability. Even considering voters in isolation, their perceptual biases about economic reality and the difficulties created by institutional complexity for identifying who really influences the economy pose severe obstacles to the electoral connection. One of the leading findings of the last decade is that, because of economic globalization and the power of trans-national corporations and trade agreements, fewer and fewer national governments can be considered responsible for their own economies' health. To sum up what economic-voting studies have to say about electoral accountability: Though a small segment of voters habitually cast their ballots for a better economy, politicians are now better able to avoid paying the electoral price than to deliver what those voters want.[8]

With positional issues, by contrast with valence issues like corruption and prosperity, voters' preferences are more varied and volatile, and elected politicians would be expected to move with them. Political science has analyzed such issues with a key distinction in mind between *congruence* and *responsiveness*. Congruence describes how close a fit we find between the public's preferred positions (e.g., on tax rates or health-insurance regulations) and the actual policy outcomes produced by elected representatives; responsiveness refers to directions of change in public opinion and policy output, when the former moves in one direction and the latter also shifts in that direction. Though research on positional issues in American politics looks, at first glance, exceedingly uncertain and disputatious, Brandice Canes-Wrone has shrewdly pointed out two underlying points of consensus beneath the superficial

---

[8]On the tendency for vote-share studies to draw less skeptical conclusions than survival-in-office studies: Healy and Malhotra (2013, 297n) and Maloy (2014, 16–17, 24). For skeptical results based on a global dataset of survival in office: Maravall (2010). On biases in economic perceptions: Healy and Malhotra (2013, 292–93). On the problem of economic responsibility under conditions of globalization: Duch and Stevenson (2008) and Hellwig et al. (2008).

appearance of contention. Most scholars agree, first, that congruence, or closeness of fit, is lower than responsiveness, or directional shifting; second, that responsiveness has been declining since the 1970s.[9]

CONSENSUS AND DEBATE

The collective verdict of academic political research on the strength of electoral accountability in democratic countries has therefore shifted noticeably in a skeptical direction since the end of the Cold War. As scholarly histories of democratic ideas began to recover the original purpose of periodic elections, which was to serve as elites' tool for obtaining consent rather than voters' tool for exercising control, empirical studies sought to establish how well elections had adapted to modern expectations that they serve "people power" after all. A useful way to see the direction of momentum is to survey several landmark studies that have promulgated the skeptical position.[10]

The first was a collection of essays edited by Adam Przeworski, Susan Stokes, and Bernard Manin in 1999, titled *Democracy, Accountability, and Representation*. Among a diverse range of views, several contributions rejected the notion that real democratic elections live up to the ideal of popular control which has long been associated with them. Przeworski and José Cheibub analyzed economic voting with a dataset covering all democratic elections in the world from 1950 to 1990, finding no consistent statistical relationship between economic outcomes and the survival in office of incumbent governments. Stokes documented several Latin American presidential elections in the 1980s and 1990s in which the winning candidates dropped their proposed economic programs and implemented *their opponents'* plans instead, facing minimal electoral consequences for such dramatic policy switches. James Fearon theorized that elections are poorly suited by nature for sanctioning politicians for past conduct and suggested that trying to select personal characteristics for the future is voters' most logical approach. José Maravall explored the theme of political manipulation and concluded that elections leave plenty of room for maneuver for politicians to stay in office

---

[9]Canes-Wrone (2015).

[10]On the intellectual history of electoral accountability: Manin (1997) and Maloy (2008).

despite failing to respect voters' wishes, intentions, or interests. Though other contributors offered less pessimistic assessments, the editors' own synthesis of the collection's findings emphasized "the ineffectiveness of elections as a mechanism of control over governments." Significant future changes in both institutional design and voter information would be required, they concluded, to make the reliable operation of electoral accountability conceivable in modern democracies.[11]

The trend of electoral skepticism was now well underway, and its progress was marked in 2007 by Christopher J. Anderson's provocatively titled review article, "The End of Economic Voting?" Anderson dwelt at length on the shortcomings of electoral accountability for economic conditions which had been uncovered by numerous studies; one year later, the next major book on the subject confirmed the skeptical trend in certain respects. Raymond Duch and Randy Stevenson's global analysis of economic voting found that some voters do consistently base their ballot choices on the goal of prosperity, but only in countries with the least exposure to and integration with the forces of economic globalization. Moreover, they concentrated their analysis on voters and vote-shares, not on survival in office or any other effort to measure electoral sanctions directly. In fact, Duch and Stevenson explicitly rejected (extending Fearon's logic from 1999) the idea that votes could be meaningfully interpreted as rewards or punishments for past governmental performance.[12]

The most recent work in this tradition of electoral skepticism is Christopher Achen and Larry Bartels' *Democracy for Realists*, published in 2016 and addressed mostly to scholars of the USA (whose skepticism has been slowest to materialize) rather than scholars of the global context (where the skeptical findings have been better received). Achen and Bartels' position first gained notoriety with an unpublished paper in 2002, informally known as the "shark attack" study. They examined voting data from across the New Jersey coastline during Woodrow Wilson's 1916 re-election bid, finding major decreases in the incumbent's

---

[11] Quotation at Manin et al. (1999b, 24). On economic voting: Cheibub and Przeworski (1999). On Latin American policy switches: Stokes (1999). On sanction vs. selection: Fearon (1999, esp. 77–81). On political manipulation: Maravall (1999). For the most optimistic contribution to this volume: Stimson (1999).

[12] Anderson (2007) and Duch and Stevenson (2008).

vote-share in areas that happened to experience a rash of shark attacks prior to election day. If it is senseless to punish elected leaders for things outside their control—sharks being things of that sort, alongside trans-national corporations—we are left with what Achen and Bartels call "blind retrospection." The book as a whole adds several other analyses of (non-shark) empirical data to reinforce the theme. Accordingly, this latest scholarly salvo puts more blame on irrational voters than on institutional structures for the accountability deficits of democratic elections.[13]

This is now the core debate, the lingering area of uncertainty and unexplored terrain, in academic research on electoral accountability: not whether it is failing, but why. The areas of consensus are clear. Voters often cannot use the vote to end corruption, nor can they control politicians on economic policy—which may be just as well, since politicians cannot really control the economy. Policy responsiveness (in the USA, at least) has been on a long and steady decline, and policy congruence is so low that many researchers have stopped bothering about it. Voters try to act rationally at the ballot box, but they often fail: Elections make fools of them. Part of the reason is that they leave "a good deal of leeway for incumbents," whose "margin to escape responsibility is large."[14]

Turning from the "whether" to the "why" of accountability deficits, naturalism vs. constructivism remains a relevant contrast within the camp of electoral skeptics. Naturalists assume that electoral events and outcomes reflect something basic and essential about voters—their ignorance, their short-sightedness, their bad judgment. Constructivists caution, on the contrary, that voters might not be the most powerful cause of what happens in an electoral system, that different institutional structures might produce different kinds of results with the same voters, and that different institutional structures might even produce different kinds of voters. For those interested in research with public purpose, naturalism vs. constructivism can determine which reforms you believe will make elections better serve the cause of democracy and which you believe are destined to become stray bullets lodged firmly in democracy's own feet. For this reason, a rather misunderstood figure from the middle twentieth century could play an important role in the debates to come.

[13] Achen and Bartels (2016, 118–28).

[14] Quotations (respectively) at Bartels (2016, 39) and Przeworski (2018, 4).

A Tale of Two Echo Chambers

V. O. Key Jr. received his doctoral training in political science at the University of Chicago, where he was supervised by the legendary Charles Merriam. A certain flair for realism was part of Chicago's in-house tradition at the time. Key's dissertation was a minute dissection of governmental corruption, titled "The Techniques of Political Graft in the United States" (1934). Much later, when Pres. John F. Kennedy invited Key to serve on a presidential commission to study the financing of American election campaigns, it could not have been because JFK only wanted to hear good news.[15]

Key died one month before the president did, in 1963, and among his surviving papers was an unfinished book manuscript that has since become a minor classic in the history of political science. After friends and colleagues of Key's made some additions and modifications to his material, *The Responsible Electorate* was published in 1966. Given Key's long history and sterling reputation as a hard-nosed political realist, readers might have been expected to latch onto the striking metaphor that was signaled in the title of the book's introductory chapter: "The Voice of the People: An Echo." He used this metaphor to explain his distinctive approach to understanding elections.

> For a glaringly obvious reason, electoral victory cannot be regarded as necessarily a popular ratification of a candidate's outlook. The voice of the people is but an echo. The output of an echo chamber bears an inevitable and invariable relation to the input. As candidates and parties clamor for attention and vie for popular support, the people's verdict can be no more than a selective reflection from the alternatives and outlooks presented to them. Even the most discriminating popular judgment can reflect only ambiguity, uncertainty, or even foolishness if those are the qualities of the input into the echo chamber.[16]

Instead of taking this framing metaphor to heart, however, many readers formed a different sort of echo around Key's last book, and therewith his posthumous intellectual legacy. The prevailing interpretation has been that *The Responsible Electorate* vindicated the rationality of voters and

[15] Lamis (2008).
[16] Key (1966, 2–3).

substantiated the effectiveness of electoral accountability. This verdict on Key has been bouncing off the inner walls of the ivory tower ever since.[17]

The image of Key as an optimist about accountability has not been fabricated out of nothing. The full title of the book was *The Responsible Electorate: Rationality in Presidential Voting, 1936–60*. No surviving evidence indicates how much of this title came from Key himself or from the colleagues who assembled the book after his death, but the words "responsible" and "rationality" were consistent with Arthur Maass's preface to the book. A former student and then a colleague of Key's, Maass offered readers this summation of the book's main conclusions: "Political man is rational, and … the political institutions that he has developed, at least those for election of the president, are rational too." Though some scholars, then and since, have regarded this as an exaggeration of Key's thesis, others consider it congruent with Key's own statement, in his introduction, that "voters are not fools." The other claim from *The Responsible Electorate* which has most often been cited in favor of electoral accountability is that "the fear of loss of popular support powerfully disciplines the actions of governments." Thanks to repeated citations of these two passages over the years, even the leading skeptics about electoral accountability have regarded Key as an obstacle to overcome rather than a launching pad. For instance, several contributors to the *Democracy, Accountability, and Representation* volume, as well as Anderson's article and Achen and Bartels' book, cite *The Responsible Electorate* as a pro-accountability tract.[18]

The puzzle is how to make this rationalist, pro-accountability image consistent with Key's interpretive framing of his book, via the metaphor of the echo chamber, as opposed to Maass's framing. Ignoring Key's echo chamber, in favor of participating in his successors' echo chamber about Key, is not an intellectually honest option because his choice of metaphor was fully consistent with what he had been writing about public opinion and voting behavior for many years.

Notice that the term "responsible electorate" is not equivalent to "accountable office-holders," and that "voters are not fools" is not

---

[17]On the influence of *The Responsible Electorate* down to the present: Healy and Malhotra (2013, 286).

[18]Quotations at Key (1966, viii, 7, 10). For skeptics' citations of Key as an optimist: Manin et al. (1999a, 42), Fearon (1999, 56), Maravall (1999, 155), Anderson (2007, 273), and Achen and Bartels (2016, 92).

equivalent to "voters control governments through elections." What is missing in each of these mistranslations are the politicians, and Key's views about the relation between voters and politicians tend to be overlooked by electoral optimists. In his magisterial *Public Opinion and American Democracy* (1961), Key explained that "mass opinion is not self-generating; in the main, it is a response to the cues, the proposals, and the visions propagated by the political activists." This constructivist premise would be widely accepted today, but Key went on to say that the "translation of opinion into actions of electoral punishment or reward is a tortuous and uncertain procedure." In consequence, "democracies decay, if they do, not because of the cupidity of the masses but because of the stupidity and self-seeking of leadership echelons." In a related article published the same year in the *Virginia Quarterly Review*, Key expanded this theme:

> the more I study elections[,] the more disposed I am to believe that they have within themselves more than a trace of the lottery. ... Even when the public in manifest anger and disillusionment throws an Administration from office, it does not express its policy preferences with precision. The voice of the people may be loud but the enunciation is indistinct.

Therefore, Key reiterated, "those who blame mass opinion for our ills hang the wrong villain. ... If the American democracy has within itself a drive toward self-destruction, we might more accurately localize the trouble by looking among the best people than at the great mass of the people."[19]

When these reflections were published in 1961, Key's final manuscript was not long in coming. The metaphor of the echo chamber that lay among his papers when he died in 1963 was therefore not the result of an ephemeral choice of words for a single, passing occasion. It was central to his mature thinking about elections. Key repeatedly stressed that public opinion is constructed by political elites because doing so made possible a second move that was evidently important to him: absolving voters from blame for failures of electoral accountability. This is the real meaning of the famous refrain in his final book that "voters are not fools," a phrasing with roots in his 1961 article. There Key had

---

[19] Quotations at Key (1961a, 557; 1961b, 487, 489, 494).

written that "public men often act as if they thought the deciding margin in elections was cast by fools; moreover, by fools informed enough and alert enough to bring retribution to those who dare not demonstrate themselves to be equally foolish." Key scoffed at this notion because it allowed political elites to deflect responsibility for their own faults. The mantra that "voters are not fools" was not a claim that rational voters succeed in holding politicians accountable; it was Key's way of saying that elections' failure to deliver accountability was not the result of folly among voters.[20]

Key was the intellectual forebear of today's skeptics, not of the optimists. His conclusions rub against both Achen and Bartels' indictment of voter irrationality and the optimists' defense of systemic rationality. Key's position was more sophisticated than either of these: Electoral accountability is weak, despite the fact that voters are not fools, to the extent that elites are dysfunctional.

Yet doubt is not equivalent, as every good skeptic knows, to absolute denial. We must remember Key's seminal publications on the politics of the southern states, which still in his lifetime featured dominant one-party regimes with little inter-party (though some intra-party) competition. From this perspective, two-party competition would clearly improve the chances for electoral accountability. Key regarded the 1936 re-election of Franklin Roosevelt as a robust popular ratification of the New Deal, for example. But the presence of two options on the ballot only makes accountability *possible*, contingent on what exactly partisan elites are offering to voters under a particular set of circumstances; two-partyism is not *sufficient* for accountability. It would only take a tweak, a logical extension, to supplement Key's brand of electoral constructivism with the insight that not only elite actors but also institutional structures can have the effect of disempowering voters. Since various types of institutions affect real electoral processes, examining several of these more closely can help us to understand why constructivists tend to be skeptics—and just how ample or narrow the scope may be for special occasions of electoral accountability.[21]

---

[20] Quotation at Key (1961b, 490).

[21] For a rebuttal to Key's optimistic account of 1936: Achen and Bartels (2016, 178–96).

(Highly) Conditional Accountability:
A Top Ten List

The phrase "mixed results" summons the thought that something appears to be conditional on something else, as opposed to robust and independent in its own right. It turns out that a host of conditions can and do weaken the electoral connection between voters and politicians. The following "top ten" list (see also Fig. 2.2) describes the most common sources of deficits of accountability, according to empirical research.[22]

1. Poor Information. The empirical reality of widespread voter ignorance about public affairs, even in relatively affluent and educated societies, is perhaps the most obvious source of accountability deficits in elections. If the vote is a tool, users should have some idea of when and how it can (and cannot) be used to good effect. Studies comparing content-rich and content-poor media environments in the USA suggest a glimmer of hope that the former are home to more responsive politicians, but these are the exception rather than the rule. Digital media are currently laboring under the stigma of "fake news," not an encouraging sign for future progress. Because the World Wide Web makes it easier for consumers of news to access exclusively partisan sources, Markus Prior concluded that "the share of politically uninformed people [in the USA] has risen since we entered the so-called information age." The vivid nickname given to the American "right-wing media establishment" by Kathleen Jamieson was "the echo chamber." This unintentional and indirect allusion to V. O. Key has since become a popular (and apt) descriptor of on-line media all over the ideological spectrum and all over the world.[23]

2. Weak Judgment. The effects of poor information can be exacerbated by various kinds of cognitive error and bias among voters, endangering accountability even when the supply of information is good. Intensive exposure to major policy issues sometimes enflames rather than tames voters' partisan misperceptions, not only in the USA but also in other democracies. Difficulty of recall leads voters to weight recent information

---

[22] The rest of this section and the accompanying Fig. 2.2 are revised (and condensed) versions of material in Maloy (2015, 80–86).

[23] Quotation at Prior (2007, 134). On voter ignorance in general: Hardin (2000). On rich vs. poor media environments: Arnold (2004, 251–53), Snyder and Stromberg (2010). On right-wing echo chambers: Jamieson and Cappella (2008).

1. POOR INFORMATION Voters have low exposure or access to evidence of political reality.	**6. PRIVATE FUNDING** Dollars can also sway politicians through legally sanctioned donations and lobbying.
2. WEAK JUDGMENT Voters distort evidence of political reality through various kinds of bias.	**7. PARTIES TOO WEAK** Political parties lack internal strength to translate votes into action.
3. MISPLACED RESPONSIBILITY Complex issues and institutions make it difficult to attribute credit and blame.	**8. PARTIES TOO STRONG** Political parties flex muscles externally to control electoral processes.
4. WEAK INCENTIVES Politicians are not deterred by electoral sanction when the rewards of office are low.	**9. ELECTORAL FRAUD** Voting results are prone to intentional skewing.
5. CORRUPTION AND BRIBERY Politicians can be swayed by dollars more than votes.	**10. ELECTORAL INACCURACY** Voting results are prone to technical or otherwise random errors.

Fig. 2.2 Top ten deficits of electoral accountability (*Source* Maloy [2015])

more heavily than information about earlier periods of a representative's term, explaining why politicians often wait until just before election day to engage in deviant behavior resembling responsiveness. As Achen and Bartels put it, based on examining elections in relation to droughts and floods, "voters consistently and systematically punish incumbents for conditions beyond their control."[24]

3. Misplaced Responsibility. On the all-important political question of who is responsible for what, partisan and ideological rationalizations enjoy particularly broad scope for playing havoc with voters' judgments. Complexity in policy issues and political institutions also contributes to misattributed responsibility. The concept of "clarity of responsibility" was devised by Bingham Powell and Guy Whitten, and extended by other researchers, to measure how easy it is for voters to identify who is responsible for economic policy. With the split authorities of "divided federalism" in the USA, for example, many voters attribute responsibility

[24]Quotation at Achen and Bartels (2016, 128). On partisan misperception and bias: Claassen and Highton (2006) and Healy and Malhotra (2013, 292–93). On weak memory and recency bias: Jacobs and Shapiro (2000, 43–44) and Huber et al. (2012).

to presidents and state governors based on partisan bias more than economic reality. Voters in Latin America blame incumbents at subnational levels of government for the effects of national policy, and vice versa, and they blame international agencies for the effects of domestic policy. The advice of Thomas Paine ca. 1776, that people power is favored by institutional simplicity and hindered by institutional complexity, has in this sense stood the test of time.[25]

4. Weak Incentives. Electoral accountability depends on the motivation of incumbents to retain their seats on election day, but politicians' incentives for actually keeping office are sometimes too weak to give voters the power of deterrence. In local governments in rural China, for example, official salaries are meager and elected officers little fearful of the consequences of disappointing their constituents' expectations. In the USA, many state and local governments offer relatively low salaries (or only part-time appointments) for elected officers. In such circumstances, the potential gains of unrepresentative behavior may over-balance the potential costs of poor electoral performance. As a study of mayors in Brazil has shown, people who become career politicians do not necessarily have risk-averse personalities when it comes to facing the threat of voters' wrath.[26]

5. Corruption and Bribery. Even healthy levels of official compensation might be overwhelmed by monetary inducements from unofficial sources. An extreme example illustrates the general problem: The Peruvian state in the 1990s played host to an elaborate scheme of bribery, operated on behalf of the elected president, Alberto Fujimori, by his intelligence chief, Vladimiro Montesinos. The monthly cost of a non-partisan judge in Peru was about $10,000; of a deputy from another party, $20,000; of the owner of a private television network, $60,000. This scheme gave members of the opposition ample incentives not to be responsive to their supporters. Whereas kick-backs and bribes may diminish a representative's incentive to be re-elected, the continued presence of the sources of these funds also lowers the probability that victorious challengers would behave differently.[27]

---

[25]For the original "clarity of responsibility" study: Powell and Whitten (1993). On lack of clarity in the American federal system: Brown (2010). On lack of clarity in Latin America: Gelineau and Remmer (2005) and Alcaniz and Hellwig (2011). For Paine's association of democracy with institutional simplicity: Paine (2003, 7–9, 248–51, 294–301).

[26]On China: Tsai (2007, 254–55). On Brazil: Pereira et al. (2009).

[27]On Peru: McMillan and Zoido (2004).

6. Private Funding. In systems where electoral campaigns are funded by private donors, lobbying and money freely mingle in ways not covered by bribery laws. A more formal, legalized inequality of influence over elected officers by donors is therefore possible. Academic research on the American federal government has found that many policy favors are dispensed through legislative amendments and regulatory directives, shielded from the usual sight-lines of journalists and voters. The economist Thomas Ferguson found evidence in the 1990s that parties and candidates switch policies after elections in response to the interests of campaign donors. His more recent research on the 2012 elections in the USA has documented interesting divergences between the support of large donors and the content of campaign rhetoric, including the surprising linkage of Wall Street donations with Tea Party candidates. Schemes of public financing and free advertising for candidates hold some potential to reduce accountability to dollars over votes. In the American states, research suggests that efforts to block or to weaken regulations on private funding tend to make state and local elections less competitive.[28]

7. Parties Too Weak. Variations in partisan institutions can have an enormous impact on electoral dynamics. Strong partisan organizations could in theory supply ideological cues to compensate for voters' limited information, yet the failure of parties actually to play this role has often been lamented. Morris Fiorina wrote in 1981 that "collective responsibility has leaked out of the system" as a result of American parties' lack of organizational and ideological coherence. A similar problem arises where a lack of partisan unity obscures "clarity of responsibility" for policy or fails to offer viable electoral alternatives, which are essential to make ballots count as sanctions. If elected, structurally weak parties may be unable to carry out a policy program that is responsive to those voters who deliberately deposed the incumbents.[29]

8. Parties Too Strong. If political parties may endanger accountability when they are too weak internally, they are also a threat when too

---

[28] On behind-the-scenes policy-making: Fellowes and Wolf (2004). On policy switches in the 1990s: Ferguson 1995. On campaign donations in the 2012 election: Ferguson et al. (2013). On American states' campaign-funding rules: Hogan (2004) and Hamm and Hogan (2008).

[29] On weak parties in the USA: Fiorina (1981, 202–210). On problems with clarity of responsibility and party unity around the world: Powell (2000, Chapter 3) and Anderson (2007, 281–86).

strong externally. In many American states, the two major parties face lower barriers to ballot access than others but may nonetheless exclude non-members from primary elections that decide nominations. As a result, nominations tend to be bestowed by a relatively small minority of ideological extremists. In addition, partisan "gerrymandering" of "safe" electoral districts is the USA's peculiar contribution to the theory of minority rule. If a small number of strong partisans can oust an incumbent in a nominating primary that excludes non-members, but a much larger number of voters cannot do the same at the general election because the district as a whole is uncompetitive, the people to whom the incumbent is truly accountable are the smaller faction, not the larger. Beyond the USA, the "cartel party" thesis holds that major parties around the world are increasingly able to sustain their positions through state support, to place control of electoral processes in the hands of partisan functionaries, and to engage in collusive behavior with one another.[30]

9. *Electoral Fraud.* Most people intuitively sense that an accurate count of votes is the sine qua non of interpreting the outcome as a popular reward or a popular punishment. One threat to an accurate count is fraud, or intentional manipulation. Classic strategies include registering fictitious, deceased, or otherwise ineligible voters; using "repeaters" to vote more than once; imprisoning eligible voters and releasing them after the polls are closed; physically blocking eligible voters from leaving home or entering a polling station; administratively purging eligible voters from voting lists; bribing or intimidating eligible voters before they cast their ballots; and tampering with ballots or otherwise miscounting them after they are cast. These techniques have been confirmed in the USA in both the nineteenth and twentieth centuries. Twenty-first-century cases of fraud have attracted attention in places as varied as Argentina, Germany, Mexico, Russia, Spain, Taiwan, the UK, and Ukraine. A centralized and professionalized electoral administration is therefore taken for granted as a prerequisite for clean elections by scholars, whereas the decentralized electoral bureaucracies in many of the less wealthy

---

[30]On hyper-partisan primaries in the USA: Jacobs and Shapiro (2000, 32–36), Lee et al. (2004), and Masket and Noel (2012). On partisan districting: Thompson (2004, 52–55). On "cartel parties" outside the USA: Katz and Mair (2009).

democracies, plus the American states, are notoriously partisan, under-paid, and under-trained.[31]

10. *Electoral Inaccuracy.* Basic facts of life mean that there are no definitive technical solutions to the problem of inaccurate electoral results—whether intentionally inaccurate (via fraud) or unintentionally so. Studies of elections in the USA suggest that voter error in any given election accounts for 1.5–2.5% of the total vote. It is well known that certain types of ballot yield lower rates of voter error than others, and that optical-scan (fill-in-the-bubble) ballots are superior in ensuring voter accuracy and leaving a paper trail in case of audits or recounts. Computer touch-screen technology promises lower error rates, but at the cost of lower recountability and higher vulnerability to hacking. Political scientists, journalists, and citizens alike have come around to the concept of recountability, or the capacity of electoral machinery to have its results publicly verified, as an essential operational component of electoral accountability. Yet computer touch-screens, the least recountable technology available, have proliferated in some jurisdictions.[32]

WHERE NEXT FOR ACCOUNTABILITY?

Put together, these ten possible routes to failure for electoral accountability may explain the weak-to-middling evidence that academic research has found for elections' causal connection to flourishing economies, reduced corruption, and representative policy-making. Each of the ten, however, also implies converse preconditions for success—a to-do list for would-be reformers and democratizers. Theoretically, the components of electoral structure (see Fig. 1.1) should also be relevant, but they do not feature heavily in our top ten list because research has not found compelling differences between, for example, proportional representation (PR) and single-seat plurality (SSP) electoral systems on questions

---

[31] On electoral fraud in the USA, yesterday and today: Argersinger (1985) and Campbell (2005). On Russia and Ukraine: Myagkov et al. (2009). On various other countries: Lehoucq (2003, 237–45). On independent and professional administrative bodies: Hartlyn et al. (2008), Kropf and Kimball (2012), and Norris (2017).

[32] For average error rates: Stewart (2010, 372). On the superiority of optical-scan systems: Saltman (2006, 189). On the vulnerability of touch-screen systems to fraud: Herrnson et al. (2008, 111–12) and Jones and Simons (2012, 153–54, 331). On the lack of a paper trail: Stewart (2010, 359, 364, 367–68).

of accountability. Though some theories expect SSP to make it easier to identify those responsible for bad policy, the congruence and responsiveness that should result from placing effective sanctions in voters' hands often seem stronger in PR (multi-seat) systems. Altering contest structure alone to raise or lower the numbers of seats filled is not, therefore, a promising strategy for boosting accountability.[33]

The traditional academic emphasis on contest structure is a distraction from the equally important factor of ballot structure. Voting for a single party list in a multi-winner contest, in most democracies, still relies on a single mark to input a voter's judgment, so that ballot structure remains the same even as contest structure varies. Since PR and SSP seem equally bad at rendering governments accountable to voters, could the one-mark ballot (1MB) structure that they have in common be at fault, leaving the alternatives to 1MB as potential solutions? The rest of this book will explore these crucial but neglected questions.

Before we proceed, however, it is worth pondering what is at stake in a democratic theory of election reform which responds to electoral skepticism. After all, some responses to the uncomfortable reality of accountability deficits would not require reforming elections or their surrounding institutions to strengthen democracy. There are options on the table for *non-electoral* accountability.

First, it is theoretically possible for a society to bring customary or informal pressures to bear on authority figures—not only elected representatives but also unelected judges, police, teachers, parents, etc.—to encourage responsive or responsible uses of their power. Some political theorists argue that the adversarial and punitive character of the sanctioning type of accountability is counter-productive, anyway, and that designing institutions to select benevolent leaders (then trusting them to govern well) is the main task at hand.[34]

A second response might notice that unelected police, teachers, and parents already face incentives to exercise authority beneficently because of punishment through the legal system, not the electoral system. Another substitute for electoral accountability, then, would bring governmental officers more deeply into the legal regime of sanctions,

---

[33]For the conclusion that PR and SSP are equally limited on accountability: Franklin et al. (2014, 395–96). For mixed findings about congruence (depending on how it is defined) in single-seat vs. multi-seat systems: Golder and Ferland (2018).

[34]Mansbridge (2009, 2014).

in effect reducing the scope of immunity or privilege for office-holders. If the criminal-justice system can deter corrupt police and abusive guardians, expanding the criminal code to cover bad governance would let courts (judges and, in some jurisdictions, juries) do the job of sanctioning political representatives.

As a third response, unique forums of non-electoral accountability outside the legal system may be appropriate for politicians. Instead of a new set of legal strictures, imagine a new set of political institutions specifically tailored to activate citizens' evaluative, sanctioning judgments. Ancient Athenians, classical Romans, and colonial New Englanders, for example, occasionally subjected political leaders to trials and audits—political affairs in which the expertise of lawyers and judges was not required for the people to punish official malfeasance. With techniques of random selection and representative sampling, new kinds of civic assemblies, political not legal juries, could hold powers of accountability on behalf of their fellow citizens.[35]

These non-electoral reforms might allow elections to play a narrower role in democratic life that has traditionally been demanded, unburdening them of the job of reducing the democratic deficits of our times. But periodic competitive elections are the traditional bedrock of modern democracy—and the neglect of ballot structure means that it may be an arena of fixable flaws. Key called the voters' voice "loud but indistinct," noting that "the vocabulary of the voice of the people consists mainly of the words 'yes' and 'no'; and at times one cannot be certain which word is being uttered." More recent scholars have stressed that votes are too "blunt" to be instruments of popular control in the complex arena of modern politics. This all-pervading assumption that ballots are crude, blunt, and clumsy—is it a cast-iron fact of life, an axiom of electoral mathematics, an empirically rock-solid observation? Or is it an assumption based on taking certain kinds of ballot structure as given, thereby ignoring or under-valuing other types of ballot?[36]

We should take seriously the possibility that voting is associated with a blunt form of power because we tend to use one type of tool rather than another to vote with. If 1MB voting is the source of bluntness, other

[35] McCormick (2006), Maloy (2008, 187–189), and Chwalisz (2015, 38–55).
[36] Quotations at Key (1961b, 487; 1964, 544). For bluntness: Manin et al. (1999a, 45–46, 50–51), O'Donnell (2003, 48–49), and Przeworski (2018, 97).

ballot structures may be sharper, or smarter. Trying to salvage the very idea of electoral accountability—that peculiar marriage of the voting mechanism with the sanctioning mode of power—may be worth another throw of the dice before the non-electoral options are seized on as a last resort. I am going to make that throw in the remainder of this book, but readers will have to judge at the end of it whether the right numbers have come up.

References

Achen, C., & L.M. Bartels. 2016. *Democracy for Realists.* Princeton: Princeton University Press.

Alcaniz, I., & T. Hellwig. 2011. "Who's to Blame? The Distribution of Responsibility in Developing Democracies." *British Journal of Political Science* 41: 389–411.

Anderson, C.J. 2007. "The End of Economic Voting? Contingency Dilemmas and the Limits of Accountability." *Annual Review of Political Science* 10: 271–96.

Argersinger, P.H. 1985. "New Perspectives on Election Fraud in the Gilded Age." *Political Science Quarterly* 100: 669–87.

Arnold, R.D. 2004. *Congress, the Press, and Political Accountability.* Princeton: Princeton University Press.

Bartels, L.M. 2016. "Elections in America." *Annals of the American Academy of Political and Social Science* 667: 36–49.

Bovens, M. 2005. "Public Accountability." *The Oxford Handbook of Public Management,* eds. E. Ferlie, L.E. Lynn, & C. Pollitt. New York: Oxford University Press.

Brown, A.R. 2010. "Are Governors Responsible for the State Economy? Partisanship, Blame, and Divided Federalism." *Journal of Politics* 73: 605–15.

Campbell, T. 2005. *Deliver the Vote: A History of Election Fraud, an American Political Tradition, 1742–2004.* New York: Avalon.

Canes-Wrone, B. 2015. "From Mass Preferences to Policy." *Annual Review of Political Science* 18: 147–65.

Cheibub, J.A., & A. Przeworski. 1999. "Democracy, Elections, and Accountability for Outcomes." *Democracy, Accountability, and Representation,* eds. A. Przeworski, S.C. Stokes, & B. Manin. New York: Cambridge University Press.

Chwalisz, C. 2015. *The Populist Signal: Why Politics and Democracy Need to Change.* Lanham, MD: Rowman & Littlefield.

Claassen, R.L., & B. Highton. 2006. "Does Policy Debate Reduce Information Effects in Public Opinion? Analyzing the Evolution of Public Opinion on Health Care." *Journal of Politics* 68: 410–20.

Crisp, B.F., S. Olivella, J.D. Potter, & W. Mishler. 2014. "Elections as Instruments for Punishing Bad Representatives and Selecting Good Ones." *Electoral Studies* 34: 1–15.

De Vries, C.E., & H. Solaz. 2017. "The Electoral Consequences of Corruption." *Annual Review of Political Science* 20: 391–408.

Duch, R.M., & R.T. Stevenson. 2008. *The Economic Vote: How Political and Economic Institutions Condition Election Results.* New York: Cambridge University Press.

Fearon, J.D. 1999. "Electoral Accountability and the Control of Politicians." *Democracy, Accountability, and Representation*, eds. A. Przeworski, S.C. Stokes, & B. Manin. New York: Cambridge University Press.

Fellowes, M.C., & P.J. Wolf. 2004. "Funding Mechanisms and Policy Instruments: How Business Campaign Contributions Influence Congressional Votes." *Political Research Quarterly* 57: 315–24.

Ferguson, T., P. Jorgensen, & J. Chen. 2013. "Party Competition and Industrial Structure in the 2012 Elections: Who's Really Driving the Taxi to the Dark Side?" *International Journal of Political Economy* 42: 3–41.

Fiorina, M.P. 1981. *Retrospective Voting in American National Elections.* New Haven: Yale University Press.

Franklin, M.N., S.N. Soroka, & C. Wlezien. 2014. "Elections." *The Oxford Handbook of Public Accountability*, eds. M. Bovens, R.E. Goodin, & T. Schillemans. Oxford: Oxford University Press.

Gelineau, F., & K.L. Remmer. 2005. "Political Decentralization and Electoral Accountability: The Argentine Experience, 1983–2001." *British Journal of Political Science* 36: 133–57.

Golder, M., & B. Ferland. 2018. "Electoral Systems and Citizen-Elite Ideological Congruence." *The Oxford Handbook of Electoral Systems*, eds. E.S. Herron, R.J. Pekkanen, & M.S. Shugart. Oxford: Oxford University Press.

Hamilton, A., J. Madison, & J. Jay. 2005 (1788). *The Federalist*, ed. J.R. Pole. Indianapolis: Hackett.

Hamm, K.E., & R.E. Hogan. 2008. "Campaign-Finance Laws and Candidacy Decisions in State Legislative Elections." *Political Research Quarterly* 61: 458–67.

Hardin, R. 2000. "Democratic Epistemology and Accountability." *Social Philosophy and Policy* 17: 110–26.

Hartlyn, J., J. McCoy, & T.M. Mustillo. 2008. "Electoral Governance Matters: Explaining the Quality of Elections in Contemporary Latin America." *Comparative Political Studies* 41: 73–98.

Healy, A., & N. Malhotra. 2013. "Retrospective Voting Reconsidered." *Annual Review of Political Science* 16: 285–306.

Hellwig, T., E. Ringsmuth, & J.R. Freeman. 2008. "The American Public and the Room to Maneuver: Responsibility Attributions and Policy Efficacy in an Era of Globalization." *International Studies Quarterly* 52: 855–80.

Herrnson, P.S., R.G. Niemi, M.J. Hanmer, B.B. Bederson, F.C. Conrad, & M.W. Traugott. 2008. *Voting Technology: The Not So Simple Act of Casting a Ballot*. Washington, DC: Brookings Institution.

Hogan, R.E. 2004. "Challenger Emergence, Incumbent Success, and Electoral Accountability in State Legislative Elections." *Journal of Politics* 66: 1283–303.

Huber, G.A., S.J. Hill, & G.S. Lenz. 2012. "Sources of Bias in Retrospective Decision-Making: Experimental Evidence on Voters' Limitations in Controlling Incumbents." *American Political Science Review* 106: 720–41.

Jacobs, L.R., & R.Y. Shapiro. 2000. *Politicians Don't Pander: Political Manipulation and the Loss of Democratic Responsiveness*. Chicago: University of Chicago Press.

Jamieson, K.H., & J.N. Cappella. 2008. *The Echo Chamber: Rush Limbaugh and the Conservative Media Establishment*. New York: Oxford University Press.

Jones, D.W., & B. Simons. 2012. *Broken Ballots: Will Your Vote Count?* Stanford: CSLI Publications.

Katz, R.S., & P. Mair. 2009. "The Cartel Party Thesis: A Restatement." *Perspectives on Politics* 7: 753–66.

Key, V.O. 1961a. *Public Opinion and American Democracy*. New York: Knopf.

Key, V.O. 1961b. "Public Opinion and the Decay of Democracy." *Virginia Quarterly Review* 37: 481–94.

Key, V.O. 1964. *Politics, Parties, and Pressure Groups*. 5th edn. New York: T. Crowell.

Key, V.O. 1966. *The Responsible Electorate: Rationality in Presidential Voting, 1936–60*, ed. M.C. Cummings. Cambridge, MA: Harvard University Press.

Kropf, M., & D.C. Kimball. 2012. *Helping America Vote: The Limits of Election Reform*. New York: Routledge.

Lamis, A.P. 2008. "Key, V.O., Jr." *International Encyclopedia of the Social Sciences*, ed. W.A. Darity. Vol. 4. 2nd edn. Detroit: Macmillan Reference.

LeDuc, L., & J.H. Pammett. 2013. "The Fate of Governing Parties in Times of Economic Crisis." *Electoral Studies* 32: 494–99.

Lee, D.S., E. Moretti, & M.J. Butler. 2004. "Do Voters Affect or Elect Policies? Evidence from the U.S. House." *Quarterly Journal of Economics* 119: 807–59.

Lehoucq, F. 2003. "Electoral Fraud: Cases, Types, and Consequences." *Annual Review of Political Science* 6: 233–56.

Maloy, J.S. 2008. *The Colonial American Origins of Modern Democratic Thought*. New York: Cambridge University Press.

Maloy, J.S. 2014. "Linkages of Electoral Accountability: Empirical Results and Methodological Lessons." *Politics and Governance* 2.2: 13–27.

Maloy, J.S. 2015. "Intermediate Conditions of Democratic Accountability: A Response to Electoral Skepticism." *Politics and Governance* 3.2: 76–89.

Manin, B. 1997. *The Principles of Representative Government*. New York: Cambridge University Press.

Manin, B., A. Przeworski, & S.C. Stokes. 1999a. "Elections and Representation." *Democracy, Accountability, and Representation*, eds. A. Przeworski, S.C. Stokes, & B. Manin. New York: Cambridge University Press.

Manin, B., A. Przeworski, & S.C. Stokes. 1999b. "Introduction." *Democracy, Accountability, and Representation*, eds. A. Przeworski, S.C. Stokes, & B. Manin. New York: Cambridge University Press.

Mansbridge, J. 2009. "A Selection Model of Political Representation." *Journal of Political Philosophy* 17: 369–98.

Mansbridge, J. 2014. "A Contingency Theory of Accountability." *The Oxford Handbook of Public Accountability*, eds. M. Bovens, R.E. Goodin, & T. Schillemans. Oxford: Oxford University Press.

Maravall, J.M. 1999. "Accountability and Manipulation." *Democracy, Accountability, and Representation*, eds. A. Przeworski, S.C. Stokes, & B. Manin. New York: Cambridge University Press.

Maravall, J.M. 2010. "Accountability in Coalition Governments." *Annual Review of Political Science* 13: 81–100.

Masket, S.E., & H. Noel. 2012. "Serving Two Masters: Using Referenda to Assess Partisan versus Dyadic Legislative Representation." *Political Research Quarterly* 65: 104–23.

Mayhew, D.R. 1974. *Congress: The Electoral Connection*. New Haven: Yale University Press.

McCormick, J.P. 2006. "Contain the Wealthy and Patrol the Magistrates: Restoring Elite Accountability to Popular Government." *American Political Science Review* 100: 147–63.

McMillan, J., & P. Zoido. 2004. "How to Subvert Democracy: Montesinos in Peru." *Journal of Economic Perspectives* 18.4: 69–92.

Myagkov, M., P.C. Ordeshook, & D. Shakin. 2009. *The Forensics of Election Fraud: Russia and Ukraine*. Cambridge, UK: Cambridge University Press.

Norpoth, H. 2001. "Divided Government and Economic Voting." *Journal of Politics* 63: 413–35.

Norris, P. 2017. *Why American Elections Are Flawed (and How to Fix Them)*. Ithaca, NY: Cornell University Press.

O'Donnell, G. 2003. "Horizontal Accountability: The Legal Institutionalization of Mistrust." *Democratic Accountability in Latin America*, eds. S. Mainwaring & C. Welna. New York: Oxford University Press.

Paine, T. 2003. *Common Sense, Rights of Man, and Other Essential Writings*. New York: Signet Classics.

Pereira, C., M.A. Melo, & C.M. Figueiredo. 2009. "The Corruption-Enhancing Role of Re-election Incentives? Counter-Intuitive Evidence from Brazil's Audit Reports." *Political Research Quarterly* 62: 731–44.

Powell, G.B. 2000. *Elections as Instruments of Democracy: Majoritarian and Proportional Visions*. New Haven: Yale University Press.

Powell, G.B., & G.D. Whitten. 1993. "A Cross-National Analysis of Economic Voting." *American Journal of Political Science* 37: 391–414.

Prior, M. 2007. *Post-broadcast Democracy: How Media Choice Increases Inequality in Political Involvement and Polarizes Elections.* New York: Cambridge University Press.

Przeworski, A. 2018. *Why Bother with Elections?* Cambridge, UK: Polity.

Saltman, R.G. 2006. *The History and Politics of Voting Technology.* New York: Palgrave Macmillan.

Snyder, J.M., & D. Stromberg. 2010. "Press Coverage and Political Accountability." *Journal of Political Economy* 118: 355–408.

Stewart, C. 2010. "Voting Technologies." *Annual Review of Political Science* 14: 353–78.

Stimson, J.A. 1999. "Party Government and Responsiveness." *Democracy, Accountability, and Representation,* eds. A. Przeworski, S.C. Stokes, & B. Manin. New York: Cambridge University Press.

Stokes, S.C. 1999. "What Do Policy Switches Tell Us about Democracy?" *Democracy, Accountability, and Representation,* eds. A. Przeworski, S.C. Stokes, & B. Manin. New York: Cambridge University Press.

Thompson, D.F. 2004. *Restoring Responsibility.* New York: Cambridge University Press.

Tsai, L.L. 2007. *Accountability without Democracy: Solidary Groups and Public Goods Provision in Rural China.* New York: Cambridge University Press.

VandeHei, J., & M.A. Fletcher. 2005. "Bush Says Election Ratified Iraq Policy." *Washington Post,* January 16.

Wattenberg, M.P. 1991. *The Rise of Candidate-Centered Politics: Presidential Elections of the 1980s.* Cambridge, MA: Harvard University Press.

CHAPTER 3

What Research Overlooks: Voters' Dilemma of Disempowerment

The 1900 presidential campaign was greeted by the American public with unusual levels of despair and consternation. The contest between W. J. Bryan for the Democrats and William McKinley for the Republicans offered up the same major-party candidates that had competed in the previous election, in 1896. Since then, the only other time that such a repeat match-up has occurred was when Adlai Stevenson made a second run against Dwight Eisenhower in 1956. Both these rematches in American history were won by the incumbent; in 1900, that was McKinley.

Despite resulting in a successful re-election bid, the 1900 outcome could hardly count as an endorsement of the Republican administration's conduct in office. The two main candidates differed on two big issues, monetary policy and foreign policy. Bryan was in favor of adding silver to the money supply and was staunchly opposed to American intervention in Philippines; McKinley pledged his faith to the gold standard while making the case for territorial expansion in Asia and the Caribbean in the wake of the Spanish-American War. According to contemporary accounts, most Americans were against Bryan's silver money but also against McKinley's imperialism. The problem, then, was the absence of any viable candidate on the ballot who occupied this position in a two-dimensional space (see Fig. 3.1). As a result, newspapers openly mocked the available options, characterizing the voters' task as "a choice between evils." It got so bad for former president Grover Cleveland that

© The Author(s) 2019   51
J. S. Maloy, *Smarter Ballots*, Elections, Voting, Technology,
https://doi.org/10.1007/978-3-030-13031-2_3

| MONETARY | FOREIGN POLICY | |
POLICY	pro-expansionist	anti-imperialist
pro-silver	[few voters, no viable candidates]	W.J. Bryan (challenger)
pro-gold	W. McKinley (incumbent)	[many voters, no viable candidates]

Fig. 3.1 Issue space in the 1900 US presidential election (*Source* Bailey [1937])

he decided, according to a reporter, to go duck-hunting on election day rather than getting bogged down in the voting booth.[1]

This was a classic case of voting for the lesser of two evils. Indeed, 1900 may have been the moment when the language of "lesser evil" elections first entered the American political lexicon. Some Republicans who opposed imperialism reluctantly cast their ballots for Bryan on that basis, and more Democrats who opposed silver crossed over to McKinley. When the votes were counted, McKinley had more—but no one could decipher the meaning of that numeric fact. The limited range of ballot options, with neither holding wide appeal, made it difficult to tell whether 1900 had seen a pro-accountability result for McKinley or a false-positive result. The incumbent, in other words, may have benefitted less from voters' evaluations of his performance than from a restrictive contest structure that happened to favor him under the circumstances prevailing on election day. Such ambiguous and disempowering results are the looming, concrete realities that underlie the quantitative results from big-data analyses in academic research. The school of electoral skepticism may be relatively young in political science, but it is old in human experience.

[1] Bailey (1937).

To make matters worse, the lesser-evil problem coexists with another electoral dynamic that also tends to spoil accountability. "Vote-splitting" describes a situation, in the words of the International IDEA (Institute for Democracy and Election Assistance), "where two similar parties or candidates split their combined vote between them, thus allowing a less popular [party or] candidate to win." The vote-splitting problem therefore creates a second difficulty that hampers any effort to address the first one, since normally a plentiful supply of options would be an obvious way to avoid the lesser-evil problem. Together these two problems create a dilemma of disempowerment for voters, partially explaining where the discouraging research findings about electoral accountability come from. Contrary to vote-splitting, lesser evils thrive in environments with restricted options—as voters in the UK and the USA were reminded in 2016.[2]

The Evils of Brexit and Trump

The ballot structure that was put before the British people in June 2016 could not have been simpler. There was one contest to be decided, a referendum proposition phrased as a question in a single complete sentence: "Should the United Kingdom remain a member of the European Union or leave the European Union?" There were two options, and only one mark was allowed to indicate the voter's answer.

Yet simplicity can be carried to such an extreme that it ceases to be a virtue. The previous year's referendum in Greece, on accepting or rejecting an international bail-out package for the nation's public debt, was billed as a decisive vote with crucial implications for Greeks' status within the Euro currency zone. Similarly, Britain's choice between "Remain" and "Leave" with respect to the European Union (EU) offered plenty of vagueness with its simplicity. In both cases, there was widespread confusion about what the likely consequences would be of one result or the other, economically and politically. In Britain, the stark, binary choice between two options left considerable doubt in the minds of voters about the "what next?" question. Some people who had a similar goal in mind, such as increasing funds for public-health services,

---

[2] Quotation at Reynolds et al. (2005, 53).

placed themselves on opposite sides of the referendum question because of disputes over the best means to achieve that end.[3]

Some observers suggested that neither option on the Brexit ballot was likely to make significant inroads on Britain's most pressing problems. Consider George Monbiot:

> The European Union is a festering cesspool of undue influence and opaque lobbying. ... By comparison to the British system, however, this noxious sewer is a crystal spring. Every stream of corporate effluent with which the EU poisons political life has a more malodorous counterpart in the United Kingdom. ... We do not release ourselves from the power of money by leaving the EU. We just exchange one version for another: another that is even worse. This is not an inspiring position from which to vote Remain. But it is a coherent one.

The reasoning here offers a poignant illustration of the "lesser of two evils" horn of the dilemma. Such a choice can only be made with nostrils closed against the "noxious" and "malodorous" options on offer.[4]

The classic expression of the lesser-evil logic can be found in Niccolo Machiavelli's *Prince* (1519), where he advised that "prudence consists in knowing how to assess risks and in accepting the lesser evil as a good." Accordingly, Machiavelli counselled leaders and citizens to harden their hearts and steel their stomachs in an imperfect world, whenever circumstances conspire against us—sound, realistic advice. The lesser-evil problem in voting, however, has a different complexion because electoral structure is neither a force of nature nor a function of blind chance. Electoral institutions are human artifacts, to some extent the products of design and choice. Whenever our elections hand us a lesser-evil dilemma, or many such dilemmas in repetitious fashion over time, we can realistically consider changing the process.[5]

Consider the 2016 presidential election in the USA. In most of the 51 separate contests (one in each state plus the capital district), unlike on the Brexit ballot, there were more than two options for the office of president: Gary Johnson of the Libertarian Party and Jill Stein of the Green Party were the most likely third and fourth options to be

---

[3] Jenkins (2017).
[4] Monbiot (2016).
[5] Quotation at Machiavelli (1994, 70).

presented on a given state's ballot. Yet media coverage of public debates, reinforced by the winner-take-all system by which state-level outcomes are translated into Electoral College votes, naturally led most voters to treat presidential ballots like Brexit ballots. They saw only two viable options, and many voters felt that they could only pick the least bad between them. This absence of adequate alternatives violated the first principle of voter empowerment.

Who defines "adequate alternatives"? A litany of pre-election polls in 2016 demonstrated the extent to which American voters saw their task as choosing the lesser of two evils. The "unfavorable" ratings for the two major candidates both exceeded 50%, and both had "highly unfavorable" ratings well in excess of historically disliked candidates (see Fig. 3.2). Roughly half of Hillary Clinton's and Donald Trump's supporters described their votes as "against" their candidate's opponent rather than as "for" their candidate (see Fig. 3.3). The incidence of what political scientists call "negative partisanship," a condition in which citizens "dislike the opposing party and its leaders more than they like their own

Candidate (Party), Year	Unfavorable	Highly Unfavorable
H. Clinton (D), 2016	13	39
Trump (R), 2016	19	42
Obama (D), 2012	13	24
Romney (R), 2012	21	22
Obama (D), 2008	13	22
McCain (R), 2008	15	20
Kerry (D), 2004	18	22
G.W. Bush (R), 2004	16	23
W. Clinton (D), 1992	18	15
G.H.W. Bush (R) 1992	24	16
Mondale (D), 1984	19	15
Reagan (R), 1984	12	18
Carter (D), 1980	15	17
Reagan (R), 1980	21	16
Carter (D), 1976	11	5
Ford (R), 1976	11	9

N.B. Data were unavailable for 1988, 1996, and 2000.

Fig. 3.2 Unfavorability ratings of US presidential candidates, 1976–2016 (*Source* Gallup [2016])

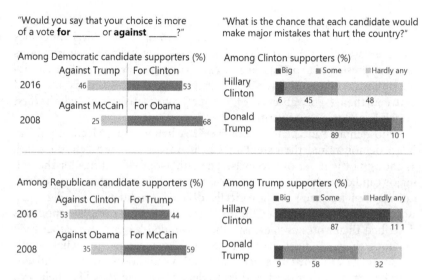

Fig. 3.3 Lesser-evil sentiment in the 2016 US presidential election (*Source* Pew [2016b])

party and its leaders," was measured at record-high levels in the 2016 election. Perhaps most telling were voters' expectations of whether their favored candidate would "make major mistakes that hurt the country." While high proportions of both Clinton's and Trump's supporters naturally called their candidate's rival "very" likely to make major mistakes in office, 45% of Clinton's and 58% of Trump's supporters considered their *own* candidate "somewhat" likely to do so.[6]

To put it another way, when Trump won the election, more than two thirds of his own voters were reasonably afraid that disaster might ensue—on top of nine out of ten of his opponent's voters. This level of fear and loathing would have been only mildly attenuated by a Clinton victory, since fewer than half of her voters were confident that their preferred candidate would avoid major mistakes. That appears to fit the extreme case of a lesser-evil election: The voters are confronted with such poor choices that a majority of them fear the very candidate whom they are supporting.

[6]On negative partisanship in 2016: Abramowitz and McCoy (2019, 146–47; quotation at 146).

Beyond American and British shores, the presidential election in France in 2017 at one point appeared to be headed for a "lesser of three evils" dynamic. When pollsters gathered early unfavorability ratings for the best-known candidates from the top three parties, Francois Hollande, the incumbent Socialist president, scored 73%; Nicolas Sarkozy, a former Republican president, stood at 66%; and Marine Le Pen, the leader of the National Front, received 63%. As it turned out, only Le Pen among these three managed to secure her party's nomination, and she indeed advanced to the second round of voting to face off against a relative newcomer: Emmanuel Macron. Voter turnout took a nose-dive as some sections of French society bemoaned a fresh lesser-evil choice: between a morally questionable nationalism, offering change in the wrong direction on social issues, and a politically inexperienced globalism, offering change in the wrong direction on economic issues.[7]

The lesser-evil problem violates the criterion of adequate alternatives in an obvious way, but it also impedes effective sanctions—implicating not only the first but also the second principle of voter empowerment (see Chapter 1). A higher number of alternatives on the ballot means a higher probability that at least one will be found acceptable to an anti-incumbent voter. But lesser-evil elections between only two or three poor options offer a "forced choice," in the words of Dennis Thompson, raising the likelihood of false positives, or electoral rewards for unpopular incumbents.[8]

What is "evil" about a lesser-evil contest is not the outcome per se. In certain ideological respects, the Trump and Macron victories represented opposite outcomes; and making the national vote for Clinton authoritative, rather than Trump's Electoral College win, would not have changed the underlying lesser-evil dynamic. From the perspective of electoral realism, outcomes matter little; structures are all-important. Elections become systematically disempowering of ordinary citizens when their institutional structure tends to make lesser-evil choices a routine possibility.

---

[7] Barkin (2016) and Willsher (2017a, b).

[8] On the necessity of ample alternatives for accountability: Mitchell (2000, 346) and McGann (2006, 148–49; 2013, 100–3). For "forced choice": Thompson (2002, 70).

MORE AND MORE OF LESSER EVILS

There are two pressing questions about the lesser-evil problem to which democratic societies should demand answers from election experts. How often do voters actually face this sort of situation? What, if anything, can be done to make it less common? There is not as much published research out there as we would want, but the available evidence suggests an answer to the first question. The lesser-evil problem appears to be on the rise in the USA while remaining less of a concern in systems with multi-party (rather than two-party) competition.

The results of surveys in which American voters were asked about the favorability or unfavorability of major-party presidential candidates (see Fig. 3.2) present one pathway to visualizing lesser-evil trends. The "highly unfavorable" ratings of Clinton and Trump were well in excess of any other candidates in history, but perhaps the bigger story is that those negative ratings have been steadily rising for *all* candidates in recent decades. More and more voters with each passing electoral cycle seem to be utterly disgusted with at least one of the main candidates. Even outside the fevered context of a presidential year, survey data indicate that increasing numbers of Americans are driven by negative partisanship, in which dislike of opponents is stronger than positive affect for the politicians they end up supporting.[9]

While contributing to the problem, however, the negative feelings of extreme partisans cannot be the whole story. After all, an election does not contain *two* evils unless large numbers of voters feel that *both* major candidates are unacceptable. The unique dynamic created by this situation is the inevitability of a negative outcome and the muddying of the winner's mandate. As V. O. Key put it, "a candidate may win despite his tactics and appeals rather than because of them. If the people can choose only from among rascals, they are certain to choose a rascal." This certainty is what gives lesser-evil voting its hand-cuffing quality. The "highly unfavorable" ratings of candidates considered one at a time do not necessarily capture the same sense of inevitable disaster. We need a better measurement tool, one that fits a more precise definition of the problem.[10]

[9]On negative partisanship: Abramowitz and Webster (2016).
[10]Quotation at Key (1966, 3).

More than three decades after its publication, Stanley Kelley's *Interpreting Elections* (1983) remains the sole work produced by a political scientist which has tackled the lesser-evil problem head-on. Like Key before him, Kelley was fascinated by the dubious nature of winners' mandates, and he was addressing the lesser-evil question within a broader study of the meanings of American presidential outcomes. But his brief foray included a precise definition of a "lesser of evils" vote as one made when *both* major-party candidates are evaluated by the voter more negatively than positively. From 1952 to 1980, Kelley found that the percentage of presidential voters who met this condition rose significantly: from an average of 7.5% of all voters (in '52, '56, and '60) to 12.3% in 1964, and again to an average of 20.2% from 1968 to 1980. Kelley also found that the winning candidates in '68, '76, and '80 (Richard Nixon, Jimmy Carter, and Ronald Reagan, respectively) received more favorable than unfavorable mentions by fewer than 50% of all survey respondents.[11]

The 1980 presidential contest was a turning point. Notwithstanding the "landslide" Electoral College tally for Reagan over Carter, voters' negative assessments were unusually intense and more evenly distributed between the two candidates. Large swathes of both Reagan voters (43%) and Carter voters (37%) reported opposition to the other side as their primary motivation. Reagan received "highly favorable" ratings from only 23% of all voters, a record-low number for any winning candidate since such data first appeared. The 1980 election inspired several political-science studies of "anti-candidate voting." One such analysis put the number of all voters who were motivated by negative feelings against one of the candidates at 46%, even higher than Kelley's figures.[12]

The problem was conceptual and methodological, however. Anti-candidate voting was measured in terms of whether a vote was more "against" one candidate than "for" the alternative, whereas voters who had negative judgments about both options were excluded from consideration. Yet these missing voters are precisely the ones of greatest interest: those who were resigned to an unsatisfactory outcome in advance of voting. As the Reagan years passed, scholarly interest in anti-candidate voting subsided, but no better measures have since emerged to track systematically the kind of "forced choice" situation that seemed to arise in

---

[11]Kelley (1983, 37–38, 172n); see also Wattenberg (1991, 66, 72).

[12]Kelley (1983, 172–90). On anti-candidate voting in the 1980s: Gant and Sigelman (1985, 329, 332–33) and Sigelman and Gant (1989, 84).

multiple countries in 2016 and after. As a result, we do not have solid grounds for saying how frequently such situations actually occur. The closest available indicators for the USA (see Figs. 3.2 and 3.3), at least, suggest that the lesser-evil problem is not lessening but strengthening.

Outside the USA, most other democracies have more viable options on the ballot and therefore a lower likelihood, theoretically, that their voters get trapped between one bad option and a second that is even worse. But the likelihood is not nil, given the growing distrust and decaying partisan feeling found in democracies all over Europe. Lesser-evil voting, in short, is a phenomenon that has been waiting a long time for a sustained research agenda to pick it up. Empirical political science can help to measure what is going on in electoral systems across the world, but democratic theory is needed to help in identifying and constructing the relevant measurement tools—not to mention designing institutional responses to reduce lesser-evil pressures on voter empowerment.[13]

Ballot Options

Since lesser-evil contests implicate two aspects of voter empowerment, electoral institutions' impact on one may spill over to the other. Adequate alternatives, in other words, may be an enabling condition for strengthening effective sanctions.

One empirical proxy for the concept of adequate alternatives already exists in an established, cross-national measurement tool: the "effective number of parties," or ENP. When a democracy's ENP value is high, multiple parties have a realistic chance of gaining some share of power in the political system. Unrestrictive rules about ballot access and generous rules about public funding for parties and candidates can raise the odds that voters see plentiful alternatives on their ballots, but other institutional features are also important. The "ENP-Votes" and "ENP-Seats" values estimate, respectively, the number of serious or viable parties that are receiving support from voters and the number that are actually

---

[13]On partisan decomposition: Mair (2013, 31–33, 70–71, 78, 83). For a perceptive and promising approach to measuring "non-optimal" voting, which may be quite close to lesser-evil voting, in a global context: Singh (2014).

Country, Year	ENP-Votes	ENP-Seats
Australia, 2016	4.47	3.07
Canada, 2015	3.33	2.50
France, 2017	6.82	3.00
Germany, 2013	6.18	4.64
India, 2014	6.82	3.45
Ireland, 2016	6.57	4.93
Italy, 2013	5.33	3.47
Japan, 2012	4.22	2.48
Mexico, 2015	4.38	3.11
Russia, 2016	3.14	1.67
Spain, 2016	5.03	4.16
U.K., 2017	2.89	2.48
U.S.A., 2016	2.14	1.98

N.B. Values are from elections for the most numerous branch of the national legislature; in the U.S.A., for example, for the House but not the Senate. Countries using only single-seat contests for such branches, with no proportional representation, are in bold.

Fig. 3.4 Effective number of parties in recent elections worldwide (*Source* Gallagher [2018])

winning seats in the national legislature (for any given country in any given election year; see Fig. 3.4).[14]

What makes the difference between countries with more ballot options and those with fewer, apart from the direct effects of rules about ballot access and public funding? Maurice Duverger famously speculated in the 1950s that, whereas an electoral system rewarding only one winner per district should tend toward a two-party system, a system assigning many legislative seats per district in proportion to each party's share of votes should see multiple parties competing. Political scientists now

[14]Farrell (2011, 160).

call these two types of system single-seat plurality (SSP) and proportional representation (PR), respectively. Duverger's logic, also called the "psychological effect" of district magnitude, is that new parties can enter the legislature (and hope to grow thereafter) when they can realistically gain a small number of seats with a small share of votes. Voters under PR therefore tend to spread their support across many parties according to the varied preferences within society. The flip-side of the psychological effect for SSP is that support for smaller parties looks likely to lead to "wasted" votes. With only one winner possible in a non-proportional election, voters will anticipate the futility of a minor-party vote and gravitate toward the largest parties, causing all but the top two to die out. According to Duverger's logic, then, a higher district magnitude (i.e., the number of seats on offer) should cause higher ENP values compared to a district magnitude of one. Subsequent research has confirmed that, though ethnic and regional diversity within a country can raise the number of smaller identity parties even in single-seat districts (India being the most prominent example), PR does tend to give seats to more parties than SSP. In many democracies, political and ideological upheavals since the Great Recession of 2008 have added new parties to election campaigns, thereby raising the most recent ENP-V values above historical norms. All in all, ENP-S offers the more reliable and intuitive approximation of the number of ballot options that voters can consider viable or realistic contenders for power in any given electoral system.[15]

District magnitude is a core feature of contest structure (see Chapter 1), and the lesser-evil problem is usually a feature of single-winner contests. The Brexit and Trump votes of 2016 were of this type: PR was not applicable because there could be only a single winner. In countries with single-seat districts and relatively low ENP values, new rules might help to lower the probability of lesser-evil elections by raising the number of ballot options. The ENP-S measure could then be a tool for monitoring changes in ballot options over time. Canada, Japan, the UK, and the USA all have two-and-a-half or fewer "effective" parties nationally, making them most prone to lesser-evil choices. (Russia has an even lower ENP-V value than these countries, but significant levels of governmental repression of political dissent make it difficult to isolate the electoral system's effects

---

[15]On Duverger's theses: Riker (1982) and Singer (2013).

there.) Australia, France, and Mexico are hovering around an ENP-V value of 3, making it likely that many individual districts are prone to lesser-evil choices, or else simply uncompetitive.

Though the USA's two-party system presents a hard case for reforms targeting lesser-evil choices, some states there employ an unusual contest structure which tends to increase the supply of alternatives for voters to choose from. This model involves a two-round system (2RS) with a "jungle" or "top two" primary. Most American states' primary elections are narrowly partisan affairs in which one nominee is selected for each seat that the two major parties plan to contest. A tiny fraction of the electorate (usually party members of the most activist type) actually votes in such contests, and the single Democrat and the single Republican who obtain plurality wins from their co-partisans then appear on the general ballot at a later date. But the states of California, Louisiana, and Washington (for certain contests) offer all voters the chance to participate in a primary open to all candidates from all parties and from no party. Every voter casts one vote, and the top two vote-getters advance to the second-round election, regardless of their party affiliation. There is no guarantee that one Democrat and one Republican will comprise the last two options in the second-round contest.

The states of California and Washington adopted their "top two" primaries relatively recently, but Louisiana has had its "jungle" primaries for several decades. A comparison with the French 2RS shows a similar breadth of ballot options but a difference of party labels. In France, where it is common to find ten or more candidates running for president in the first round, each candidate must have a unique party affiliation. Creating a new party around any particular candidate and securing a line on the ballot are relatively easy, as Macron showed when he won in 2017 as the nominee of a party created in 2016. In America's jungle-primary states, by contrast, voters typically encounter two, three, or four different Democrats and similar numbers of Republicans on the jungle ballot, in addition to some independents and minor-party candidates. The outcome rules are exactly the same in both systems: The top two vote-getters advance to the run-off election. In California, Louisiana, and Washington, but not in France, it is logically possible for the second round to pit two candidates from the same party against one another.

The jungle primary strikes some observers as odd in its by-passing of exclusive nominations to a final-round ballot and, consequently, the possibility of an intra-party face-off there. From the perspective of voter empowerment, however, the jungle primary offers a distinct benefit for a rigidly two-party context. This particular contest structure creates a high-stakes, high-visibility race in the first round which presents the largest range of voters (the whole electorate, with no partisan gatekeeping) with a relatively high number of ballot options. Other American contests tend to present smaller numbers of voters with larger numbers of options (in partisan primaries) or larger numbers of voters with smaller numbers of options (in general elections).[16]

This advantage is a serious one, for the sake of empowering voters with adequate alternatives. But of course there is another side of the coin with plentiful ballot supply. Is the vote-splitting problem the inevitable price to be paid for democracies that want to mitigate the lesser-evil problem through increasing ballot options?

VOTE-SPLITTING

The dangers of vote-splitting are obvious in any single-winner contest, and Americans are familiar with the related phenomenon of "spoiler" candidates in famous presidential elections. Woodrow Wilson benefitted from a split between Theodore Roosevelt and (the incumbent) W. H. Taft in 1912, when Wilson won with less than a majority of all votes cast. George Bush the younger became a minority winner in 2000 in a crazy contest in which, on the left, Ralph Nader's voters could have given victory to Al Gore in the states of Florida and New Hampshire; and, on the right, Pat Buchanan's voters could have made Bush the winner of Iowa, New Mexico, Oregon, and Wisconsin. British voters are also keenly aware of vote-splitting in their single-member parliamentary constituencies, as the Liberal Democrats and the Labour Party often fail to stop a plurality winner from the Conservatives, while the Conservatives and the UK Independence Party sometimes fail to stop a plurality winner

[16]On "top two" primaries in California: McGhee and Krimm (2012) and McGhee et al. (2014). In the tangled terminology of primary elections in the USA, "blanket" primaries provide plentiful ballot options for the first contest but then count candidates' vote totals only against their co-partisans, sending exactly one nominee from each party (potentially more than two) to the final round of voting. The main difference between "top two" and "jungle" is that the former always runs a second round even if one candidate gets majority support in the first, whereas the latter awards the seat to a first-round majority winner.

from the center-left. In the British election of 2017, according to the (possibly wishful) estimate of some Labour and Green Party politicians, vote-splitting on the left could have gifted over 100 constituencies to the victorious Tory government, which earned only 42% of all votes and just under half of all seats in Parliament.[17]

In response to such outcomes, the obvious response is to sing the praises of a rigid two-party system with fewer options on the ballot— leading back to lesser evils. This is the essence of the dilemma: Taking concrete steps to make one problem less likely mathematically makes the other problem more likely. To put this vicious trade-off in the terms of voter empowerment, the dilemma is between having the power to select a good government undermined (by a lesser-evil choice) and having the power to punish a bad government blown up (by vote-splitting). Is there no way out of the dilemma of disempowerment for voters?

Managing the number of options on the ballot cannot banish both problems at once, but perhaps other features of contest structure can be leveraged. One intuitive option is the two-round contest structure, with potentially many options on the first ballot (hence no lesser-evil choice) and only the top two (hence no vote-splitting) on the second ballot. Many single-winner elections in many jurisdictions around the world use 2RS. In a way, American presidential elections also resemble 2RS, albeit in an unusually drawn-out form, with a wide variety of candidates in a multi-tiered primary-election stage and only two viable candidates in the general election. Far from striking a blow for voter empowerment, however, the 2016 primary process made things look even more perverse.

Before winning the presidency with 46% of the *national vote*, Trump won the right to appear on the ballot by collecting an even smaller share (44.9%) of *his own party's support* in the primary elections. For comparative purposes, consider that Bernie Sanders won 43% of all votes in the Democratic Party primaries, in a failed effort at nomination, while Trump had received just 40% of all Republican votes when his last two rivals withdrew from the race in May.[18]

---

[17] For historical US presidential results: Berg-Andersson (2017). On vote-splitting in the UK in 2017: Lewis and Lucas (2017). On the relation between vote-splitting, fear of "wasted votes," and lesser-evil voting: Amy (2000, 17–18, 43).

[18] For vote totals from the Republican Party nominating process: Berg-Andersson (2017).

This plurality result on the Republican side was produced by vote-splitting among anti-Trump voters within the party. In the earliest primaries, in chronological order, Trump "won" New Hampshire with 35% of the vote, South Carolina with 33, Alabama with 43, Arkansas with 33, Georgia with 39, Massachusetts with 49, Tennessee with 39, Vermont with 32, Virginia with 35, Louisiana with 41, Michigan with 37, Mississippi with 47, Florida with 46, Illinois with 39, Missouri with 41, North Carolina with 40, and Arizona with 46. In the same period, he lost Oklahoma with 28%, Texas with 27, Idaho with 28, Ohio with 36, and Wisconsin with 35. He then won his first majority victories in a spate of northeastern states: his native New York plus Connecticut, Delaware, Maryland, Pennsylvania, and Rhode Island. These gave him the momentum to win Indiana with 53%, after which John Kasich and Ted Cruz stood down. Trump therefore profited from not only the lesser-evil dilemma (in the general election) but also the vote-splitting dilemma (in the nominating primaries).[19]

Collectively, the presidential primaries of 2016 presented a fascinating picture of the American political system in a cameo role as a European-style multi-party democracy. Among Cruz, Kasich, and Trump on the Republican side; between Clinton and Sanders on the Democratic side; and with Johnson claiming the Libertarian mantle and Stein that of the Greens, Americans discovered that there are as many as seven distinct parties in public opinion. Now consider a hypothetical scenario in which all seven of these leaders appeared on the presidential ballot in a jungle primary. If we assume that Stein's support gravitates toward Sanders on the basis of ideological affinity, a simplified but plausible way to imagine the result is to say that Clinton and Sanders would have finished first and second because they were splitting the left-wing vote only two ways, while Cruz, Kasich, Johnson, and Trump would have been splitting the right-wing vote four ways. If Clinton and Sanders had faced off in the second round, a sizeable plurality of American voters would still have regarded it as a one-party affair and a lesser-evil election.

[19]Berg-Andersson (2017).

DOUBLE TROUBLE

The Republican Party primaries in 2016 illustrate the double trouble of two-round systems: Vote-splitting in the first round can impose lesser-evil choices in the second. France and its former colony in Louisiana furnish additional examples of double trouble in more traditional two-round contests. All these examples provide depth to just how serious the dilemma of disempowerment can be.

France suffered a notable instance of vote-splitting in its presidential election of 2002, with more than a dozen candidates on the first-round ballot, including several who were identifiably left-wing in orientation. The leading center-left candidate, Lionel Jospin, finished the first round with less than 1% fewer votes than Jean-Marie Le Pen (father of Marine, his political heiress) of the National Front, an extreme right-wing party. Le Pen's second-place finish put him in a run-off contest against the center-right incumbent and first-round leader, Jacques Chirac. This was a classic case of vote-splitting within a two-round system: Spreading a lot of left-wing votes across many candidates in the first round resulted in no left-wingers in the run-off. As a result, tens of millions of left-of-center voters went into the decisive round with a choice between a more extreme and a more moderate right-wing candidate for chief executive of the nation. Remarkably, with 63% of all votes still up for grabs in the second round (Chirac had initially received 20% of votes to Le Pen's 17%), Le Pen barely managed to raise his share of the vote in the second round, to 18%. Chirac trounced him with an astonishing 82% of all votes, and voter turnout actually increased from 72% in the first round to 80% in the second round.[20]

It is obvious that the French left, as well as many centrists, turned out in force to give Chirac his landslide victory and to repudiate the National Front. It is also obvious that this second round was an extreme case of a lesser-evil vote. Referring to a corruption investigation against Chirac, which was on hold because of his immunity as the incumbent president, a motto circulated on French streets in 2002: "vote for the crook, not the fascist." Wittingly or not, this phrasing echoed that of thousands of bumper-stickers that had appeared in Louisiana during the 1991 election

---

[20]Farrell (2011, 50) and Miguet (2002).

for governor: "vote for the crook; it's important." Edwin Edwards had been indicted for corruption, but his second-round rival, David Duke, was a white supremacist and former grand wizard of the Ku Klux Klan. As in France nine years later, the campaign for "the crook" was successful.[21]

The 2RS scheme has the notable virtue, by winnowing down the field of candidates for the second round, of raising the probability that the final winner will have majority support (i.e., 50% plus one). But this system also proves that an abundant number of ballot options can make lesser-evil voting more likely in the second round as a result of vote-splitting in the first—as when Duke, ideologically a fringe candidate, managed to take second place in the first round of voting in 1991.

Lest we be lured into the assumption that the dilemma of disempowerment always afflicts left-wing voters, to the benefit of right-wing candidates, consider the 2015 edition of the Louisiana governor's race. Three Democrats, three Republicans, and three independents appeared on the jungle ballot in the first round: an admirably diverse menu of choice, by American standards. Because two of the Democrats were notably deficient in name recognition and campaign funding, whereas all the Republicans were potentially serious candidates, there was little doubt that the leading Democrat, John Bel Edwards, would make the run-off. The vote-splitting was happening on the right wing, among Scott Angelle, Jay Dardenne, and David Vitter. The one with his nose in front of the other two happened to be Vitter, despite a sex scandal swirling around him at the time. Supporters of Angelle and Dardenne then confronted a lesser-evil choice in the second round, with the weakest of the Republican candidates representing their side. As it turned out, Louisiana elected a Democratic governor in the run-off—in a jurisdiction where Republicans typically win more than 60% of votes in statewide races.

The alteration of contest structure that leads to 2RS or run-off elections, then, is not a solution to the dilemma of disempowerment; it may even make things worse. Insincere voting is fairly significant in French presidential elections, estimated at 15% of voters in a survey before the first round of the 2012 contest. Even then, vote-splitting remains a risk. The first of two rounds leads voters to think in terms of three

[21] On Duke vs. Edwards: Poundstone (2008, 20).

viable candidates for the two highest positions, and after guessing the likely identities of those three, they must decide which of their favorites (or least disliked) needs their vote less and which needs it more. Jospin in 2002 likely suffered the penalty for left-wing voters' wrong guesses about how many votes he needed to advance and which other candidate was most likely to take his place if he did not. Even the advantages of numerous options on the ballot lose some of their appeal when they are accompanied by vote-splitting.[22]

Horns of a Dilemma

Since one alteration of the contest structure, adding a second round of voting, cannot offer a way out of the dilemma of disempowerment, perhaps another alteration of contest structure can: holding elections with more than one winner per contest or multiple seats per legislative district.

Recent empirical studies, for instance, have shown that PR electoral systems with relatively high numbers of seats per contest are a key ingredient in structural complexes of "institutionalized popular inclusion," which tend to reduce elites' institutional room for maneuver vis-a-vis ordinary citizens. Proportionally constituted parliaments are accustomed to awarding a half-dozen or more parties with some legislative seats but no single party with a majority of all seats. Voters in such a scheme are supposed to seize on a healthy range of options, spreading their votes around with blissful immunity to the lesser-evil problem; at the same time, the award of seats proportionally to each party's vote-share is also supposed to alleviate vote-splitting concerns. The reason is that, even if no single party wins a majority, a governing coalition can be formed that collectively represents a majority. Coalition-building after the voters have their say should remove the problem of minority rule and the inability of a voting majority to remove an incumbent government.[23]

But theory and evidence tend to undermine the multi-seat solution to the dilemma of disempowerment. The inter-locking horns of

---

[22]On insincere and strategic voting in France: Blais et al. (2015, 433) and Hoyo (2018, 680–81).

[23]On PR as a component of "popular" more than "elite" democracies: Joshi et al. (2015, 2019).

vote-splitting and lesser-evil choices are found not only in SSP but also in PR electoral systems.

Even where voters are not picking a single winner per contest, the fear of vote-splitting, vote-wasting, and electoral spoilers can still find fertile ground. The prime reason is that, in a system where voters consider a single-party majority unlikely to emerge, a great deal is at stake for the largest (plurality) party in the wake of a PR election. Whether by formal rule or informal custom, the plurality party generally gets first option to act as *formateur*, or leader of a coalition government. This role naturally includes privileged access to most executive positions, including prime minister. Mathematically, the largest party also has less work to do to form a majority coalition than any other party. Because voters are aware of these advantages, especially the *formateur* role, there are bound to be anxieties about vote-splitting even in multi-seat contests. Casting a wasted vote for a small spoiler cannot give 100% of executive power to a voter's least favored party, but it can deprive a lesser-evil party of the opportunity to replace the worst option as *formateur*. This fear of vote-splitting under PR can have the same hand-cuffing effects as in a presidential poll, with the same adverse consequences for accountability.

Though no empirical studies of European elections have pursued the phenomenon of lesser-evil voting by name, plenty of evidence exists for the related phenomena of "insincere" and "strategic" voting, which can serve as proxies for the fear of vote-splitting. An analysis comparing voters in the USA and Mexico (single-seat) with voters in Israel and Netherlands (multi-seat) found no significant difference in the levels of insincere voting between the two types of contest structure. A survey of Dutch voters in 2002, after asking respondents to evaluate all the political parties on a 10-point scale, found almost 30% of them intending to vote for a party that was not their highest or tied-for-highest. As André Blais and Arianna Degan concluded after reviewing these and related analyses, "contrary to conventional wisdom, there is as much strategic voting under PR as under the plurality rule." The persistence of such psychological effects even in multi-seat elections might be related to the democratic deficits that helped to spawn populist upheavals after 2008. According to William Galston, European democracies before then generally exhibited "a duopoly of the center-left and the center-right that kept important issues off the public agenda"—a characterization that could apply to PR systems like Germany, Italy, Spain, and perhaps others. The duopolistic mind-set, of course, is at the heart of lesser-evil voting.[24]

Elections in Spain since the Great Recession help to illustrate the broader problem among Europe's proportional-parliamentary systems. Before 2008, Spanish politics appeared to be shifting toward a bipolar system, anchored by the center-left Socialist Worker Party and the center-right Popular Party. Both had been steadily increasing their vote-shares as supporters of smaller parties resorted more and more to "useful votes" and "fear votes"—particularly on the left, where such votes gravitated toward the Socialists in an effort to keep the Populars out of power. Once the full force of the financial crisis hit Spain, however, the popularity of the major parties plummeted in tandem. Given relatively easy access to the ballot, third and fourth parties—Podemos ("We Can") and Ciudadanos ("Citizens")—joined the fray and became overnight contenders. Parliamentary elections in late 2015 produced a massive loss for the incumbent Populars, but a widely scattered distribution of votes left no single party with a majority to form a government. When coalition negotiations broke down on all sides, new elections were held only six months later, in 2016. Yet the second outcome was little different from the first, with no majority winner, though a modest recovery by the incumbents enabled them to arrange a coalition. Though Spain's revitalized multi-party system, with ostensibly adequate alternatives from which to choose, gave voters the ability to reject the lesser-evil logic by voting for new options, vote-splitting kept the unpopular Populars from being deposed. The majority of Spaniards therefore lost their power of sanction as soon as they started refusing to back the lesser of two evils (i.e., the Socialists).[25]

Spain's electoral system, to be fair, contains some disproportional features that make it less than a typical European PR system. Because of the way districts are drawn, many rural areas are significantly

---

[24] Quotations at Galston (2018, 8) and Blais and Degan (2018, 305); see also Schmitter 2012, 44–5. For the comparison of USA, Mexico, Israel, and Netherlands: Abramson et al. (2010). On Netherlands in 2002: Irwin and Van Holsteyn (2012, 185).

[25] On traditional vote-splitting in Spain: Colomer (2005, 150). On tactical voting in the 2008 election: Field (2009, 156). On the background and results of Spain's 2015–2016 elections: Castillo-Manzano et al. (2017). The interpretation of these elections in terms of vote-splitting and lesser-evil choices is my own.

over-represented in parliament, giving the Populars consistently more seats than their proportion of votes would strictly allow. This feature may generally increase pressure on the left to cast lesser-evil votes for the Socialists, perhaps more than in a less disproportional system. But the fact that insincere or strategic voting is a significant factor in other PR systems—especially Israel and Netherlands, generally considered the standard-bearers of strict proportionality—suggests that Spanish struggles with the dilemma of disempowerment are typical rather than idiosyncratic. After all, Spain's malapportioned districts were not enough to give the plurality party a majority of seats in either 2015 or '16, putting the voters in a position familiar to those in other PR systems.[26]

What has happened to beleaguered Spanish voters in recent elections, then, is generalizable. In response, we could take the ultra-pragmatic step of talking about which horn of the dilemma cuts more deeply and which less. Maybe systems that offer multiple parties and candidates from which to choose have simply chosen to live with the vote-splitting problem (and diminished accountability for unpopular incumbents) in exchange for avoiding the lesser-evil problem. And maybe systems with only two viable parties have come to terms with the lesser-evil problem as the price to be paid for avoiding the vote-splitting problem. A realist could certainly find something noble and praiseworthy in societies that have faced terrible trade-offs and have made hard choices. More is the pity, then, that the examples of the USA and Spain in 2016 undermine this hope of pragmatism. Whereas both cases should in theory have been able to avoid one of the two horns of the dilemma, in practice both sets of voters got doubly gored.

The two parts of the dilemma of disempowerment work in tandem and therefore must be unlocked in tandem. The choice of one to avoid the other, in terms of designing institutions, is a fool's errand. We have now considered three different ways of trying to get out of the dilemma of disempowerment. Changing rules to increase the number of options on the ballot will not work, nor will changing the contest structure from one-round to two-round elections (even when accompanied by more adequate alternatives), nor will changing the contest structure by increasing the number of seats up for grabs. What else is there?

---

[26]On the malapportionment of Spanish legislative districts: Lancaster (2017, 926) and Riera and Montero (2017, 369).

BACK TO THE BALLOT

Consider again the Spanish results of 2015 and '16. The two largest right-wing parties together amassed about 43% of votes in the first poll and 46% in the second; the two largest left-wing parties combined for 46% and then 44%. In each election, about 10% of voters for smaller parties could in theory have decided on which side majority coalitions would be formed, if they had any discriminating views between the members of the two largest blocs. This question could have received some sort of institutionalized answer, rather than being the subject of armchair speculation, if Spanish voters had been allowed to express more than one preference as they cast their votes for the primary assembly in parliament.[27]

The missing ingredient is ballot structure: the input and output rules according to which voters' judgments are inserted and then processed to construct electoral results. The single- and multi-seat electoral systems which have been considered so far share something fundamental about ballot structure: a single vote per voter per contest. What if each voter had more than one vote to use in one contest?

There is an established form of two-level voting aside from the 2RS or run-off method, with first and second rounds of voting for the same seat. This is the "mixed member" or "parallel" system, which lets voters cast one vote to choose a single representative for their local constituency and a second vote to choose a preferred party for the legislature overall. The party-list votes are used to fill out the rest of the seats after the district winners are in place, in proportion to the percentages of support that each party receives. Any voter can therefore express judgments about a personal representative and a policy-oriented party on the same ballot, and the constituency member does not have to be of the same party as a voter's party-list preference. The German federal legislature is elected in this manner, and places as far apart as Scotland and New Zealand have reformed their single-member elections by adopting similar schemes (the former is not a sovereign state but has a regional legislature).[28]

An oft-neglected fact about these versions of two-level voting is that the ratio of votes to contests is effectively still one-to-one. What makes the system "parallel" is that the two votes apply to different tiers of legislative seats. Yet having one vote for each of two parallel contests leaves

---

[27] For Spanish election returns: Castillo-Manzano et al. (2017, 159).
[28] On "mixed" and "parallel" electoral systems: Reynolds et al. (2005, 90–91).

voters vulnerable to vote-splitting and the lesser evil in either or both. The contests remain separate as far as the voter's inputs are concerned, even if the seat outcomes in the two contests might be mutually dependent to some degree (for the sake of maintaining proportionality). As we have seen, we cannot assume that party-list voting on one side of the ballot will be immune to the logic of the dilemma operating on the candidate vote on the other side simply because proportional outcomes are guaranteed. What these parallel elections have in common with 2RS is giving two votes for what are, logically and structurally, two separate contests. They all therefore respect the rule of a single vote per contest.

Intriguingly, surveys suggest that some German voters think of their second (party-list) vote as the expression of a second preference for the legislature overall. These voters may not understand that their two votes are kept parallel in two separate contests, rather than merged into one contest, but their intuitive wish to express varied preferences or nuanced judgments is eminently understandable. Probably some of the small-party voters in Spain also had preferences about the larger parties that they would have liked to incorporate, if the ballot structure had not required them to desert their preferred party altogether in order to do so.[29]

If we change our assumptions about what sorts of ballots voters should work with, and consider the possibility of expressing more than one judgment per contest, the apparent futility of different tweaks to contest structure may no longer apply. In particular, using jungle primaries to increase ballot options need not be abandoned because of the problems of vote-splitting that may arise. France and Louisiana are currently inadequate models for resolving voters' central dilemma, but they may be half-right. If they do not appear to work well under one type of input rule, we cannot necessarily rule out their provision of a high number of ballot options when in conjunction with another scheme of ballot inputs.

Instead of trying and failing to operate cleverly within the dilemma of disempowerment's basic parameters, then, we must consider getting outside those parameters by changing the ballot itself. Expressive judgments, the third component of voter empowerment, can have a fundamental impact on salvaging the other two, selection and accountability. Making

---

[29] On German voters' second preferences: Sartori (1997, 19). On voters' choices in parallel systems worldwide: Plescia (2016, 68, 113).

the ballot more expressive could allow us to sharpen it up as a tool for voters. But what would it mean to have more than one vote per contest? Australia, Ireland, and Malta use one kind of multi-mark ballot for elections to their national legislatures. But the range of multi-mark options is considerably broader. We now turn to voting theory to explore the possibilities.

REFERENCES

Abramowitz, A.I., & J. McCoy. 2019. "United States: Racial Resentment, Negative Partisanship, and Polarization in Trump's America." *Annals of the American Academy of Political and Social Science* 681: 137–56.

Abramowitz, A.I., & S. Webster. 2016. "The Rise of Negative Partisanship and the Nationalization of U.S. Elections in the 21st Century." *Electoral Studies* 41: 12–22.

Abramson, P.R., J.H. Aldrich, A. Blais, M. Diamond, A. Diskin, I.H. Indridason, D.J. Lee, & R. Levine. 2010. "Comparing Strategic Voting under FPTP and PR." *Comparative Political Studies* 43: 61–90.

Amy, D.J. 2000. *Behind the Ballot Box: A Citizen's Guide to Electoral Systems.* Westport, CT: Praeger.

Bailey, T.A. 1937. "Was the Presidential Election of 1900 a Mandate on Imperialism?" *Mississippi Valley Historical Review* 24: 43–52.

Barkin, N. 2016. "Who Do You Hate the Least? The Dilemma for French Voters." *Reuters,* August 17 (Accessed on December 29, 2016 at www.reuters.com/article/us-france-politics-column-idUSKCN10P0FY).

Berg-Andersson, R.E. 2017. "The Green Papers" (Accessed on August 13, 2017 at www.thegreenpapers.com).

Blais, A., & A. Degan. 2018. "The Study of Strategic Voting." *The Oxford Handbook of Public Choice,* eds. R.D. Congleton, B. Grofman, & S. Voigt. Oxford: Oxford University Press.

Blais, A., J.-F. Laslier, F. Poinas, & K. Van der Straeten. 2015. "Citizens' Preferences about Voting Rules: Self-Interest, Ideology, and Sincerity." *Public Choice* 164: 423–42.

Castillo-Manzano, J.I., L. Lopez-Valpuesta, & R. Pozo-Barajas. 2017. "Six Months and Two Parliamentary Elections in Spain." *Electoral Studies* 45: 157–60.

Colomer, J.M. 2005. "The General Election in Spain, March 2004." *Electoral Studies* 24: 149–56.

Farrell, D.M. 2011. *Electoral Systems: A Comparative Introduction.* 2nd edn. Basingstoke, UK: Palgrave Macmillan.

Field, B.N. 2009. "The Parliamentary Election in Spain, March 2008." *Electoral Studies* 28: 155–8.

Gallagher, M. 2018. "Election Indices Dataset" (Accessed on December 17, 2018 at www.tcd.ie/political_science/staff/michael_gallagher/elsystems/index.php).

Gallup. 2016. "Trump and Clinton Finish with Historically Poor Images" (Accessed on January 18, 2017 at www.gallup.com/poll/197231/trump-clinton-finish-historically-poor-images.aspx).

Galston, W.A. 2018. "The Populist Challenge to Liberal Democracy." *Journal of Democracy* 29: 5–19.

Gant, M.M., & L. Sigelman. 1985. "Anti-candidate Voting in Presidential Elections." *Polity* 18: 329–39.

Hoyo, V. 2018. "Electoral Systems in Context: France." *The Oxford Handbook of Electoral Systems*, eds. E.S. Herron, R.J. Pekkanen, & M.S. Shugart. Oxford: Oxford University Press.

Irwin, G.A., & J.J.M. Van Holsteyn. 2012. "Strategic Electoral Considerations under Proportional Representation." *Electoral Studies* 31: 184–91.

Jenkins, S. 2017. "Hardliners Won't Like this Soft Brexit Plan." *Guardian* (London), July 27 (Accessed on July 27, 2017 at www.theguardian.com/commentisfree/2017/jul/27/hardliners-soft-brexit-tough-negotiate-properly).

Joshi, D.K., J.S. Maloy, & T.M. Peterson. 2015. "Popular vs. Elite Democratic Structures and International Peace." *Journal of Peace Research* 52: 463–77.

Joshi, D.K., J.S. Maloy, & T.M. Peterson. 2019. "Popular vs. Elite Democracies and Human Rights: Inclusion Makes a Difference." *International Studies Quarterly* 63: 111–26.

Kelley, S. 1983. *Interpreting Elections.* Princeton: Princeton University Press.

Key, V.O. 1966. *The Responsible Electorate: Rationality in Presidential Voting, 1936–60*, ed. M.C. Cummings. Cambridge, MA: Harvard University Press.

Lancaster, T.D. 2017. "The Spanish General Elections of 2015 and 2016: A New Stage of Democratic Politics?" *West European Politics* 40: 919–37.

Lewis, C., & C. Lucas. 2017. "A True Progressive Alliance Would Have Made Jeremy Corbyn Prime Minister." *Guardian* (London), June 13 (Accessed on June 13, 2017 at www.theguardian.com/commentisfree/2017/jun/13/true-progressive-alliance-made-jeremy-corbyn-prime-minister).

Machiavelli, N. 1994. *Selected Political Writings*, trans. D. Wootton. Indianapolis: Hackett.

Mair, P. 2013. *Ruling the Void: The Hollowing of Western Democracy.* London: Verso.

McGann, A. 2006. *The Logic of Democracy: Reconciling Equality, Deliberation, and Minority Protection.* Ann Arbor: University of Michigan Press.

McGann, A. 2013. "Fairness and Bias in Electoral Systems." *Representation: Elections and Beyond*, eds. J.H. Nagel & R.M. Smith. Philadelphia: University of Pennsylvania Press.

McGhee, E., & D. Krimm. 2012. "California's New Electoral Reforms: How Did They Work?" Public Policy Institute of California. June Report.

McGhee, E., S.E. Masket, B. Shor, S. Rogers, & N. McCarty. 2014. "A Primary Cause of Partisanship? Nomination Systems and Legislator Ideology." *American Journal of Political Science* 58: 337–51.

Miguet, A. 2002. "The French Elections of 2002: After the Earthquake, the Deluge." *West European Politics* 25: 207–20.

Mitchell, P. 2000. "Voters and Their Representatives: Electoral Institutions and Delegation in Parliamentary Democracies." *European Journal of Political Research* 37: 335–51.

Monbiot, G. 2016. "The European Union Is the Worst Choice, Apart from the Alternative." *Guardian* (London), June 15 (Accessed on January 5, 2017 at www.theguardian.com/commentisfree/2016/jun/15/european-union-eu-britain-sovereignty).

Pew Research Center. 2016b. "Clinton, Trump Supporters Have Starkly Different Views of a Changing Nation." August Report.

Plescia, C. 2016. *Split-Ticket Voting in Mixed-Member Electoral Systems: A Theoretical and Methodological Investigation*. Colchester, UK: ECPR Press.

Poundstone, W. 2008. *Gaming the Vote: Why Elections Aren't Fair (and What We Can Do about It)*. New York: Hill & Wang.

Reynolds, A., B. Reilly, & C. Ellis. 2005. *Electoral System Design: The New International IDEA Handbook*. Stockholm: Institute for Democracy and Election Assistance.

Riera, P., & J.R. Montero. 2017. "Attempts to Reform the Electoral System in Spain: The Role of Experts." *Election Law Journal* 16: 367–76.

Riker, W.H. 1982. "The Two-Party System and Duverger's Law: An Essay on the History of Political Science." *American Political Science Review* 76: 753–66.

Sartori, G. 1997. *Comparative Constitutional Engineering: An Inquiry into Structures, Incentives, and Outcomes*. 2nd edn. New York: New York University Press.

Schmitter, P.C. 2012. "A Way Forward?" *Journal of Democracy* 23: 39–46.

Sigelman, L., & M.M. Gant. 1989. "Anti-candidate Voting in the 1984 Presidential Election." *Political Behavior* 11: 81–92.

Singer, M.M. 2013. "Was Duverger Correct? Single-Member District Election Outcomes in Fifty-Three Countries." *British Journal of Political Science* 43: 201–20.

Singh, S.P. 2014. "Not All Election Winners Are Equal: Satisfaction with Democracy and the Nature of the Vote." *European Journal of Political Research* 53: 308–27.

Thompson, D.F. 2002. *Just Elections: Creating a Fair Electoral Process in the United States.* Chicago: University of Chicago Press.

Wattenberg, M.P. 1991. *The Rise of Candidate-Centered Politics: Presidential Elections of the 1980s.* Cambridge, MA: Harvard University Press.

Willsher, K. 2017a. "Fear of Neofascism Keeps Emmanuel Macron ahead of Marine Le Pen." *Guardian* (London), April 29 (Accessed on May 2, 2017 at www.theguardian.com/world/2017/apr/29/france-election-neofascism-le-pen-macron).

Willsher, K. 2017b. "Macron Is En Route to the Elysée, but May Find It Hard to Govern." *Guardian* (London), May 6 (Accessed on May 6, 2017 at www.theguardian.com/world/2017/may/06/macron-french-presidential-election-2017-future-govern-effective).

CHAPTER 4

Lessons from Theory:
The Blunted Blade of One-Mark Ballots

The French presidential election of 2017 showed that the pathologies of 2016 were no fluke. The centrist Emmanuel Macron's victory over the far-right Marine Le Pen in the second round may have been prematurely toasted in some quarters as the official end of the Brexit-Trump electoral trend, but many French voters were still hurting from the dilemma of disempowerment. Not unlike the American presidential election of 1900, this contest featured yawning gaps on the ideological spectrum (see Fig. 4.1). Macron and Le Pen had captured 45.3% of first-round ballots between them, but three other candidates who were excluded from the run-off represented slightly more voters, at 46%: Benoit Hamon and Jean-Luc Melenchon on the left and Francois Fillon on the right. This plurality of voters had no clear pathway to an honest second-round vote.[1]

Macron offered a blend of socially liberal and economically austere (neo-liberal) policies, while Le Pen offered a mixture of cultural nationalism and economic welfarism or protectionism. There can be little wonder that a popular motto on the streets and over digital media was *ni patrie, ni patron*—vote for "neither the fatherland [Le Pen] nor the boss [Macron]." The far right's benefit from vote-splitting on the left was reminiscent of 2002. Unlike the earlier contest, though, when voter turnout surged in the second round so that people could raise their voice

[1] For first-round vote-tallies: Conseil (2017a).

© The Author(s) 2019
J. S. Maloy, *Smarter Ballots*, Elections, Voting, Technology,
https://doi.org/10.1007/978-3-030-13031-2_4

CULTURE	ECONOMICS	
	protectionist, welfarist	neo-liberal
pluralist	B. Hamon, J.-L. Melenchon [eliminated, 1st round]	E. Macron [run-off]
nationalist	M. Le Pen [run-off]	F. Fillon [eliminated, 1st round]

Fig. 4.1 Issue space in the 2017 French presidential election

against Le Pen's father, a million and a half fewer voters participated in the 2017 run-off. Even more telling, the proportion of blank and spoiled ballots rose from 2.6% in the first round to 11.5% in the run-off. There was a record-high increase in spoiled ballots between the two rounds, and turnout as a whole was the lowest of any previous presidential run-off. The French electorate was yet again beset by double trouble: the vote-splitting problem in the first round followed by the lesser-evil problem in the second.[2]

Seven years before and less than 100 miles to the west of Macron's victory party in Paris, an international gathering of scholars had conducted a small election of their own. They were being hosted by a major British charity in a Norman castle that has been converted to a hotel and now advertises its proximity to the killing fields of the Second World War. Some two-dozen theoreticians from both sides of the Atlantic Ocean had been talking about the theme of "Voting Power in Practice," and now they were going to do some voting of their own. No fewer than 18 different voting systems were put on a ballot for selecting a single answer to the question, "What is the best voting rule for your town to use to elect the mayor?" The system known as "Plurality," in which

---

[2] For turnout and valid votes: Conseil (2017a, b). The official figures do not include a separate line for spoiled ballots, but these can be calculated by subtracting blank votes and valid votes from total votes. On the record-high and record-low numbers: Hoyo (2018, 690).

voters make only one mark on the ballot, and the winner is the candidate with more marks than any other, received no marks at all from the assembled theorists. The winner of this election, a voting system called "Approval," lets voters make a single mark for as many or as few options as they like.[3]

Could the answer really be as simple as allowing voters to make multiple marks on their ballots instead of one only? The voting-theory community, including dozens if not hundreds of scholars around the world who were not at the Normandy conference in 2010, is largely united on this point. They have spent decades pummeling "first past the post," the plurality-winner system in single-round, single-seat contests which is used to elect members of the national legislatures of the USA, the UK, and Canada. For the voting theorist, the reason typically has to do with the value of majority rule and the merciless beating that it takes in such elections. For a realist, however, the goal of breaking out of the dilemma of disempowerment is primary, and this may be an overlapping agenda but not an identical one. We need to reconstruct the theory of ballot structure, with a conceptual map of the possible alternatives, and to subject it to assessment by realist criteria.[4]

VOTER EMPOWERMENT AND BALLOT STRUCTURE

The triad of voter empowerment consists of adequate alternatives, effective sanctions, and expressive judgments (see Fig. 1.2). The first principle means that voters need a decent supply of options on the ballot, to reduce the likelihood of a "lesser of two evils" choice, and the second means that voting outcomes need to deliver effective rewards and punishments to make politicians accountable to voters. The third principle is the foundation of the other two, since voters need sharp enough tools for expressing their judgments to make selection and accountability meaningful.

The electoral system as a whole can affect the triad of voter empowerment in a variety of ways, but the theory of ballot structure is primarily

---

[3]For details of the voting-theory conference: Laslier (2011a). For the definitive exposition and defense of the Approval voting system: Brams and Fishburn (2007).

[4]For a brief and accessible indictment of plurality voting's crimes against basic political equality: McLean (1991, 177).

concerned with the third and foundational component of voter empowerment. Ballot structure refers to the combination of input rules and output rules that take voters' judgments and turn them into election results. We need a conceptual map of the different kinds of ballot structure that may be used in a single-winner election as a starting point for thinking about reform. Several criteria for assessing ballot types can be derived from the imperative of expressive judgments, and four of these will guide our search for smarter ballots throughout the second half of this book.

1. *Expression across options.* Input rules should allow the voter the possibility of giving non-zero support to more than one option on the ballot.
2. *Expression within options.* Input rules should allow the voter to choose from different levels of support which may be delivered to any one option.
3. *Accessibility.* Input rules should make it easy to cast a valid ballot.
4. *Alternatives.* Input rules should not create incentives for political actors to manipulate the number of options presented to voters, in the hope of systematically raising their own electoral prospects or lowering their rivals'.

These four criteria will be used as the electoral realist's scorecard. Several different ballot types will be assessed on a preliminary, theoretical basis by the end of this chapter, and then more fully on the basis of experimental and empirical evidence in the next chapter. First, however, a deep dive into conceptual and taxonomical issues is required to develop the menu of ballot types to be assessed.

This is normally the terrain of voting theory—a territory that many empirical scholars and even democratic theorists have been reluctant to enter. Electoral realism is bound to feel rather out of place here. But it is still territory worth seeing and learning about, even if (perhaps especially if) your guide is not entirely at ease with the local customs.

TOWERS TOO SHORT

Economists, mathematicians, and a handful of political scientists have examined a wide range of voting methods in terms of certain logical and mathematical properties. They have come up with formal rules about how inputs should lead to outputs, which they believe reflect basic values of rationality and justice. But a strong dose of realism and a relentless focus on voter empowerment are not easy to come by in this scholarly literature, making the novel conceptual map-making effort in this chapter potentially non-redundant.

Academia, and especially any field with the word "theory" attached to it, is easily derided as an ivory tower: a privileged and secluded place that is too far off the ground to be of any service to real people and real problems. But the metaphor of a tower also indicates one of the great potential strengths of scholarship, since observers who are stationed on high can see things that people on the ground cannot. The social purpose of academia is supposed to have less to do with the fine or exotic building materials than with the height of the buildings—indeed the metaphor of a fire-tower might do just as well. When academics build their towers too short, however, they cannot see much and therefore have little to offer to a ground-level audience.

In the massive scholarly literature on democratic elections which has been produced in the last half-century or so, the problem of building towers too short is a familiar one. Theorists have generally been focussed on the criteria of a perfectly fair and rational "social choice," as embodied in the ideal of a "Condorcet winner"—the one option on the ballot that would prevail over most of the other options in hypothetical head-to-head contests. Named after a French mathematician of the later eighteenth century, the ideal of the Condorcet winner is the moral and intellectual pole-star for many professional voting theorists. Though it sounds reasonable enough and sheds interesting light on the extremely complicated problem of designing voting rules, it suffers from a basic limitation. In the real world of democracy, voting rules affect far more than whether the next electoral result will be rational or fair. They also affect the incentives for participation, the habits of doing politics, and the institutionalized means of distributing power which pervade a whole political system. In other words, ballots are structures of power, for realists, which may be more important in the long term than what the most rational and just outcome should have been in the last election.

Scholars in comparative electoral studies, through gathering and analyzing evidence from real elections across time and space, are well placed to appreciate that voting systems are not just results factories; they are institutional structures of power with long-term, on-going effects. But empirical researchers, until relatively recently, have not been greatly concerned with issues of voter empowerment. Their natural audience over the past half-century has been professional politicians, and their primary objects of concern have been political parties and party systems. As research has indicated increasing disenchantment with party loyalties and disgust with party organizations, the field of electoral studies has shifted in the past decade or two toward voters' freedom of choice as a property worth studying, a value that some electoral systems appear to serve better than others. Paulo Pereira and Joao Andrade have explained the new paradigm in terms strikingly similar to our triad of voter empowerment: "voters' freedom of choice is greater when they have more candidates and political platforms to choose from [and] more possibility to express their preferences." From this perspective are emerging new theories and findings about more "preferential" and "personalized" systems as compared with more traditional, party-oriented ones.[5]

The problem with electoral studies is that the personalized-vs.-partyfied dimension of analysis fails to get to the point that electoral realism cares about. The dilemma of disempowerment operates in both highly personalized (e.g., presidential) and highly partyfied (e.g., proportional-parliamentary) contests. Extremely personalized and extremely partyfied systems often share an essential similarity in ballot structure: Most instances of both systems allow voters to make only a single mark per contest—for one person in a presidential election, for one party in a parliamentary election. We therefore need a root-and-branch review of how to categorize the possible types of ballot structure to get to the bottom of the dilemma of disempowerment.

INPUTS, COUNTS, AND WINNERS

Two things have been missing from academic theories of ballot structure, from a realist's perspective. First, a democratic theory of election reform needs to know which ballot types are possible, not just which are observable today. Second, we cannot distinguish which are possible and which are not unless we take account of the interaction of input rules with output rules, since some input-output combinations simply cannot fit together to yield a stipulated number of winners. Previous classifications have treated "ballot structure" as only a matter of input rules,

---

[5] Quotation at Pereira and Andrade (2009, 102); see also Bowler et al. (2018, 93–94). For the scholarly shift: Farrell (2011, 169–70) and Renwick and Pilet (2016). On the decline of voters' attachments to parties: Mair (2013, 31–33, 70–71, 78, 83).

obscuring how identical input rules can fit easily or uneasily with different output rules. At the same time, output rules should themselves be distinguished into rules for counting and winning, since inputs may be processed or aggregated in more than one way before criteria of victory are applied.

On a conventional ballot in an American presidential election (within a state) or a British parliamentary election (within a constituency), the input rule allows one mark per voter per contest. The mathematical meaning of this input rule is that one candidate or party receives 100% of a voter's support while all others necessarily receive zero. The counting rule is straight addition of all marks by all voters across all candidates. The winning rule is what leads many to call the American and British methods the Plurality Vote: The candidate with more votes than any other single candidate—a plurality but not necessarily a majority—is pronounced the representative of the community.

Breaking down ballot structure in this way clarifies that the two-round system (2RS) differs on the winning rule but not on either the input or counting rules. The winning rule of 2RS eliminates all but the top two vote-getters and places them in a second contest; both the first and second contests follow exactly the same input and counting rules as the Plurality Vote in the Anglo-American examples.

Once we distinguish input, counting, and winning rules, 2RS can be appreciated as a relatively minor change from the Anglo-American system of single-seat plurality (SSP). The common input rule in both cases was called a "categorical" ballot structure by Douglas Rae in *The Political Consequences of Electoral Laws* (1967). Rae perceptively indicated that this classification included a single vote for a candidate as well as a single vote for a party; both are of the all-or-nothing type. Even in a system of proportional representation (PR), where voters are asked to support one party in a multi-seat district, the input rule is typically categorical despite the fact that a different winning rule is used to fill multiple seats rather than one.[6]

Yet many other alternative ballot structures are conceivable because several different input and output schemes can be matched in different combinations. The range of input rules alone extends well beyond Rae's classification, which had the "ordinal" (i.e., ranking) ballot structure as

[6] Rae (1967, 16).

the sole alternative to the categorical. Many scholars have noticed Rae's errors and proposed different taxonomies of ballot structure, but without appreciating the real range of input types and without taking inputs' interface with various output rules as seriously as I do here.[7]

In the analysis that follows, I will refer interchangeably to "candidates" and "parties" as the objects of voters' judgment and choice and will often place them under the general term "options." An important conceptual disclaimer is that I take a single-winner contest structure as given while elaborating my new taxonomy of ballot structure. The reason is that additional types of output rule beyond the three discussed here would be available for multi-winner contests (see Appendix), rendering the discussion and accompanying visual aids considerably more cluttered than they are already destined to be.

BALLOT INPUT RULES

Because the normative and analytic core of modern democratic voting is equality, each voter is assumed to have the same package of support, per contest, to be delivered according to the voter's choice. Input rules are what give the voter the tools for delivering that support through the ballot. An *exclusive* input rule treats the voter's package of support as one that must be delivered in bulk, all 100% of it, at one destination: The whole vote goes to a single option on the ballot. Once the entire package is delivered, there is nothing left to distribute elsewhere. Since the voter is allowed (and required) only a single mark on the ballot to deliver a package in bulk to one location, this type of input rule fits the logical and expressive structure of a "one-mark ballot" (1MB).

A *distributive* input rule, by contrast, liberates the voter's package of support from the rules of exclusive delivery, in one or both of two ways. First, the package of support is not destined for a single location but can be distributed to more than one; second, it may also be possible to divide the package into pieces smaller than 100% before delivery to multiple locations. In short, a distributive input scheme either keeps the voter's support whole while delivering it to more than one option in sequence, or else divides the voter's support into multiple parcels of

---

[7]Rae (1967, 17–18). More detailed analysis of alternative schemes for classifying ballot structure appears in the Appendix of this book, in the section on "Ballot Structure and Voting Theory."

varying sizes for delivery to multiple options at once. Because it is impossible for a voter to indicate how such multiple distributions should proceed without being allowed to make multiple marks on the ballot, we have now moved from a one-mark to a "multi-mark" ballot.

These are the two main categories of ballot inputs: exclusive (or 1MB) and distributive (or multi-mark). Because of its capacity to deliver parcels of support (i.e., votes) to more than one location (i.e., parties or candidates), the distributive type of input structure might be considered polytheistic rather than monotheistic. Exclusive ballot inputs, by contrast, require the voter to pronounce that "there is no god but God" in any given contest. In addition to this major difference of input categories, there are three different kinds of distributive input rule based on three different sets of structural parameters for distributing voting support.

A truly "ordinal" input scheme allows voters to rank their preferences as first, second, third, and so on, through the whole list of options for any given contest. Ranking ballots are well known to political scientists and voting theorists alike from their use in Australia and Ireland, among other jurisdictions. Uniquely, rankings differentiate fractions of the voter's total support in a strict linear order: Only one candidate may receive each distinct level or degree of support, and no two candidates may be judged equal when a ranking ballot is in use (unless a voter refuses to indicate any support at all to more than one candidate).

A second kind of distributive input rule divides the total package of support into equal parcels and lets the voter pick one or more destinations for all the parcels. This is the essence of the Cumulative Vote system in some American cities and counties as well as two regional legislatures in Germany. A town that elects five councilors, for example, would give each voter five votes to spread around to as many or as few candidates as desired; other versions may give a lower number of votes than there are seats. Regardless of magnitude, the cap on the number of votes that each ballot can distribute, forcing the voter to make arithmetic choices, is the property that makes a cumulative ballot unique among distributive input systems. The Cumulative Vote has always been applied to multi-seat contests in the real world, but in principle it could elect a single winner.[8]

---

[8]On Cumulative in American local governments: Bowler et al. (2003, 23, 32–33). On Switzerland: Lakeman (1974, 105, 154). On Cumulative in Germany, as adopted in two regions in 2011: Bowler et al. (2018).

One-Mark Ballots (**1MB**), a.k.a. "categorical" (Rae 1967)
  1. The voter must deliver maximal support to one option, nothing to all the others.

Multi-Mark Ballots
  2. **Ranking**, a.k.a. "ordinal" (Rae 1967)
  The voter can indicate a hierarchic order of preference among all options, thereby distributing a unique degree of support to each one marked.

3. **Cumulative**
The voter can distribute variable quantities of support to one or more options, subject to an upper limit on the total quantity of support distributed.

4. **Grading**
The voter can distribute variable quantities of support to one or more options, subject to an upper limit on each option's quantity of support received.

Fig. 4.2   Ballot input rules: two categories, four types

A third and final version of distributive inputs places a different kind of constraint on voter support: a ceiling on the number of votes that any one candidate may receive. Instead of giving all votes to one option, which is allowed with cumulative input rules, the voter can give up to a certain maximum to any and every option; what is given to one does not affect what can or cannot be given to another. Such a scheme would be similar to a classroom grading system: No student can receive more than 100 points, or a grade of A, or what have you, and the instructor can give any amount beneath that limit to any student. Voting theorists have advocated several versions of this type of input rule, which is not used in any public elections but does operate in many other contexts (e.g., rating films or other types of performance in competitions). The difference between limiting voters' ability to give, as with cumulative inputs, and candidates' ability to receive is significant, and calling the latter a *grading* input structure makes intuitive sense.

The main alternatives to exclusive inputs can now be distinguished according to their three unique distribution rules, giving us a comprehensive list of ballot input types (see Fig. 4.2).

Are Distributive Inputs Smarter?

The three kinds of multi-mark inputs can be visualized in respective ballot templates. Imagine a contest among five colors: black, white, yellow, red, and blue. If only one of these can be used as the background color

Ranking

	1st	2nd	3rd	4th	5th
Black					
White					
Yellow					
Red					
Blue					

Place no more than one mark in each row and column. Any row or column with no marks or more than one will not count.

Comulative

	5	4	3	2	1
Black					
White					
Yellow					
Red					
Blue					

The total number of votes given cannot exceed five (5). Excess votes will be deducted and may invalidate the ballot.

Grading A B C D F

	5	4	3	2	1
Black					
White					
Yellow					
Red					
Blue					

Place no more than one mark in each row. Rows with no marks or more than one will not count.

Fig. 4.3 Multi-mark (distributive) ballot templates

on the street signs in our town, which should it be? An exclusive ballot, of course, would require you to be monotheistic about the colors of street signs, with five rows for each of the candidates but only one column to leave blank or to fill in. The distributive options, by contrast, offer more columns to mark various levels of support (see Fig. 4.3).

It is now clear that all the elections that we have been considering as illustrations of the dilemma of disempowerment were using exclusive, 1MB rules. Logically, 1MB voting appears to be a crucial enabling factor for both ends of the dilemma of disempowerment. The lesser-evil problem arises when voters fear wasting their whole packages of support on a high-quality loser and have no ability to deliver their package, or any fraction of it, to more than one candidate. The vote-splitting problem arises when like-minded voters have no choice but to assign their whole packages of support to one party, depriving others of any share of it. The multi-mark alternatives therefore offer possible solutions.[9]

At the very least, it is obvious that distributive input rules give the voter, in theory, a metaphorically sharper or smarter tool—a less dull or blunt instrument—with which to wield power vis-a-vis parties and candidates. We still have to do some probing with the criteria derived from voter empowerment in mind before we can be confident that 1MB voting—an empirically large category indeed—is the bete noire of democratic realism.

---

[9]For a similar distinction between "uninominal" and "plurinominal" ballots made by the French economist Antoinette Baujard: Laslier (2011a, 11).

EXPRESSION VS. ACCESSIBILITY

Among our four realist criteria of assessment, three can be partially addressed on the basis of input rules' structural characteristics alone, even before their combinations with output rules are considered. Expression across options, expression within options, and accessibility will receive further attention now, and the criterion of alternatives will be taken up later.

Among input types, exclusive ballots impose a high degree of constraint on expression across options by limiting the voter's delivery of support to a single destination. By contrast, both grading and ranking allow non-zero support for each and every option on the ballot. Cumulative inputs fall in the middle, since the voter's need to distribute a finite number of votes across candidates means that all available support may be exhausted before all options are considered. The continuum from best to worst for expression across options therefore runs from grading and ranking, more or less together, to cumulative to exclusive.

For expression within options, there is a clear one-dimensional continuum of voter constraint. Ranking inputs impose the constraint of a linear, hierarchic order, meaning that no two options may receive equivalent levels of support. In addition, no single option may receive a level of support that is simultaneously much greater than some and much lesser than other options' support. Grading imposes neither of these constraints on how one option's support received may vary from another's. Cumulative inputs impose the lesser constraint that voters must husband their total package of votes to distribute. Both cumulative and grading inputs leave voters a free hand to minimize or maximize the differential between one option's support and another's, but grading is unique in not reducing the share available to distribute once an option has received non-zero support. For this criterion, from best to worst, the continuum runs from grading to cumulative to ranking to exclusive ballots.

The formal properties of distributive input rules clearly give them an advantage over 1MB voting in terms of expressive potential. But do smarter ballots require smarter voters? Making several marks undoubtedly requires more time, effort, and thought than only a single mark per contest. Would a realist therefore expect a terrible trade-off in which the most expressive ballots are also the least accessible, cognitively and practically? These questions deserve consideration in light of the empirical record of smarter ballots (see Chapter 5), but there are also some theoretical considerations that caution against assuming a zero-sum trade-off between expression and accessibility. We should consider two kinds of hurdles to accessible voting: how difficult it is, cognitively, to use a ballot as a tool for expression, and how easy it is to break the rules (i.e., to cast an invalid ballot).

The cognitive difficulty imposed by distributive input rules does not seem immense in light of the fact that humans in non-political contexts express varying levels of support all the time. When shopping, most people identify second- or third-preference items to buy if their first preference is out of stock: This is ranking. Having a limited budget with which to make more than one purchase requires making similar judgments to those required by a cumulative ballot. Watching films or Olympic athletes, and grading them against one another on a common scale, is also a widely shared experience in the twenty-first century. The notion that large numbers of voters would be disfranchised by having the opportunity to use distributive ballots seems unlikely, to put it mildly.

The second issue, ballot error, may be more serious. Given the rules placed immediately beneath the templates for ranking, cumulative, and grading ballots (see Fig. 4.3), how would the three vary in the numbers of invalid ballots generated by real voters? The cumulative ballot has one cardinal rule, simple in form but also potentially requiring precise arithmetical reasoning. An error of under-voting would not present any need to throw out the entire ballot, but over-voting might. The grading ballot is relatively difficult to invalidate: The only way to do so is to mark more than one grade per candidate (by marking more than one box across any given row). Even then, that invalidates only the one candidate's grade, not any other's. The ranking ballot recognizes an error in case either a row or a column gets more than one mark (horizontally or vertically). That makes two ways to spoil a ballot compared to one way with cumulative and grading. Grading's advantage over cumulative, ultimately, is the absence of any need to calculate fractions of a total vote budget.

All these multi-mark ballots, of course, are more complex than 1MB. The exclusive input rule may be constraining, but it is accessible. Simplicity may be its strongest virtue, for the democratic realist. Even so, there is undoubtedly some portion of voters in every contest who find the requirement to rank a single option above all other options rather demanding, cognitively; whereas a grading ballot would allow them simply to give equally high grades to a few of the better options and equally low grades to a few of the worse ones.

BALLOT OUTPUT RULES

The output side of ballot structure gives us winning rules which must work hand-in-hand with input rules through the medium of counting rules. The winner of a single-seat contest can be determined by types of rules that correspond to three basic concepts in statistics: mean, median, and mode. The mean is a value equal to the sum of all values divided by the number of values summed; the median is the single value that has equal numbers of values on either side of it, both higher and lower; the mode is the single value that appears more frequently than any other.

The three output rules and their differences can be most easily illustrated with an example in which voters have to choose among a range of quantitative options. Imagine that nine residents of a building must decide the mandatory monthly contribution that each must make toward garbage collection. Each resident is asked to set a specific level of contribution, and it is understood that higher levels of contribution will see the garbage hauled away more frequently. The residents' votes must be aggregated to yield a representative output. Imagine the following distribution of votes (see Fig. 4.4): Two prefer to spend nothing, three prefer to spend $10 per month, and four prefer to spend $30 per month.

Different output rules have the power to construct different decisions of the community. The modal value is the easiest to identify: More votes came in for $30 than for any other amount, so the modal output rule says that everyone should pay that amount per month. The mean value

[Preferred contribution]	0	$10	$20	$30
[Number of votes]	2	3	0	4

Mean output = $16.67
   $[(0 \times 2) + (10 \times 3) + (20 \times 0) + (30 \times 4)] / 9$

Median output = $10
   (the value with the same number of lesser-or-equal and greater-or-equal values in the distribution)

Modal output = $30
   (the value voted for more frequently than any other single value)

Fig. 4.4   Examples of three output rules

is the average of all proposed contributions, in this case equal to $16.67 (or $150 divided by nine voters). The median value is the one in the middle of the distribution: Here, the value of $10 is the median because it has four others on the lesser-or-equal side (two for $10 and two for zero) and four others on the greater-or-equal side (four for $30). Three different output rules, each with an intuitively plausible claim to being fair and representative, would yield three different levels of garbage collection.

When we are considering elections of personnel rather than, say, of budget policies, the three basic output rules are still applicable if we shift our perspective slightly to parties or candidates as the ballot options. Reducing a large group to a single judgment requires identifying the choice of the most representative voter. Winning rules based on the mean voter, the median voter, and the modal voter are simply three different ways of operationalizing which one counts as most "representative."

The modal voter is the one who belongs to the largest bloc of supporters, so that the party or candidate who has more supporters than any other candidate is by definition the winner in a modal outcome. The mean voter is a statistical fiction, in the sense that no real resident voted for $16.67 in our example about garbage fees, but this fiction is valuable because it can "split the differences" among any number of real voters. The median voter is initially difficult to conceptualize but is usually found intuitively appealing once understood: Placing equal numbers of voters (about half) on each side of a distribution, the median voter is the one voter left standing in the middle of that distribution.

If the options on the ballot are, like candidates or parties, not themselves true quantities, both mean and median output rules require some numeric scale on which to measure the most representative voter for each option on the ballot. All the representative (whether mean or median) voters are then compared before determining a winner. For this reason, multi-mark input rules are well suited to mean and median output rules: They create a numeric scale on which ballot options are ranked, graded, or otherwise evaluated. If all the rankings, grades, or other evaluations can be assembled together (per candidate), the mean counting procedure would be straight aggregation or averaging. The median counting procedure would be sorting the whole distribution (per candidate) into two halves and identifying the one value in the middle. After either of these counts, different though they are, the winner would be the candidate whose representative voter had bestowed the highest rank, grade, or other unit of value.[10]

In an election with only two options on the ballot, a single exclusive vote could determine the mean, median, and modal winners all at once. With distributive inputs, choices about combinations get more interesting. Matching up the two components of ballot structure in different combinations will allow us to complete our taxonomy.

INPUT–OUTPUT COMBINATIONS

There are three alternatives to the traditional exclusive ballot, on the input side of our taxonomy, but the diversity of output rules (for single-winner contests) results in six main families of ballot structure (see Fig. 4.5).

A 1MB structure with exclusive input rules basically fits only one set of counting and winning rules. The mode (largest bloc) and the mean (largest average support per candidate) necessarily give the same result when each voter can support only a single candidate at only one level (100%). The voting is all-or-nothing, and the outcome is "first past the post," crowning the candidate whose nose is in front at the finish line. The winner may have a majority of votes but may also have only a plurality, depending on the number of candidates and the distribution of votes among them. For this reason, the use of 1MB inputs in single-seat contests is often called Plurality Vote.

Ranking ballots are more versatile in their range of compatible counting and winning rules. The most common such system in the real world of elections is the Single Transferable Vote (STV), in which candidates with low levels of support are eliminated and their votes are transferred to more viable candidates. The rankings for different candidates, then, serve to express conditional support. A second-choice ranking does not assign a fractional parcel of support; instead, it specifies that a voter's whole package of support will be shifted if the first-choice candidate proves non-viable across the electorate as a whole. On condition that the

[10]On the "median voter theorem," a famous concept in political science which is unrelated, strictly speaking, to median output rules within the concept of ballot structure: McLean et al. (1996, xi–xii).

	Mode	Mean	Median
Exclusive	1MB	1MB	
Ranking	STV	BC	
Cumulative		CV	
Grading		GPA	MG

1MB = One-Mark Ballot
BC = Borda Count
CV = Cumulative Vote

GPA = Grade-Point Average
MG = Median Grade
STV = Single Transferable Vote

N.B. Proportional formulas and quota-based rules belong to fourth and fifth output columns, applicable only to multi-winner contests.

Fig. 4.5 Taxonomy of ballot structure

second choice also drops out, the third choice then receives the whole package, and so on. With this counting system, the modal voter in a system of ranking inputs is the voter whose whole support, after eliminations and transfers are completed, has been delivered to the candidate with the largest number of supporters (i.e., the modal winner). STV was well named in the nineteenth century. The fact that only whole, "single" votes are counted indicates how the output rule ends up being modal, and the fact that these single votes are "transferable" indicates how unique the counting process must be to get a modal output from ranking inputs.

Ranking inputs can also be combined with mean outputs, provided that each rank is given a numeric value by being converted into a unique number of votes received. Some pre-defined maximum quantity of support is usually allotted to the first choice, a lesser quantity to the second preference, and so on: In a field of four, the first preference receives three votes, the second receives two, the third receives one, and the fourth receives none. Each candidate's total is summed, and the mean voter selects the one with the highest average. This combination of ranking and the mean is known as the Borda Count, so named after an eighteenth-century Frenchman who was a rival to Condorcet.

Both cumulative and grading inputs can easily find the mean voter, provided that votes are cast on a true numeric scale: Sum up all the points and divide by the number of valid votes, as in the Cumulative Vote already mentioned above. Combining grading inputs with mean outputs yields what I call the Grade-Point Average (GPA) system, after the American system of academic evaluations. GPA is often called the Range Vote or the Evaluative Vote in voting-theory circles.

Combining any of the distributive input systems with median outputs is plausible, in theory, because they can all supply a one-dimensional range of values on which to place candidates. Only the system that I call Median Grade has been fleshed out procedurally and tested in voting experiments. The counting system is less familiar than modal or mean outputs. By counting all ballots and noting the percentages given at each level of support for each candidate, the median grade for each candidate can be quickly identified by locating the column that has 50% or more of all votes both lesser-or-equal and greater-or-equal. The trick is how to break ties, in case more than one candidate has a median voter at the same level. Various tie-breaking rules have been considered, but these do not make a large difference for the ballot type's underlying dynamics.[11]

Having seen that 1MB schemes offer the least scope for voter expression, we can now envision the main alternatives at a glance. All the important voting-system proposals of our times, and perhaps some that have yet to appear, could in theory be placed in our taxonomy of ballot structure (in Fig. 4.5). For example, the voting theorists' favorite in Normandy in 2010 (called Approval by them) is a version of GPA that offers only two values, zero and one, on the input scale. All five of the multi-mark families in our taxonomy have either been used in actual political elections or have been experimentally tested in the field during such elections, and we will turn to examine the results of such tests later (in Chapter 5).

[11]For the Median Grade system's proposal and experimentation, under the name "Majority Judgment": Balinski and Laraki (2010; see also 2014, in briefer form).

PRELIMINARY ASSESSMENT OF BALLOT STRUCTURES

The interface between input and output rules is key to assessing elites' incentives to manipulate the options on the ballot. The main question to address is how threatening a plentiful range of alternatives would be those with the power to tilt rules toward limited ballot access.

Cumulative rules make the prospect of a new entrant on the ballot appear rather threatening. With a per-voter limit on how many votes may be delivered per contest, any votes given to the new candidate automatically reduce what is available for every other candidate. The most powerful players would therefore face strong incentives, as with 1MB, to limit voters' range of choice.

The same kind of scarcity does not exist for grading or ranking inputs. In the abstract, ranking (including the Borda and STV ballot types) should pose greater risks to an established candidate who fears losing support to a newcomer on the ballot, while grading (including GPA and Median Grade) should create little or no such fear. The reason is that an additional candidate in a ranking system threatens every existing candidate with being knocked down exactly one level in the rankings. With grading, by contrast, voters have the logical possibility of giving the new option a high (or low) grade without altering the others' grades in any way. Since the new option poses no danger, politicians' incentives to restrict the number of ballot options should be nil, theoretically.

Being realistic about human psychology, however, muddies the clarity of the abstract logic. The reason is that voters often judge individuals through implicit comparisons. Suppose that, in the 2016 Democratic primaries, Hillary Clinton was considered far superior to Bernie Sanders by some bloc of voters who were inclined to grade Clinton at the A level (4 votes out of 4) while giving Sanders only a D (1 out of 4). Now imagine that Joe Biden enters the race and is considered a breath of fresh air by some Clinton voters. The grading ballot would allow giving 4 votes to both Clinton and Biden, in theory. But some of them would start to view Clinton less favorably when Biden joins the fray: Clinton seemed to be an excellent candidate compared to Sanders, but the new option now makes them re-evaluate. Some of this voting bloc therefore drops Clinton from 4 votes to 3, reserving the maximum grade for Biden alone. In such a case, Clinton would have every reason to fear new options on the ballot. Anticipating it before it happened, the Clinton camp might already have lobbied for rules that make it difficult for Biden and others to get ballot access.

If this line of reasoning is compelling, the grading type of ballot cannot altogether remove established powers' incentives to make ballot access difficult for new faces. In fact, the STV ballot type (often called Ranked-Choice Voting, or RCV, in single-winner contests) may be even less threatening to the powers-that-be than GPA or Median Grade because conditional votes for fringe candidates can return, 100%, to more viable candidates after transfers. With grading, by contrast, the entry of a new name on the ballot might have the effect of lowering support for one or more of the other candidates after voters have re-evaluated the field as a whole. Ranking ballots have an advantage, theoretically, in mitigating politicians' temptation to tamper with ballot access.

THE UNIMPORTANCE OF BEING EARNEST

The four criteria that we have been using to assess different types of ballot structure end with the incentives for manipulation by politicians but not by voters. The question of "insincere," "strategic," and manipulative voting may be second only to the Condorcet winner on the list of voting theorists' abiding concerns, principally because the presence of the former can defeat the goal of the latter. By their lights, voters' incentives for manipulation must be carefully weighed before endorsing any voting system.

The general mark of insincere voting is to push a voter's judgment of ballot options to extremes, through either over-stating or under-stating support. Under 1MB this behavior is reactive and defensive, a badge of the dilemma of disempowerment. Voters who are alive to the danger of vote-splitting deliberately over-state in favor of one candidate (with 100% support) while under-stating their support for their sincere favorite by leaving that option blank. Experimental studies that compare different voting systems' performance on this issue have consistently concluded that the STV family—the most constrained form of multi-mark input, with its linear order of levels of support—promotes more sincere voting than Borda and GPA. (Similar studies have yet to be done that include the Cumulative Vote or Median Grade.) The question is whether Borda and GPA should therefore be ruled out.[12]

---

[12] On STV's low manipulability in general: Bowler and Grofman (2000, 268–89). On its lower levels of tactical voting than other systems: Chamberlin (1985), Laslier (2016), and Van der Straeten et al. (2016). On tactical voting under binary, Pass-Fail schemes of grading: Van der Straeten et al. (2016, 451–53) and Granic (2017, 32). For the argument that over-stating and under-stating should be considered legitimate expressions of intense preferences: Poundstone (2008, 241).

Compared to the reformists in voting theory, the realists in comparative electoral studies tend to be dismissive of concerns about the potential excesses of strategic or manipulative behavior by voters. They note that, though a clever minority may launch a systematic and co-ordinated scheme of votes to improve one candidate's chances or subvert another's, such a scheme would require a sizeable bloc of schemers (10% or more of the total electorate, according to some estimates) and an ability to predict the voting intentions of many of the other 90% (across multiple candidates and multiple levels of support). It would also require an absence of other blocs of schemers that take counter-measures. Some theoreticians work overtime to design elaborate conspiracies of this kind; real voters seem unlikely to follow suit.[13]

The empiricists' attitude is derived not only from an assumption that successful schemes of strategic manipulation would be very unlikely to materialize or very difficult to consummate but also from a normative attitude of acceptance or permissiveness about their fellow citizens' motives for insincere voting. Some empirical scholars scarcely hide their satisfaction in taking the second of these precepts even further by endorsing strategic voting as a rational response to conditions and thus a normatively flattering aspect of democratic citizenship.[14]

The position of realistic reform on this question is distinct from the other two. On the one hand, a democratic realist tends to credit the more skeptical estimates of the odds of successfully changing an outcome through strategic manipulation. Moreover, even if the odds were higher, we should consider that over- and under-stating within the relatively confined realm of voting activity appears to be purposeful behavior—and purposefulness is a kind of sincerity, part-and-parcel of an authentic judgment. On the other hand, rationalizing strategic voting (as the empiricists tend to do) suggests a severe detachment from the realities of power within institutional structures, as if lesser-evil choices have nothing coercive about them—thrilling opportunities rather than disgusting ordeals. We should not be surprised when, as researchers in France found, "voters who vote insincerely are less prone to prefer the existing two-round

---

[13]On the practical difficulties that accompany the theoretical possibilities of manipulation: Chamberlin (1985), Nurmi (1987, 117–18, 192), and Emerson (2007, 88).

[14]For a brief normative defense of strategic votes, nestled in a review of dozens of empirical studies of the phenomenon: Gschwend and Meffert (2017).

system, which suggests that at least some people do not appreciate being 'forced' to support a party or candidate that is not their preferred option."[15]

In short, the perspective of electoral realism suggests that theoretical dwelling on "manipulative" voting and empirical dwelling on "strategic" voting are both peripheral to the main action—distractions from the dilemma of disempowerment and its institutional supports. What matters is less the insincerity of the vote than the structural compulsion behind the insincerity, reflecting a dramatic discrepancy in the institutional room for maneuver of partisan elites compared to voting citizens. For this reason, the politicians' incentives toward manipulation are more consequential in electoral systems than the voters', and more worthy of close attention theoretically (in this chapter) and empirically (in Chapter 5).

DILEMMA RESOLVED (IN THEORY)

Our new conceptual map for analyzing ballot structure has laid out the menu of options, preliminary assessments of which (see Fig. 4.6) yield two major theoretic conclusions. First, multi-mark inputs are generally superior to 1MB on three of the four criteria for founding voter empowerment on expressive judgments: expression within options, expression across options, and alternatives. Only accessibility gives 1MB any advantage, theoretically, pending empirical assessment of potential trade-offs between expression and accessibility. Second, based on these same criteria, the grading family of ballots (including GPA and Median Grade) is the strongest version of multi-mark ballot, in theory; it is as good as or better than ranking on expression within options, expression across options, and accessibility, though ranking is stronger on the incentives related to adequate alternatives.

What exactly do the conceptual menu and the preliminary assessments mean for resolving the dilemma of disempowerment? The upper-level distinction between 1MB and multi-mark ballots confirms that 2RS has something essentially in common with both SSP and party-list voting with PR. Two rounds of voting represent a variation in contest structure, just like the dual ballot in Germany and the multi-winner contests in

---

[15]Quotation at Blais and Degan (2018, 306). For the conclusion that, in parallel PR systems with two votes for one legislative election, supposedly strategic choices probably reflect "either sincere misaligned preferences for parties and candidates or ... a limited vote-choice menu": Plescia (2016, 115).

1. **EXPRESSION ACROSS OPTIONS** Input rules allow support for more than one option.
   *Grading and Ranking better than Cumulative. (1MB worst.)

2. **EXPRESSION WITHIN OPTIONS** Input rules allow variable levels of support.
   *Grading best, Cumulative and Ranking good. (1MB worst.)

3. **ACCESSIBILITY** Input rules allow easy use of ballots.
   *Grading best, then Ranking, then Cumulative. (1MB equal or superior to Grading.)

4. **ALTERNATIVES:** Politicians are not incentivized to manipulate ballot options.
   *Ranking best, then Grading, then Cumulative. (1MB worst.)

Fig. 4.6   Preliminary, theory-based assessment of smarter ballots

Spain, but the exclusive inputs remain the same across all these examples. They are all prone to the dilemma of disempowerment (see Chapter 3). Could it be that our taxonomy has uncovered, in the 1MB structure, a reason for the shared tendency of these three kinds of elections toward vote-splitting and lesser-evil choices?

Recall that voters get caught between the lesser-evil and vote-splitting problems when the delivery of support to options on the ballot has an all-or-nothing quality. Distributive inputs change the logic of the vote by allowing variable levels of support across two or more ballot options. In the 2017 presidential election in France, for example, some supporters of Benoit Hamon or Jean-Luc Melenchon may have viewed Emmanuel Macron as a lesser evil than Marine Le Pen in the second round. But what if, in the first round, Hamon's and Melenchon's anti-globalization voters had been able to give one another's candidates nearly equally high levels of support, combined with nearly equally low levels to Macron and Francois Fillon? To take another bloc of voters, what if Fillon's and Le Pen's nationalist voters had been able to give one another's candidates nearly equally high levels of support, combined with the lowest possible level to the eventual winner? And what if multi-mark inputs had allowed all these interactions to be played out in a single round of voting?

With the STV ballot structure, the count first distinguishes the more viable from the less viable candidates and then transfers votes from the latter to the former. Voters do not have to convert guesses about viability into tactical votes because they can shift their entire package of support as many times as necessary until it reaches a viable option. When this system was first installed for political elections, in Australia about 100 years ago, the specific purpose was to end vote-splitting. With the fear of vote-splitting neutralized, the lesser-evil problem can then be safely tackled through steps to ensure adequate alternatives on the ballot.[16]

Grading holds out the potential to solve the dilemma even more directly, since giving your favorite a high mark has no effect on your ability to give high or low marks to other candidates. You simply grade as many candidates as possible according to your judgment. With no zero-sum game between any two candidates, and vote-splitting off the table, the syndrome of misincentives around "wasted" votes and "spoiler" candidates never appears.

The Borda Count and Cumulative Vote both allow a voter's package of support to be subdivided into smaller parcels and spread around; this is their essential likeness with the grading-input systems. On the other hand, because the first decision in either Borda or Cumulative about delivering a specific level of support logically reduces the options for how much support additional candidates can receive, the implications for vote-splitting are ambiguous. The all-or-nothing logic of 1MB is gone, but guesses about viability might still determine whether a voter puts Hamon first and Melenchon second or vice versa (under Borda), or whether Hamon gets five votes to Melenchon's zero or three to two, and so on (under Cumulative).

Having uncovered the essential characteristics of the six major families of ballot structure, it is clear that, in theory, multiple marks have the potential to fix what a single mark cannot. From the realist perspective of voter empowerment, it appears that GPA and Median Grade are closest to our goal, that STV is next in proximity, and that Borda and Cumulative are farther off. With a new map for navigating ballot structure, the next move toward smarter ballots is to turn from the lessons of theory to the lessons of experience.

REFERENCES

Balinski, M., & R. Laraki. 2010. *Majority Judgment: Measuring, Ranking, and Electing*. Cambridge, MA: MIT Press.

Balinski, M., & R. Laraki. 2014. "What Should 'Majority Decision' Mean?" *Majority Decisions: Principles and Practices*, eds. S. Novak & J. Elster. New York: Cambridge University Press.

---

[16]On the introduction of STV in Australia: Sawer (2004, 481).

Blais, A., & A. Degan. 2018. "The Study of Strategic Voting." *The Oxford Handbook of Public Choice*, eds. R.D. Congleton, B. Grofman, & S. Voigt. Oxford: Oxford University Press.

Bowler, S., & B. Grofman. 2000. "Conclusion: STV's Place in the Family of Electoral Systems." *Elections in Australia, Ireland, and Malta under the Single Transferable Vote: Reflections on an Embedded Institution*, eds. S. Bowler & B. Grofman. Ann Arbor: University of Michigan Press.

Bowler, S., T. Donovan, & D. Brockington. 2003. *Electoral Reform and Minority Representation: Local Experiments with Alternative Elections.* Columbus: Ohio State University Press.

Bowler, S., G. McElroy, & S. Muller. 2018. "Voter Preferences and Party Loyalty under Cumulative Voting: Political Behaviour after Electoral Reform in Bremen and Hamburg." *Electoral Studies* 51: 93–102.

Brams, S.J., & P.C. Fishburn. 2007. *Approval Voting.* 2nd edn. New York: Springer.

Chamberlin, J.R. 1985. "An Investigation into the Relative Manipulability of Four Voting Systems." *Behavioral Science* 30: 195–203.

Conseil Constitutionnel. 2017a. "Declaration du 26 Avril 2017." Decision no. 2017-169, April 26 (Accessed on August 15, 2017 at presidentielle2017.conseil-constitutionnel.fr).

Conseil Constitutionnel. 2017b. "Proclamation des Resultats de l'Election du President de la Republique." Decision no. 2017-171, May 10 (Accessed on August 15, 2017 at presidentielle2017.conseil-constitutionnel.fr).

Emerson, P.J. 2007. "The Art or Science of Manipulation." *Designing an All-Inclusive Democracy: Consensual Voting Procedures for Use in Parliaments, Councils, and Committees*, ed. P.J. Emerson. Berlin: Springer.

Farrell, D.M. 2011. *Electoral Systems: A Comparative Introduction.* 2nd edn. Basingstoke, UK: Palgrave Macmillan.

Granic, D.-G. 2017. "The Problem of the Divided Majority: Preference Aggregation under Uncertainty." *Journal of Economic Behavior and Organization* 133: 21–38.

Gschwend, T., & M.F. Meffert. 2017. "Strategic Voting." *The SAGE Handbook of Electoral Behaviour*, eds. K. Arzheimer, J. Evans, & M.S. Lewis-Beck. London: SAGE Publications.

Hoyo, V. 2018. "Electoral Systems in Context: France." *The Oxford Handbook of Electoral Systems*, eds. E.S. Herron, R.J. Pekkanen, & M.S. Shugart. Oxford: Oxford University Press.

Lakeman, E. 1974. *How Democracies Vote: A Study of Electoral Systems.* 4th edn. London: Faber.

Laslier, J.-F. 2011a. "And the Loser Is … Plurality Voting." Cahier no. 2011–13. Paris: Ecole Polytechnique.

Laslier, J.-F. 2016. "Heuristic Voting under the Alternative Vote: The Efficiency of 'Sour Grapes' Behavior." *Homo Oeconomicus* 33: 57–76.

Mair, P. 2013. *Ruling the Void: The Hollowing of Western Democracy.* London: Verso.

McLean, I. 1991. "Forms of Representation and Systems of Voting." *Political Theory Today*, ed. D. Held. Oxford: Oxford University Press.

McLean, I., A. McMillan, & B.L. Monroe. 1996. "Introduction." *A Mathematical Approach to Proportional Representation: Duncan Black on Lewis Carroll*, eds. I. McLean, A. McMillan, & B.L. Monroe. Boston: Kluwer.

Nurmi, H. 1987. *Comparing Voting Systems.* Dordrecht: D. Reidel.

Pereira, P.T., & J. Andrade e Silva. 2009. "Citizens' Freedom to Choose Representatives: Ballot Structure, Proportionality, and 'Fragmented' Parliaments." *Electoral Studies* 28: 101–10.

Plescia, C. 2016. *Split-Ticket Voting in Mixed-Member Electoral Systems: A Theoretical and Methodological Investigation.* Colchester, UK: ECPR Press.

Poundstone, W. 2008. *Gaming the Vote: Why Elections Aren't Fair (and What We Can Do about It).* New York: Hill & Wang.

Rae, D.W. 1967. *The Political Consequences of Electoral Laws.* New Haven: Yale University Press.

Renwick, A., & J.-B. Pilet. 2016. *Faces on the Ballot: The Personalization of Electoral Systems in Europe.* Oxford: Oxford University Press.

Sawer, M. 2004. "Australia: Replacing Plurality Rule with Majority-Preferential Voting." *Handbook of Electoral System Choice*, ed. J.M. Colomer. New York: Palgrave Macmillan.

Van der Straeten, K., J.-F. Laslier, & A. Blais. 2016. "Patterns of Strategic Voting in Run-Off Elections." *Voting Experiments*, eds. A. Blais, J.-F. Laslier, & K. Van der Straeten. Heidelberg: Springer.

CHAPTER 5

Lessons from Experience: The Cutting Edge of Ranking and Grading Ballots

Jean Quan had virtually the entire establishment against her. The dominant political party, the major newspapers, the chamber of commerce: Most of the big players in the game of local government presented a formidable wall of opposition. She was a little like the legendary Mr. Smith of Hollywood's creation—except that Mr. Smith wasn't an Asian-American woman, and Quan wasn't going to Washington. She was running for mayor of Oakland, California.

After the initial count in the 2010 mayoral election, the Bay Area establishment's influence over Oakland voters was provisionally vindicated. Don Perata had a healthy lead of 33.7% of valid ballots to Quan's 24.5, a difference of over 11,000 votes in total. Because Oakland uses Ranked-Choice Voting (RCV) for mayoral elections, voters can also register support for their second and third preferences in case their first choice proves non-viable, and the counting does not stop until either one candidate secures majority support or only two candidates are left. One by one the less popular candidates in the field were eliminated from contention, and their supporters' next-ranked preferences were transferred. When only three were left, Quan was still 10,000 votes behind, but Perata was still well short of an overall majority. At that point, third-placed Rebecca Kaplan held almost 33,000 votes whose transfers would decide the contest. Remarkably, Kaplan's supporters ranked Quan above Perata by a ratio of almost three to one. The first ethnically Asian woman

© The Author(s) 2019
J. S. Maloy, *Smarter Ballots*, Elections, Voting, Technology,
https://doi.org/10.1007/978-3-030-13031-2_5

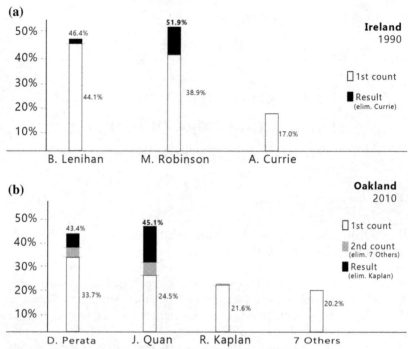

Fig. 5.1 Two examples of leap-frog results in RCV elections

ever elected mayor of a large American city finished with a margin of victory of over 2000 votes.[1]

Quan's achievement mirrored the victory of Mary Robinson in Ireland two decades before (see Fig. 5.1) and not just because of gender. Robinson had become the first female president of the Republic of Ireland in 1990 after an election using RCV (also called "AV" for Alternative Vote or "IRV" for Instant Runoff Voting). Like Quan, Robinson owed her victory in part to the ballot structure itself, to the kinds of inputs that voters were able to contribute and to the way those inputs were translated into results. She was trailing Brian Lenihan in first

---

[1] Romney (2010). Official count data were retrieved from Alameda (2018).

preferences by 44.1% to 38.9, but she overcame that margin when the third-place candidate's supporters favored her over her rival by a stonking ratio of more than five to one. In both Ireland in 1990 and Oakland in 2010, the use of a single mark with a plurality winner would have stopped the counting after the first preferences. Lenihan would then have become president of Ireland, and Perata would have become mayor of Oakland.[2]

Robinson's and Quan's historic wins were leap-frog results that took into account a broader base of support than could have been measured with exclusive or one-mark ballots (1MB). The ranking ballots in Ireland and Oakland allowed voters to plug more accurate and more informative representations of their political judgments into the electoral process, while at the same time hedging their bets with expressions of support for multiple candidates regardless of viability. Ranking ballots are one type of multi-mark or distributive ballot, among others, which offer significant gains in voter expression. Distributive ballots are smarter, sharper tools for voters compared to 1MB. But there are many alternatives to consider and many opportunities for experimentation and reform. This chapter will sort through the pro's and con's of different kinds of smarter ballot by considering the lessons of experience from around the world.

QUESTIONS OF EXPERIENCE

A lack of experience is often viewed as an intuitive drawback in a job candidate or a political candidate, and the case is no different with reform proposals in the realm of political institutions. Why would we expect any given change to be anything but a disaster? As job-seekers everywhere know, a lack of experience can be a catch-22: No one ever gained new experience without some initial step, or leap, into the unknown. In the case of multi-mark ballots, dismissing the "change" candidate for lack of experience is the easiest possible response.

Just as successful job candidates often make the case that easily overlooked experiences of theirs are nonetheless directly relevant to the advertised position, many varieties of distributive input rules have serious claims of relevant experience. The examples of Ireland's presidential and Oakland's mayoral elections show that ranking ballots already have

---

[2]On Robinson's victory: Gallagher and Mitchell (2005, 580–81) and Sinnott (2010, 119–20). Count data for Ireland were retrieved from Took and Donnelly (2018).

real-world political applications: RCV is the single-winner version of the Single Transferable Vote (STV) type of ballot structure. In Australia, this system goes back 100 years. Another kind of ballot structure based on ranking inputs, the Borda Count, was adopted for political elections in some former Australian territories in the South Pacific after they gained independence in the 1960s and 1970s. The Cumulative Vote has been used in a variety of real-world political contexts and is most prominent today in some American city and county elections. In addition to these three types of multi-mark ballot structure, there are some less experienced options that use grading inputs. These include the Grade-Point Average (GPA) system and the Median Grade system, neither of which has ever been applied in a public election.

If experience is your prime criterion of selection, then, you could be forgiven for thinking that all grading-input ballots should be immediately shelved. Yet this reaction overlooks potentially relevant experience with GPA and the Median Grade—of a kind that academic research is in a unique position to provide. It is easy to forget that the English words "experience" and "experiment" come from the same Latin root: *experiri*, meaning "to attempt" or, more literally, "put fear out." In Spanish, for instance, a person who is experienced is called *experimentado*. These linguistic origins remind us that every experience is a kind of experiment, and every experiment adds experience.

Scholars have been conducting more and more experiments on different ballot types in the last decade or two, covering four types of ranking and grading ballot in particular: RCV, Borda Count, GPA, and Median Grade; a version of GPA with a limited, binary scale (like a pass-fail grading system but usually called the Approval Vote) is frequently among these. Voting experiments come in three flavors (from least to most realistic): simulations, laboratory experiments, and field experiments. The first kind can forecast outcomes using partially or fully fictionalized voters and candidates. Second, lab experiments place real humans in a controlled setting and ask them to cast votes for real or fictionalized candidates under different sets of rules. The laboratory environment gets a little more realistic, but it still struggles to simulate campaign effects and fails to give subjects a gut feeling that the stakes are real. Third, field experiments invite actual voters into alternate polling stations on an actual election day, after the real voting has taken place. These offer a higher dose of realism, with a notable reservation: The people who volunteer to participate (in effect, taking the trouble to vote twice) are unlikely to be representative of all voters in key characteristics like education and ideology.[3]

Each of these kinds of experiment can provide valuable insights into voters' behavior and electoral outcomes; for parties' or politicians' behavior, it is extremely difficult to construct valid experimental situations of any kind. Even so, academic voting experiments should be considered relevant experience, albeit for some but not all the questions to which reformers need answers.

SINGLE-WINNER CUMULATIVE DISQUALIFIED

Ranking and grading ballots are currently at the center of most academic and policy discussions about reforming voting systems, and no version of the Cumulative Vote has been proposed for single-winner contests. It turns out that strong reasons from theory and evidence tend to disqualify that reform option, whatever the input rule's merits for multi-seat contests.

A cumulative election for one contest with one winner would give every voter the same package of support—say, equal to five votes. A voter who judges one candidate far superior to all others could give all five votes to that favorite. If one candidate is only slightly better than another, give three to the first and two to the second. Another voter might give two votes each to two good candidates, plus one to an acceptable third, and so on. In this way, a candidate's average score per voter would be a more precise and nuanced reflection of the judgment of the community than the same election on Plurality Vote principles, with only one mark per voter per contest.

Ultimately, however, a single-seat cumulative election would offer much less improvement in voter empowerment than the other multi-mark options. Cumulative input rules mean that no voter may use more than a maximum number of votes per contest, requiring more voting-booth arithmetic than other ballots. As a result, some voters may be discouraged from attempting to use the system to its full expressive effect, while others may make errors that would have been impossible

---

[3] For academic voting experiments in recent years: Dolez et al. (2011), Laslier and Sanver (2011), and Blais et al. (2016).

with 1MB, invalidating their ballots. Moreover, many voters may be discouraged from trying to spread their support precisely because of the extra cognitive labor required, instead plumping all their votes on a single candidate in the same way as (involuntarily) with 1MB. None of these voters would achieve a good balance of expression and accessibility.

Even with no additional cognitive burdens, cumulative inputs might still trap voters in the dilemma of disempowerment. In a multi-winner contest, voters use multiple votes to fill more than one seat, and it seems natural to spread votes around when electing several office-holders. In a single-winner contest, though, the strategic incentive to plump would be greater. If political parties and media pundits succeeded in elevating only two candidates to viable status in the public mind, voters would feel the same lesser-evil pressure that already operates under 1MB. They might still fear that, by doling out fractions of support, they could be handicapping the lesser evil and handing victory to the worst option. The attendant guilt and anxiety over "spoiler" candidates and "wasted" votes would then limit the number of voters who actually spread their support across several attractive options. After all, Ralph Nader voters would not have been hammered any less by Al Gore voters in 2000 if they had been able to give Gore two votes and Nader three; they would still have been accused of depriving Gore of his five-vote birthright. Despite its potential to reflect fine-grained judgments, then, the cumulative ballot's real-world effects would likely leave us feeling as though the world of blunt ballots had never passed.[4]

Once cumulative inputs are ruled out, the four single-seat alternatives to Plurality are RCV, Borda Count, GPA, and Median Grade (see Fig. 5.2). RCV is the system of ranking inputs with modal outputs, integrated by a unique counting system of eliminations and transfers: Weaker, non-viable candidates are eliminated in stages, and their ballots are transferred to the voters' next preferences until a majority winner emerges or a plurality winner remains when only two are left. Borda is the system of ranking inputs and mean outputs, with a counting

---

[4]For analysis of a local election in the USA where multi-seat Cumulative fared well on basic measures of accessibility such as voter confidence and satisfaction: Kimball and Kropf (2016). But 34% of respondents in this study reported plumping all their votes for a single candidate, and this figure would likely increase under single-seat Cumulative.

	Mode	Mean	Median
Ranking	RCV	Borda Count	
Grading		GPA	Median Grade

GPA = Grade-Point Average   RCV = Ranked-Choice Voting

Fig. 5.2   Reform options for single-winner elections

system that assigns a greater number of votes to higher-ranked candidates and a lesser number to lower-ranked candidates; the candidate with the highest average support per voter is elected. GPA has similar counting and winning rules to the Borda Count, but with grading rather than ranking inputs: Each voter may deliver any number of votes up to the per-candidate maximum. Median Grade is the system of grading inputs with median outputs, in which all candidates' median levels of support are measured by the voters that are exactly in the middle of their distributions, and the candidate with the highest median level wins (with special provisions for tie-breaking rules).

As we concentrate on these four ballot structures, recall that our preliminary, theory-based assessment indicated grading's superiority in terms of expression and accessibility, but ranking's in terms of alternatives (see Chapter 4). A number of good minds have come to similar conclusions in favor of grading over ranking. William Poundstone's compelling and wide-ranging analysis concluded in favor of GPA (a.k.a. the Range Vote) over RCV and Borda. Soon thereafter, in 2010, the most notable contribution to voting theory in recent years proposed the Median Grade system. Michel Balinski and Rida Laraki's self-styled "Majority Judgment" procedure was cogently presented as an antidote to voting theory's obsession with "comparing" options on the ballot, when what voters really need are methods for "evaluating" them. Perceptive as Poundstone's and Balinski and Laraki's pro-grading arguments are, neither approach is geared to the electoral-realist criteria of voter empowerment which I have been employing.[5]

We must now reassess the criteria of accessibility and alternatives in light of empirical evidence before accepting the theoretical advantages of grading over ranking as definitive. The task of consulting the lessons of experience is assisted by a body of evidence from real-world political elections for the ranking-input family (RCV and Borda Count) and from academic experiments for the grading-input family (GPA and Median Grade).

THE CELTIC MODEL OF RANKING BALLOTS

The largest political units that use ranking ballots are found in Australia, Ireland, and the UK. In the English-speaking world, the system of ranking ballots where multiple winners emerge from the same district is called STV; where a single winner comes from each district, the STV system tends to be called AV, IRV, or RCV.

Australia uses RCV for elections to its primary assembly and STV for its second house. Ireland uses STV for its parliamentary and RCV for its presidential elections. Within the UK, the regions of Scotland and Northern Ireland use STV for local elections, while major cities in England use a modified, two-rank form of RCV for mayoral elections. The easiest examples for illustrating the dynamics of ranking ballots are single-seat elections. Whenever a death or resignation occurs in a multi-member STV district, Ireland, Scotland, and (until recently) Northern Ireland have used special single-seat elections to fill the vacancy. Two such "by-elections" offer a handy illustration of how the Celtic model of ranking ballots works in practice—and specifically what happens to the vote-splitting problem under this model.[6]

A by-election for a seat on the Edinburgh city council, in the City Centre district, witnessed a cliff-hanger in 2011 (see Fig. 5.3). With six candidates in the race, a remarkably even spread of votes left only one of them below 10% after first-choice votes were counted. Ian McGill of the Conservative Party (the British Tories) led the initial count with 24.2% of votes, followed by Alasdair Rankin of the Scottish National

[5] Poundstone (2008) and Balinski and Laraki (2010).

[6] On STV and its single-seat variants within the UK: Lundberg (2018, 636–38). Ireland will be addressed in this section, and Australia further below.

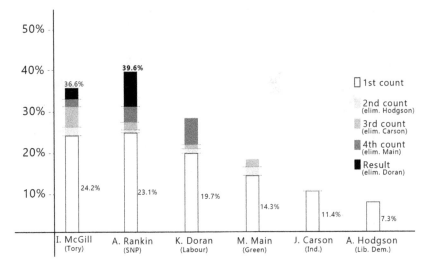

Fig. 5.3   By-election for Edinburgh City Centre (Scotland), 2011

Party with 23.1% and Karen Doran of the Labour Party with 19.7%. The exclusion of the two lowest-placed candidates left the overall order unchanged but increased the Tory's lead. Next to be excluded was the Green Party candidate, whose left-wing supporters broke heavily for the Labour and Nationalist options over the front-runner. But the Green transfers to Labour were not enough to overtake Rankin in second, so the third-place Doran was excluded next. Most of her center-left voters had marked no further preferences, but those who did favored the Nationalists over the Tories by an almost two-to-one ratio. As a result, Rankin leap-frogged McGill in dramatic fashion, at the last stage of counting. Having led the field for the previous four stages, McGill ruefully invited his supporters to his "victory, victory, victory, victory, defeat" party. The logic of RCV means that everyone's lower-ranked choices may be called into play, unless and until the leading vote-getter manages to secure a majority. In the absence of any such majority, when all who initially favored the less viable options had been heard, Rankin's support rose faster and further than McGill's.[7]

[7] Count data from Edinburgh were graciously provided by Chris Highcock of the city's elections office, and I owe a debt to Marco Biagi for his first-hand account of election night.

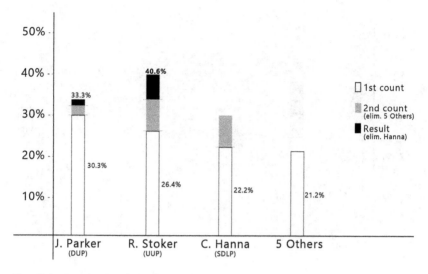

Fig. 5.4   By-election for Balmoral (N. Ireland), 1995

A second example illustrates the use of ranking ballots to deliver a discernible electoral sanction. In Balmoral, Northern Ireland, a town councilor died in 1995, leaving a vacancy that his widow attempted to fill on behalf of the incumbent party, the Democratic Unionists (DUP). With eight candidates contesting this by-election (see Fig. 5.4), three were still viable after first preferences were counted: Joan Parkes of the DUP led with 30.1%, Robert Stoker of the Ulster Unionist Party (UUP) was in second place with 26.4%, and Carmel Hanna of the Social Democratic Labour Party (SDLP) was in third with 22.2%. The DUP and UUP are right-of-center, Protestant parties; the SDLP is a left-of-center, Catholic party. The bottom five candidates' supporters, most of them from the center-left, transferred more votes to the SDLP's Hanna than to either of the unionist candidates, but not enough for Hanna to reach second place. More significantly, the excluded candidates' transfers also gave the UUP more votes than the DUP by a considerable margin, vaulting Stoker into first place and leaving Parkes in second. Thereafter Hanna's transfers would decide the contest. The SDLP votes favored the more moderate UUP, thereby padding Stoker's new lead and deciding the contest. With a clear majority of all votes on the unionist, Protestant side of the spectrum, the minority bloc none-theless was enabled to make a crucial intervention through their lower rankings.[8]

There is a particular lesson about ballot structure and electoral accountability in the Balmoral case. These special elections by definition do not include the sitting representative on the ballot (precisely because the incumbent has vacated the office), but the DUP's Parkes was run-ning as nearly as an incumbent as possible, with the same party label and surname as the previous holder of the seat. If 1MB inputs had been used, Parkes would have won the seat with a plurality of less than a third of all votes—perhaps even claiming a ratification of the previous holder's per-formance. Yet the ranking ballots not only suggest that this would have been a false-positive result; they actually helped to deliver the alternative, negative result.

Real-world experience with the Celtic model of STV/RCV, there-fore, yields a body of evidence relevant to the criteria of voter empower-ment. Feeling coerced into casting a single vote for a lesser evil is never a threat, since the vote-splitting problem is circumvented by rankings and transfers. A first-choice vote cannot be wasted because, if your favorite proves non-viable among the electorate as a whole, your vote is trans-ferred to next-best options. Diversity on the ballot is encouraged because minor parties and candidates cannot be credibly accused of spoiling for someone else. And leap-frog results, though in fact they only occur in a fraction of all contests that use the STV family of ballots, exemplify the danger that polarizing parties and candidates face, with a sizeable core of loyal supporters but little appeal beyond them. Political profession-als do not have to experience a leap-frog defeat before they can grasp that the system makes it possible, and they tailor their approach to voters accordingly.

RANKING BALLOTS IN AUSTRALASIA

In addition to Australia's STV and RCV elections, Borda elections (ranking inputs with mean outputs) are found in the island state of Nauru's legislative contests, and nearby Kiribati uses the Borda Count to

---

[8] Count data from Northern Ireland were graciously provided by Nicholas Whyte.

nominate presidential candidates. Several political parties in other parts of the world use it in their internal elections.[9]

The essence of the Borda Count, as a ranking-mean combination, is to assign larger numbers of votes to higher-ranked candidates on each ballot. The mean winner is the candidate with the highest sum or average. Nauru's small population of around 10,000, plus its non-partisan political system, makes it an unlikely model for emulation by large nation-states, but many municipal and regional jurisdictions in the USA, in addition to the state of Nebraska, already conduct non-partisan elections.

The standard critique of the ranking-mean input-output combination is that it incentivizes voters to attempt manipulation through insincere voting, based on evidence from computer and laboratory experiments. Borda leads some voters to give low-level support to a less preferred but more viable candidate while insincerely giving mid-level support to an even less attractive but also less viable candidate. Successful manipulation, however, requires a significant bloc of voters (around 10%) who all pull the same trick at the same time, with no counter-measures from anyone else. Moreover, with practice, voters may realize that gambling with viability in this way could be a fool's errand. Viability ultimately depends on actual votes, and inflating non-viable options with positive support is self-defeating if it makes them more viable. The most recent experimental results suggest that the Borda Count represents group preferences better than other systems, after a minority of voters' tactical efforts at manipulation cancel one another out.[10]

In real politics, the 1991 nominations for president in Kiribati have been cited as an example of Borda-enabled manipulation because two stooge candidates were successfully advanced ahead of a highly visible opposition leader. Kiribati is different from Nauru in having more inhabitants (100,000) and a multi-party political system. By law, either three or four presidential nominees are selected by members of parliament from among their own ranks. In 1991, two factions in parliament colluded to give second and third rankings to relatively obscure members, advancing them ahead of another, more prominent member who had

[9] Reilly (2002) and Reynolds et al. (2005, 118).

[10] For the conventional wisdom against Borda voting: Dummett (1997, 85–86) and Laslier (2011a, 14). For experimental critiques: Chamberlin (1985) and Laslier (2011b). For more positive experimental results: Granic (2017).

more first-place votes. The members with the second- and third-place votes revealed themselves as stooges when they subsequently failed to conduct any sort of campaign. This sort of thing seems a far cry from fair play, but ultimately the voting patterns merely revealed that the excluded opposition leader who finished fifth, according to the mean voter, was not very popular among his colleagues. A voting system that excludes such a figure should cause neither surprise nor alarm. If the voters of Kiribati were disempowered, if the fifth-place candidate would indeed have been viable in the general election for president, the fault obviously lies with allowing parliament rather than the voters to control the presidential ballot—and not with parliament's choice of voting method to select its nominees.[11]

The ranking-modal combination of STV/RCV is more prominent in the region, and Australia's legislative elections offer many more examples of ranking ballots in single-winner elections than do the Celtic jurisdictions. The primary assembly there is elected through hundreds of district-level RCV elections every few years. But the Celtic model is the only one worth considering, within the STV family, because some peculiarities of the Australian system render it unfit for emulation.

The prime reason is that federal elections there, unlike ranking ballots in Ireland, the UK, and the USA, impose rules for compelled rankings. Voters are required to indicate a preference for every single candidate before their ballots can be considered valid; no blanks are allowed (except for the last-place candidate). As a result, many Australian voters resort to one of two short-cuts: Either the "donkey vote," in which those candidates who are unfamiliar to the voter get ranked in an arbitrary fashion (usually alphabetically), or (in separate Senate elections only) the party vote, in which the voter makes a single mark accepting one of the political parties' predetermined rankings of all candidates for a particular contest.[12]

The Australian rule about compelled rankings has one benefit and several disadvantages. The benefit is that, when all valid ballots contain rankings for all candidates, the winner in a single-seat election is mathematically certain to reach 50% plus one. For this reason, RCV is sometimes touted as more majoritarian than 1MB. RCV in American cities,

[11] Reilly (2002, 367–68).
[12] Farrell and McAllister (2005, 86–87).

however, either follows the Celtic model, with optional rankings, or even places a limit on how many rankings voters can make (e.g., three in San Francisco, given the technical parameters of older voting machines). With optional or limited rankings, a larger field of candidates (good for voter choice, up to a point) entails a larger chance of a winner below the 50% level. Majority support is therefore not an ironclad selling point for RCV unless the system is going to follow the Australian model of discarding anyone's ballot who does not rank every single candidate.[13]

The drawbacks of Australia's compelled rankings, and mathematical majoritarianism, are significant. Requiring real-world voters to mark every single candidate, including feigned judgments about lesser-known ones, results in many votes that are either meaningless or else dictated (in Australian Senate elections) by the elites who formulate the parties' official rank-orders. The party list is usually considered a distinctive feature of "closed" PR. But Aussie rules convert elections that are supposed to be about individual candidates into votes for parties: In Senate elections, more than 90% of all voters consistently take the easy route of making only one mark to endorse a particular party's choice of rankings. Back-room negotiations about how one party's list ranks candidates from another party then come to determine electoral outcomes as much as voters' voices do. Anecdotal evidence from practicing politicians in Australia suggests that unpopular incumbents may benefit from forced rankings—presenting a clear danger of false-positive accountability results.[14]

Nor have compulsory rankings been popular with voters. A national survey in 1979 (admittedly, a long time ago) showed that Australians preferred optional over compelled rankings by a whopping margin of 72% to 26%. But the major parties could not be moved on the issue until 2016, when a slight modification was made to the rule for Senate elections. Instead of ranking all options to keep their ballots valid, voters now have to mark either more than five party lists or more than 11 individual candidates. In the elections of 2016, compared to 2013, the percentage of Senate voters making marks for parties' rankings rather than for candidates took a barely noticeable dip from 96.5 to 93.5. House

[13]For the finding that plurality (not majority) winners in RCV elections in four California cities are associated with voters' truncated rankings: Burnett and Kogan (2015).

[14]On the possibility of false-positive results: Sawer (2004, 483). For the 95% figure: Reilly and Malley (2000, 52).

elections' rankings remain fully compelled, and the comment of Ben Reilly and Michael Malley remains mostly intact: "there has never been a time when [optional rankings] seemed close to being implemented for federal elections in Australia."[15]

The somewhat surprising conclusion from a realist's look at the Australasian region, then, is that Nauru and Kiribati may actually have a more promising version of distributive ballots than Australia. This verdict comes from the perspective of voter empowerment, at least, which finds the Celtic model of STV/RCV, by virtue of its optional rankings, more congenial to a structural restoration of institutionalized accountability.

GRADING EXPERIMENTS IN EUROPE

What experience is at our disposal for assessing the grading type of ballot in comparison with ranking ballots? No major political election has ever used grading ballots, but a variety of experiments have been conducted in France during the 2002, 2007, and 2012 presidential elections. The official system in use there is 2RS, using 1MB voting in a two-step contest structure. These French experiments give the clearest idea that we have so far of how grading ballots work in practice.

Several different types of grading have been tested in France, the simplest of which is the Approval Vote, with only two possible grades (pass-fail) to give any candidate. Two other variants of GPA, with a three-point system, have also been tried: one with possible values of 0, 1, and 2, and another with −1, 0, and +1 as the options. In addition to these minimalist scales, a maximalist scale from 0 to 20 has also been tested. The one clear headline from these results, across three separate elections, is that grading ballots produce different outcomes from the exclusive input rules that real French elections impose.

The 2002 presidential election in France produced a shocking result in the first round when Jean-Marie Le Pen of the far-right National Front finished in second place (with 16.9% of votes) and advanced to the run-off against incumbent Jacques Chirac (19.9%). Le Pen narrowly surpassed Lionel Jospin (16.2%) of the Socialist Party, followed by the centrist Francois Bayrou (6.8%)—plus a menagerie of leftists and greens whose totals added up to more than 20% of votes. In a simulation on

---

[15] Quotation at Reilly and Malley (2000, 48). On the 2016 Senate reform: McAllister and Makkai (2018, 767–69).

the day of the first-round vote, voters in two districts used Approval and were able to give a grade of either zero or one to every candidate. When the results from this sample of voters were extrapolated to simulate a national vote, Chirac remained in first place with the highest number of approvals, but Jospin and Bayrou leap-frogged Le Pen into second and third place, respectively, leaving the far-right candidate in fourth. Freed from an all-or-nothing vote for a single candidate, voters encountered more freedom of choice. Le Pen's place among the top two was shown to be an artifact of the 1MB structure.[16]

The 2007 race produced a less surprising run-off between the center-right Nicolas Sarkozy (with 31.2%) and the center-left Segolene Royal (25.9%); Sarkozy then prevailed by 53% to 47% in the second round. Bayrou and Le Pen ran again, this time with the centrist taking third (18.6%) and the nationalist taking fourth (10.4%). Experimental simulations were done not only with the Approval Vote but also with three-point GPA scales, but the main results were the same for all. Bayrou in third would have swapped places with Sarkozy in first, with Royal remaining in second—a remarkable change in the outcome of the vote. Also impressive was the result that Le Pen would have dropped from fourth place to seventh when voters were able to grade every option on the same scale. As in 2002, centrist and leftist candidates appeared to have broader support than the right-of-center options.[17]

Running as the incumbent in 2012, Sarkozy was narrowly beaten in both the first and second rounds by Francois Hollande. The first-round votes gave Hollande 28.6% to Sarkozy's 27.2%, followed by Marine Le Pen (daughter and political heiress of Jean-Marie) with 17.9%. Bayrou ran yet again and now placed fifth (9.1%), one slot below the far-left Jean-Luc Melenchon (11.1%). The same-day voting simulations in 2012 added a GPA scale of zero to 20 to the pass-fail and three-grade scales of previous experiments. Hollande still won in all simulations. The binary Approval method yielded no change in the top two but did allow both Melenchon and Bayrou to leap-frog Le Pen, dropping the National Front candidate to fifth place. On this occasion, the ballots that offered voters more than two grades to assign produced distinctive results, dropping Sarkozy and Le Pen even lower while raising Melenchon

[16]On the 2002 experiment in Gy and Orsay, conducted by Michel Balinski and several colleagues: Baujard and Igersheim (2010, 381).

[17]Baujard and Igersheim (2010, 382).

and Bayrou even higher. There is important information about (and for) French voters in these numbers. Grading ballots constructed both Sarkozy and Le Pen as widely disliked outside their respective groups of core supporters, whereas Melenchon and Bayrou were constructed as comparatively "inclusive" candidates.[18]

The Approval Vote was also tested in Germany in 2008 and 2009, again with same-day simulated balloting by real voters. There the vast majority of voters chose to give approvals to one, two, or three parties (in districts whose ballots offered as few as six and as many as seventeen options), with the average number of marks being a little over two. The results showed the center-right and center-left parties (the Christian Democrats and the Social Democrats, respectively) remaining in the top two positions, but the support of minor parties went up dramatically. Parties like the left-wing Greens and the right-wing Free Democrats received many more votes when voters were freed from exclusive input rules.[19]

The distinctive Median Grade system, combining grading inputs with median instead of mean outputs, has been tested in the field during the first-round presidential voting in France in 2007 and 2012. Three voting precincts were used as sites for the first experiment, with real voters who volunteered to vote a second time with the alternative ballot; the second experiment involved an on-line survey just before election day (making it something between a lab and field experiment). In 2007, the centrist Bayrou won the Median Grade vote (over Sarkozy, the real-world plurality winner) in two out of the three precincts. In 2012, Hollande won the Median Grade vote (like the real vote), but Bayrou leap-frogged Sarkozy into second place. However, no detailed data on voter behavior were reported to shed further light on the balance between expression and accessibility.[20]

COMPLICATED BALLOTS, CONFUSED VOTERS?

Experiences with ranking and grading ballots in laboratory experiments, field experiments, and real-world elections collectively supply a body of evidence for testing with the criteria of voter empowerment.

[18] Baujard et al. (2014).
[19] Alos-Ferrer and Granic (2012).
[20] Balinski and Laraki (2014, 116–19).

A frequently heard argument against multi-mark ballots in reform debates is that they would discourage voters with low levels of formal education, civic engagement, and political knowledge from participating in the democratic process. If the voting system were to become any more complicated than 1MB, the argument goes, more voters will either mis-handle their ballots and void their votes or stop voting altogether.

In the case of grading ballots, experimental data from France and Germany have been encouraging about accessibility. Voters have had lit-tle difficulty in understanding and using the input rules, showing high levels of reported satisfaction with the alternative systems and low lev-els of invalid ballots. The percentage of rejected ballots is generally well below 1%. In the French simulations, where the binary Approval scale has been tried alongside three-point and zero-to-20 versions of GPA, participants have consistently shown enthusiasm for being able to express more fine-grained judgments than all-or-nothing. Participants in 2007 even gave the three-point scale higher marks for clarity of understand-ing than to the ostensibly simpler two-point scale, by a margin of 79% to 67%. Unlike 1MB, where plumping for one option is the voter's only option, grading ballots make plumping the exception rather than the rule. Only around 20% of voters using Approval have restricted their support to a single candidate or party, and fewer than 10% of vot-ers using more graded scales (zero-to-two or zero-to-20) have given the maximum score to a single favorite and the minimum score to all other options.[21]

For ranking ballots, we have evidence from actual public elections. Scotland is a good test case because all local councils there switched to ranking ballots at the same time in 2007. In addition to the percent-age of rejected ballots, the percentage of ballots using multiple marks can shed light on voter accessibility. In the first three elections of their use, Scottish ranking ballots showed rejection rates of 1.8%, 1.7%, and 1.9%. These figures have been consistently higher than the 0.8% rejected at the 2003 election, the last to use 1MB. For comparison, local elec-tions in Northern Ireland showed rejection rates of 1.5%, 0.9%, and 2.0% in 2003, 2007, and 2011; in Ireland (with much longer experience) the rejection rate is typically under 1%. Neighboring jurisdictions' experience

[21]On rejected ballots: Alos-Ferrer and Granic (2012, 177). On clarity of understand-ing: Baujard and Igersheim (2010, 377). On plumping: Baujard and Igersheim (2011, 81), Alos-Ferrer and Granic (2012, 178–79), and Baujard et al. (2014, 142).

implies that Scotland's rejection rate should go down with time but may still remain somewhat higher than under 1MB. Some evidence suggests that the 1% of voters adversely affected are more likely to come from lower-income, lower-education, and more elderly districts. As for the 98% still casting valid ballots, around four out of five voters in Scotland marked at least two candidates in 2007 and 2012, a little over half marked three or more, between 20% and 30% marked at least four, and between 10% and 20% marked five or more.[22]

The challenge is how to interpret these numbers. Does an increase of 1% represent too many invalid ballots? Does over 50% represent too few voters ranking three or more candidates? There does appear to be some trade-off between expression and accessibility in Scotland, but few have demanded an urgent return to 1MB. The rejection rate, and the possibility that it has an age-, income-, or education-related bias, can plausibly be considered remediable by time and by further efforts at voter education. If these remedies fail within a reasonable period of time, Scotland will have to decide whether the ability of 80% to make two or more marks should be revoked in favor of the ability of 1% to make one valid mark.

The evidence from American cities is also of interest, and several studies have been done on RCV in San Francisco. There the percentage of "over-votes," or ballots invalidated by giving the same ranking to more than one candidate, has averaged around 0.5% over more than ten years. The comparable rejection rate in a conventional plurality contest is typically only around 0.2%. Given that blacks, immigrants, and the elderly are more likely to over-vote with either ballot, the extra 0.3% invalidated in RCV elections are more likely to come from those groups. Still, when under-votes (i.e., blank ballots) are combined with over-votes in San Francisco, the overall rejection rate has actually been lower in RCV elections than previously under 1MB.[23]

A sensible conclusion from this varied body of evidence about expression vs. accessibility is that there has indeed been a trade-off in early post-reform elections, but not one that is now or is likely to become widespread. Even the most pessimistic view of the matter would concede that the accessibility problem applies to a small fraction of the electorate. The problem can be mitigated rather easily, in principle, because whoever

[22] Denver et al. (2009), Clark (2013), and Curtice and Marsh (2014).
[23] On San Francisco: Neely and Cook (2008) and Neely and McDaniel (2015).

was voting validly under 1MB has the opportunity to continue making only a single mark on either ranking or grading ballots: Find your favorite, mark the highest available value, and go home. The same could not be said for the much larger numbers of voters using multi-mark ballots to good effect, if those ballots were taken away and 1MB were reinstated. This asymmetry between who gains and who loses from a change of ballot structure is rarely noticed by the opponents of multi-mark reform.

THE PRELIMINARY ASSESSMENT, REVISITED

Given that ranking ballots currently have more real-world experience while grading ballots have to be tested experimentally, direct comparisons are elusive. Surprisingly, the recent surge in voting experiments has included very few analyses that attempt controlled comparisons between ranking- and grading-input schemes on a specific question of interest, such as expression, accessibility, or alternatives.

The available lessons of experience supply modest support for the expressive advantages of grading inputs over ranking. When presented with a seven-point grading scale, a remarkable 30% of all voters across two of the French experiments gave equally high grades to their top two candidates, thereby taking an expressive option that would have been denied to them by a ranking ballot. Anecdotal evidence from those who staffed other French field experiments suggests that "voters are particularly favorable to" grading scales with multiple possible levels of support, beyond the binary choice offered by an Approval ballot. Researchers have also found that voters need a means of expressing unique disapproval. With the Celtic model of optional rankings, voters have been observed using blanks for both indifference and disapproval in the same contest (having no input option for sensibly distinguishing the two). With grading ballots, voters use 0 for both indifference and disapproval when it is the lowest value on the ballot. When -1 is at the bottom of the grading scale instead, voters in the French experiments used 0 to express indifference and -1 to express disapproval. Again, the structure of the grading ballot allows a bit more expressive capacity than the ranking ballot does.[24]

---

[24]Quotation at Baujard et al. (2014, 132). On disapproval on grading ballots in France: Igersheim et al. (2016, 265–66). On disapproval on ranking ballots in Ireland: Laver (2004, 524–25, 530–34). On equally high grades in France: Balinski and Laraki (2010, 113; 2014, 116).

Expression, for a realist, must be balanced against accessibility: the voter's ease of comprehension and use of the input opportunities on the ballot. Whereas ranking and grading both have intuitive parallels in non-political areas of life, like shopping and education, ranking theoretically demands more cognitive effort in a multi-candidate context. Putting all the options in hierarchic order requires multiple comparisons while assigning grades can be done one option at a time. In 2008, Poundstone reported that one company on the World Wide Web recorded faster response times by users when they were asked to give grades compared to rankings: Independent evaluations seemed to take less effort than comparisons. Voting experiments and empirical political research have not attempted to isolate this kind of comparison.[25]

The pro-grading hypothesis is also supported by its structural property of offering fewer ways for the voter to err. While both types of distributive input will invalidate a ballot with more than one level of support marked for the same candidate, only the ranking ballot is also rejected for the same level of support given to more than one candidate. In France, where the political culture is deeply imbued with 1MB voting, separate experiments with ranking and grading ballots suggested a higher rejection rate for the former.[26]

This comparison cannot be carried to a satisfying conclusion without considering one further wrinkle. Though a grading ballot does, structurally, allow larger possibilities for expressing evaluations of each candidate, there is reason to think that some voters would not take advantage. In particular, where voters see some candidates about whom they have little knowledge or interest, grading inputs offer a tantalizingly easy default: give equally low (or perhaps high!) scores to the unfamiliar options. This default would be responding to a supply-side incentive to complete the voting process quickly without much thought. Consider, by contrast, the voter who confronts a ranking ballot, with no option of giving equal levels of support to two candidates. Any candidate who receives any mark at all has to be either above or below every other candidate. This logical structure nudges voters toward making comparisons as the price to be paid for making more than one mark. The ballot may then act as a lure toward more intensive thought and deliberation

---

[25] Poundstone (2008, 246–47).

[26] For a 6% rejection rate under RCV in France: Farvaque et al. (2011).

compared to a grading ballot. If you believe that two candidates are generally good enough, ranking inputs require you to think harder about similarities and differences between them. Some voters might reach more solid and authentic judgments after being prompted in this way.

Given the reality of disengaged and disgusted voters, the nudge toward comparisons on a ranking ballot could have either or both of two contrary effects. Some voters would respond to the challenge by paying more attention; others would walk away from the process altogether. Quite a lot may turn on the comparative magnitudes of these two groups under ranking, and their counterparts under grading, in terms of reform efforts. A realistic provisional case for ranking over grading could even rest on a presumption, pending further evidence, that its modest disadvantage in accessibility can be overcome by a significant advantage in deliberation prior to expression.

Politicians' strategic incentives for manipulating ballot options, whether restricting candidate entry or recruiting stooge options to dilute opponents' support, comprise the last of our criteria of assessment. The interaction of input and output rules is what structures this sort of elite incentive.

In the Celtic model of STV, ballot access is not a serious concern. Party elites worry more about which candidates to sponsor on the ballot for particular races than promoting stooge candidates for tactical purposes. Adding a stooge candidate to split an opponent's votes will not work when votes are both single and transferable: They merely move to the stronger candidate when the stooge is eliminated. Under 1MB in the USA, by contrast, the recruitment of Green Party candidates by Republican operatives for the purpose of splitting Democratic votes is one of several ways that stooge candidacies have exposed the incentives for manipulating the pool of alternatives.[27]

The real world of the Borda Count is much smaller than that of RCV, and manipulation of a 1991 election in Kiribati is worrisome. But this was a case of members of parliament who rigged a Borda election inside

[27] On stooge candidates in local elections in the American state of Washington in 2001: Hill (2002, 267). I owe a debt to several academics (Alistair Clark, David Farrell, Michael Gallagher, Michael Marsh, and Thomas Lundberg) and elections staff (Chris Highcock and David Miller) for conversations about ballot access for ranking-ballot elections in Ireland and Scotland.

their own body, not of either restricting or expanding ballot options before a national vote. The Kiribati experience therefore does not tell us much about elite behavior in managing ballot access in public elections under Borda rules.

Perhaps the democratic realist's most serious concern about all these smarter ballot structures is that politicians' behavior is not easily observed in experimental settings. With grading inputs and mean outputs, how might real parties and candidates try to signal voters, and for what potentially manipulative purposes? This consideration alone might induce reformers to feel more warmly toward the STV family than other options less experimented with. But the academic community should do more to intensify the process of building experiences, even if only experimental at first, for the other options.

REAL RANKING VS. REAL GRADING

In the realm of theory, we saw (in Chapter 4) that grading ballots are as good or better than ranking ballots in the versatility provided for expression within and across options. When the expectations of theory come into contact with experience and experiments, the theoretic advantages of grading over ranking are diminished. While both distributive input types retain significant potential for overcoming the dilemma of disempowerment which is institutionalized by exclusive ballots, no clear advantage can be awarded to either one, at least not on the grounds of electoral realism.

On the criterion of accessibility, though the grading inputs of GPA and Median Grade are probably easier for some voters to use than the ranking inputs of RCV and Borda are, the difference may not be large. On the criterion of politicians' incentives for manipulating the supply of alternatives on the ballot, RCV is demonstrably able to get mainstream parties and politicians to live with multiple competitors because of its unique counting rules. Otherwise, we are left with theory, for now, about the Borda Count, GPA, and Median Grade on this point. The mean output rules of Borda make it tempting to would-be manipulators, and the grading inputs of GPA and Median Grade might incentivize powerful incumbents to discourage high-quality candidates from running against them—but such incentives will exist at some level regardless of the input rule.

On balance, each of the four reform options for multi-mark, distributive ballot structures offers a plausible voting system for meeting the criteria of voter empowerment, given the lessons of experience that have been considered here. More, and more directly comparative, evidence between ranking and grading ballots is needed on the important questions. Since grading ballot types are unobservable in public elections, the relevant research designs must be experimental in nature. I have offered in this book a conceptual framework with theoretic expectations (in Chapter 4) as well as a literature review (in this chapter) to anchor such studies in future. We turn now to original examples of one kind of voting experiment that can be used to learn about variations in ballot structure: the retrospective election simulation.

References

Alameda County. 2018. "County of Alameda, CA: Elections" (Accessed on December 31, 2018 at www.acgov.org/government/elections.htm).

Alos-Ferrer, C., & D.-G. Granic. 2012. "Two Field Experiments on Approval Voting in Germany." *Social Choice and Welfare* 39: 171–205.

Balinski, M., & R. Laraki. 2010. *Majority Judgment: Measuring, Ranking, and Electing.* Cambridge, MA: MIT Press.

Balinski, M., & R. Laraki. 2014. "What Should 'Majority Decision' Mean?" *Majority Decisions: Principles and Practices,* eds. S. Novak & J. Elster. New York: Cambridge University Press.

Baujard, A., & H. Igersheim. 2010. "Framed Field Experiments on Approval Voting: Lessons from the 2002 and 2007 French Presidential Elections." *Handbook on Approval Voting,* eds. J.-F. Laslier & M.R. Sanver. Berlin: Springer.

Baujard, A., & H. Igersheim. 2011. "Framed-Field Experiment on Approval Voting and Evaluative Voting: Some Teachings to Reform the French Presidential Election System." *In Situ and Laboratory Experiments on Electoral Law Reform,* eds. B. Dolez, B. Grofman, & A. Laurent. New York: Springer.

Baujard, A., H. Igersheim, I. Lebon, F. Favrel, & J.-F. Laslier. 2014. "Who's Favored by Evaluative Voting? An Experiment Conducted during the 2012 French Presidential Election." *Electoral Studies* 34: 131–45.

Blais, A., J.-F. Laslier, & K. Van der Straeten, eds. 2016. *Voting Experiments.* Heidelberg: Springer.

Burnett, C.M., & V. Kogan. 2015. "Ballot (and Voter) 'Exhaustion' under Instant Runoff Voting: An Examination of Four Ranked-Choice Elections." *Electoral Studies* 37: 41–49.

Chamberlin, J.R. 1985. "An Investigation into the Relative Manipulability of Four Voting Systems." *Behavioral Science* 30: 195–203.

Clark, A. 2013. "Second Time Lucky? The Continuing Adaptation of Voters and Parties to the Single Transferable Vote in Scotland." *Representation* 49: 55–68.

Curtice, J., & M. Marsh. 2014. "Confused or Competent? How Voters Use the STV Ballot Paper." *Electoral Studies* 34: 146–58.

Denver, D., A. Clark, & L. Bennie. 2009. "Voter Reactions to a Preferential Ballot: The 2007 Scottish Local Elections." *Journal of Elections, Public Opinion, and Parties* 19: 265–82.

Dolez, B., B. Grofman, & A. Laurent, eds. 2011. *In Situ and Laboratory Experiments on Electoral Law Reform.* New York: Springer.

Dummett, M.A.E. 1997. *Principles of Electoral Reform.* Oxford: Oxford University Press.

Farrell, D.M., & I. McAllister. 2005. "Australia: The Alternative Vote in a Compliant Political Culture." *The Politics of Electoral Systems*, eds. M. Gallagher & P. Mitchell. Oxford: Oxford University Press.

Farvaque, E., H. Jayet, & L. Ragot. 2011. "French Presidential Election: A Field Experiment on the Single Transferable Vote." *In Situ and Laboratory Experiments on Electoral Law Reform*, eds. B. Dolez, B. Grofman, & A. Laurent. New York: Springer.

Gallagher, M., & P. Mitchell. 2005. "The Mechanics of Electoral Systems." *The Politics of Electoral Systems*, eds. M. Gallagher & P. Mitchell. Oxford: Oxford University Press.

Granic, D.-G. 2017. "The Problem of the Divided Majority: Preference Aggregation under Uncertainty." *Journal of Economic Behavior and Organization* 133: 21–38.

Hill, S. 2002. *Fixing Elections: The Failure of America's Winner-Take-All Politics.* New York: Routledge.

Igersheim, H., A. Baujard, F. Gavrel, J.-F. Laslier, & I. Lebon. 2016. "Individual Behavior under Evaluative Voting: A Comparison between Laboratory and *In Situ* Experiments." *Voting Experiments*, eds. A. Blais, J.-F. Laslier, & K. Van der Straeten. Heidelberg: Springer.

Kimball, D.C., & M. Kropf. 2016. "Voter Competence with Cumulative Voting." *Social Science Quarterly* 97: 619–35.

Laslier, J.-F. 2011a. "And the Loser Is … Plurality Voting." Cahier no. 2011–13. Paris: Ecole Polytechnique.

Laslier, J.-F. 2011b. "*In Silico* Voting Experiments." *Handbook on Approval Voting*, eds. J.-F. Laslier & M.R. Sanver. Berlin: Springer.

Laslier, J.-F., & M.R. Sanver, eds. 2011. *Handbook on Approval Voting.* Berlin: Springer.

Laver, M. 2004. "Analysing Structures of Party Preference in Electronic Voting Data." *Party Politics* 10: 521–41.

Lundberg, T.C. 2018. "Electoral Systems in Context: United Kingdom." *The Oxford Handbook of Electoral Systems*, eds. E.S. Herron, R.J. Pekkanen, & M.S. Shugart. Oxford: Oxford University Press.

McAllister, I., & T. Makkai. 2018. "Electoral Systems in Context: Australia." *The Oxford Handbook of Electoral Systems*, eds. E.S. Herron, R.J. Pekkanen, & M.S. Shugart. Oxford: Oxford University Press.

Neely, F., & C. Cook. 2008. "Whose Votes Count? Undervotes, Overvotes, and Ranking in San Francisco's Instant-Runoff Elections." *American Politics Research* 36: 530–54.

Neely, F., & J. McDaniel. 2015. "Overvoting and the Equality of Voice under Instant Run-Off Voting in San Francisco." *California Journal of Politics and Policy* 7: 1–27.

Poundstone, W. 2008. *Gaming the Vote: Why Elections Aren't Fair (and What We Can Do about It)*. New York: Hill & Wang.

Reilly, B. 2002. "Social Choice in the South Seas: Electoral Innovation and the Borda Count in the Pacific Island Countries." *International Political Science Review* 23: 355–72.

Reilly, B., & M. Malley. 2000. "The Single Transferable Vote and the Alternative Vote Compared." *Elections in Australia, Ireland, and Malta under the Single Transferable Vote: Reflections on an Embedded Institution*, eds. S. Bowler & B. Grofman. Ann Arbor: University Press of Michigan.

Reynolds, A., B. Reilly, & C. Ellis. 2005. *Electoral System Design: The New International IDEA Handbook*. Stockholm: Institute for Democracy and Election Assistance.

Romney, L. 2010. "Bay Area Races Increase Scrutiny of Ranked-Choice Voting." *Los Angeles Times*, November 20 (Accessed on August 24, 2017 at articles. latimes.com/2010/nov/20/local/la-me-ranked-choice-20101120).

Sawer, M. 2004. "Australia: Replacing Plurality Rule with Majority-Preferential Voting." *Handbook of Electoral System Choice*, ed. J.M. Colomer. New York: Palgrave Macmillan.

Sinnott, R. 2010. "The Electoral System." *Politics in the Republic of Ireland*, eds. J. Coakley & M. Gallagher. 5th edn. London: Routledge.

Took, C., & S. Donnelly. 2018. "Electionsireland.org" (Accessed on December 31, 2018 at www.electionsireland.org).

CHAPTER 6

America Re-votes, 2016:
Retrospective Simulations
with Smarter Ballots

There was one clear loser in the American elections of 2016. The beating that the principle of majority rule sustained was severe even by the imposing standards of the oldest, most malapportioned, most supermajoritarian of the world's democratic constitutions. The one-mark ballot (1MB), for which the US Constitution bears no responsibility, was the chief culprit. Neither of the two main candidates for the presidency of the USA in that year would have come within rock-throwing distance of power if different ballots had been used which showed greater respect for the triad of voter empowerment.

How can such outlandish claims be verified or disproven? The method of retrospective election simulation (RES) is one of the tools that researchers have at their disposal to illustrate the difference that ballot structure can make. RES involves taking a past electoral contest that was decided under one set of rules and rerunning it under different rules to reveal variations in process and outcome—instead of election forecasting, this is "back-casting." In some places, the RES method faces a significant methodological obstacle for learning about multi-mark ballots, one which academic research could do more to overcome. Information about citizens' preferences beyond their first-choice candidate is often difficult to locate or to construct, as existing opinion surveys leave gaps in our knowledge about degrees of support or lesser preferences for most contests.

© The Author(s) 2019
J. S. Maloy, *Smarter Ballots*, Elections, Voting, Technology,
https://doi.org/10.1007/978-3-030-13031-2_6

There have been three phases of RES in modern political science. In what we might call SimVote 1.0, information about voters' preferences is so limited that the researcher has no choice but to make educated guesses about how alternative input rules would have been handled. In SimVote 2.0, some information from opinion surveys around a past election is available which can be used directly or indirectly to fill in alternative ballots. For example, responses to questions about voters' judgments of multiple parties or candidates could be used to construct different degrees of counter-factual voting support. In SimVote 3.0, researchers effectively put the alternative ballots in the opinion surveys themselves, by asking voters directly how they would vote under different rules. This third approach can be a kind of field experiment, with real voters using hypothetical ballots on a real election day, or a laboratory experiment. In modern political science, the UK went from 1.0 in the 1970s to 2.0 in this century, and France has led (with Canada and Germany following) the move to 3.0 since 2007. The USA is stuck between 1.0 and 2.0 because publicly available opinion surveys usually, though not always, lack items about more than two candidate preferences per contest.[1]

Below I report the results of several RES analyses related to the 2016 presidential elections in the USA. These tend to hover on either side of SimVote 2.0, making the best of fairly limited data on what Americans thought about candidates other than the two major parties' nominees. Recall that smarter ballots are designed to have greatest impact on contests with more than two candidates and that plentiful ballot options are a key part of the formula for avoiding lesser-evil elections. The presidential field as a whole certainly had that feature prior to the end of the major parties' nomination processes, and the Republican Party's primary elections in particular presented a diverse supply of candidates. I will review a previously published simulation of a hypothetical one-round, national vote and then conduct replications thereof with different data and ballot structures. I will also present an original RES analysis of eleven state-level contests from the Republican primaries, using Ranked-Choice Voting (RCV).

---

[1] For election simulations in the UK: Steed (1974, 328) and Abramson et al. (2013). For France: Baujard and Igersheim (2010, 2011), Farvaque et al. (2011), Baujard et al. (2014), and Igersheim et al. (2016). For Canada: Blais et al. (2012). For Germany: Alos-Ferrer and Granic (2012) and Granic (2017).

Grading the Candidates

Michel Balinski and Rida Laraki, expositors and advocates of the Median Grade ballot structure, simulated the 2016 presidential election as a whole with this system. They relied on a poll that asked voters, in the heat of the primary season in March, to rate what kind of president each of various candidates from both parties would become, on a five-point scale. The response options in the Pew Research Center's survey were "great," "good," "average," "poor," and "terrible." Armed with these data, whose structure mimics grading inputs, Balinski and Laraki used median output rules to locate the level of support offered by the median voter for each of five candidates: Donald Trump, Ted Cruz, John Kasich, Hillary Clinton, and Bernie Sanders. They found that all but Trump were graded as "average" by the median voter, and that Trump came in last place with a median grade of "poor." As the only candidate among the top four who had more voters grading him above "average" than below that level, Kasich emerged as the winner of the Median Grade simulation. The other candidates could be ordered by the difference between the percentage of voters grading them higher than their median and the percentage grading them lower: With that tie-breaking rule in place, Sanders came second, Cruz third, and Clinton fourth.[2]

I have revised Balinski and Laraki's simulation with the Grade-Point Average (GPA) ballot structure: the same grading inputs but mean rather than median outputs. The data from the Pew survey have been transplanted onto a GPA ballot similar to the American scheme of school grades, with a high value of four and a low value of zero (see Fig. 6.1). The order of finish is exactly the same as in Median Grade: Kasich is first, followed by a middling pack of Sanders, Cruz, and Clinton, and Trump is well adrift in last place. The most notable result may be that the two eventual major-party nominees, Clinton and Trump, finish fourth and fifth in both grading simulations (before securing the actual nominations).

Such similar results across two output systems place a question-mark over the value added by Median Grade, given its relatively unfamiliar output rules. Balinski and Laraki have argued in general that median output rules should have beneficial effects on voters compared to GPA. Mathematically, extremely high or low grades from a small number of "cranks" can have less of an impact on an outcome decided by median

---

[2] Balinski and Laraki (2016).

	A	B	C	D	F	
	4	3	2	1	0	mean
Clinton	11	22	**20**	17	30	1.67
Cruz	7	22	**31**	21	19	1.77
Kasich	5	28	**39**	21	7	2.03
Sanders	10	26	**26**	17	21	1.87
Trump	10	16	12	**18**	44	1.30

N.B. Each box shows the percentage of voters assigning one grade to one candidate. The percentages in bold mark the median grade per candidate.

Fig. 6.1 Simulation of a hypothetical presidential vote in March 2016 (*Source* Balinski and Laraki [2016])

winning rules, which should thereby diminish incentives for strategic manipulation.[3]

If this argument for Median Grade is sound, the nature of the voters' inputs themselves would have varied depending on which output rules they believed were being used before the voting started. The electoral constructivist, of course, is less interested in a metaphysical claim about voters' true pre-electoral judgments and more interested in a comparison of ballot types' constructions of judgment. Experimental research has found that voters find Borda Count (ranking inputs, mean outputs) more tempting than other ballot types as an inducement to attempt strategic or manipulative voting, but grading scales with more than two grades available have not figured prominently in such studies. More experimental research on how voters respond to GPA and Median Grade would not only fill that gap but also facilitate a comparison that holds input rules constant but varies output rules. Such a research design would help to isolate what role output rules play in voters' incentives.[4]

---

[3] Balinski and Laraki (2010, 5, 8, 134).
[4] On Borda Count and manipulative voting: Bassi (2015).

FEELING THE CANDIDATES

I conducted further simulations with the same two ballot types but different data and a slightly different slate of candidates. The quadrennial American National Election Study (ANES) allows respondents to indicate "feeling thermometer" (FT) scores on a scale from 0 to 100 for a variety of candidates, parties, and causes. Low scores indicate "cold" feelings, and high scores are for "warm" feelings. In 2016, the main ANES study was administered in September and featured only the two major-party nominees for president in the FT items, but the pilot study of January 2016 contained FT items for eight different presidential candidates, two Democrats and six Republicans.

The 101-point FT scale allows us to simulate the effects of both GPA and Median Grade ballot structures on a hypothetical one-round election with eight candidates. This time the grading scale is much broader than the five-point scale in the Pew study of March 2016, on which Balinski and Laraki's simulation was based. The ANES data have significant limitations. The January survey responses were taken before any real elections had occurred, therefore drawing largely on respondents' attention to numerous candidate debates. The views captured were therefore partial and immature compared to the March data used by Balinski and Laraki. Another problem with the ANES data is the difficulty of constructing 1MB ballot responses for an open ballot that includes both parties' candidates. There are questions about respondents' favorite candidate in each party but no question about a single favorite for the office of president. There are questions about five different hypothetical match-ups for the top job, each one pitting Clinton against a different Republican. Results from such survey items would have been useful for the Clinton campaign at the time, but not for our purposes here.

Still, it is striking how little the FT survey responses look like the judgments constructed by exclusive ballots in real elections, which force voters to give 100% support to one option and zero to all others. Comparing evaluations of the Democratic candidates, Clinton and Sanders, only 5.5% of respondents gave one of them 80 or more points while simultaneously grading the other at 20 or less. The situation is even starker on the Republican side. Fewer than 1% (10 out of 1200) gave one of the Republican candidates 80 points or higher while simultaneously giving the other five 20 points or lower. In short, only a tiny fraction of the adult population appears to have been well served by the

	mean voter	median voter
J. Bush	35	37
B. Carson	44	48
H. Clinton	42	41
T. Cruz	41	43
C. Fiorina	39	46
M. Rubio	44	49
B. Sanders	**47**	**50**
D. Trump	40	35

N.B. Individual respondents' scores were given on a scale from zero to 100.

Fig. 6.2   Feeling thermometer scores for 2016 candidates

1MB structure for the internal party primaries, in terms of expression. The mere fact that over 90% of all respondents took advantage of the FT scores to express significantly distributed preferences among candidates within each party defies the fear that large numbers of real voters would be incapable of using anything more complex than a one-mark ballot.

We can also use the 2016 FT data to replicate the previous two RES analyses with different, much more graded preference data. Based on the 1200 responses given in January 2016, Sanders would have been the winner of a national vote with either type of output rule, whether mean (GPA) or median (Median Grade) (see Fig. 6.2).[5]

The fact that the mean and median scores are similar for most candidates indicates that roughly equal numbers of voters were on either side of their average grade. Only the discrepancy for Carly Fiorina, whose median score is seven points higher than her mean score, seems marginally significant on a 101-point scale. Mathematically, the implication is that Fiorina's average got dragged well below her median by a relatively tight cluster of low-scoring respondents which was not off-set by a similar concentration of respondents scoring her well above her median.

[5]Because the January ANES survey was conducted on the World Wide Web, and the respondents were not representative of the population of American adults, I computed means and medians with the weighting variables provided in the ANES data file to get more representative results.

	A = 4	B = 3	C = 2	D = 1	F = 0	mean
J. Bush	6.0%	13.1%	30.0%	**19.5%**	31.4%	1.43
B. Carson	16.1%	15.2%	**26.0%**	14.3%	28.6%	1.76
H. Clinton	20.8%	14.8%	**14.9%**	8.9%	40.5%	1.67
T. Cruz	12.4%	14.8%	**26.8%**	14.3%	31.8%	1.62
C. Fiorina	7.6%	15.1%	**32.9%**	13.4%	31.2%	1.55
M. Rubio	11.2%	16.9%	**31.3%**	16.2%	24.3%	1.74
B. Sanders	21.0%	13.3%	**25.9%**	13.1%	26.8%	1.89
D. Trump	21.1%	13.5%	13.8%	**9.6%**	42.0%	1.62

N.B. All grades have been rescaled, from zero-to-100 to zero-to-four. Values in bold indicate the location of the median voter for each candidate.

Fig. 6.3 Simulation of a hypothetical presidential vote in January 2016

Median Grade is usually conducted with a simplified scale that is less expansive than 0 to 100, allowing a cleaner vantage on the distribution of judgments for each candidate. If we rescale all the FT scores to a five-point scale (0 to 4), we can view the distribution in terms of quintiles or blocs of 20 FT points. The distributions from a rescaled simulation (see Fig. 6.3) show that Trump had the largest bloc of fervent support among all eight candidates, at 21.1%, to go with the largest bloc at the lowest possible grade. He was a polarizing candidate. But the other major-party nominee, Clinton, had a remarkably similar distribution on the zero-to-four scale (and had a median voter that was only 0.6% away from a grade of D).

Incidentally, the zero-to-four scale mimics the typical American system of high-school and university grades, offering some confidence that voters in that cultural context would use such a scale in relatively consistent and commensurable ways. Comparing results for the GPA and Median Grade systems on this shorter scale, we find that Sanders (unsurprisingly) still wins the GPA result while tying with five other candidates for the median grade of 2 (or C, in American school-grade terms). None of the six candidates who are tied has more voters above the median than below it, but Sanders is the only one whose deficit here is in single digits (at −5.6%). Once again, if we were to compute the tie-breaker scores of the top six, we would find that they shake out in the exact same order as given by the GPA scores.

So far I have presented four RES analyses, two for GPA and two for Median Grade, one each with two different slates of candidates and sources of voter data. Altogether, their most striking result is the poor performance of the eventual major-party nominees, Clinton and Trump, when voters' electoral judgments are reconstructed through grading ballots. Though Kasich, widely perceived as a moderate on the right, won both simulations that were based on March data, the January simulations crowned Sanders, an ideologue from the other side of the spectrum. Significant differences in the timing and context of the two data sources limit the utility of comparisons across the two sets of simulations. But it is noteworthy that, within each set of two, the simulations gave identical results regardless of output rules when the grading was done on a five-point scale.

To probe how robust this similarity may be between GPA and Median Grade, better research designs with appropriate data would be necessary for better comparative analysis. The January and March surveys used here were asking voters for their judgments with no explicit expectation that they would be aggregated as votes with a single-winner outcome. The next step for research would be to compare GPA and Median Grade with separate sets of response data, each elicited with its own particular ballot structure in respondents' minds.

Multi-mark Ballots and Polarizing Candidates

The American presidential primaries within each party also deserve attention because the RES method can use them to exploit actual electoral data rather than running an entirely hypothetical election. The Republican nominating primaries of 2016 are particularly useful because of the plentiful options on the ballot, compared to only two major candidates in the Democratic primaries. The Republican contests also accentuate the pitiable state of the principle of majority rule in the American elections of 2016, making them ripe for "back-casting" with multi-mark ballots. At the moment when Trump's last intra-party rivals announced their withdrawal from the contest, after the Indiana primary in May, the presumptive nominee had received the support of barely 40% of the Republican Party's voters. Before Trump became a minority president, thanks to the Electoral College, he was a plurality nominee with almost 60% of his own party against him.[6]

---

[6]For official voting results from the Republican primaries: Berg-Andersson (2017).

There was no Electoral College in the primaries, of course. Was ballot structure a key factor paving Trump's path to victory there? Theoretically, multi-mark ballots could have either constructed Trump as a majority winner or constructed a different majority winner against Trump. Which was more likely?

Previous experimental research speaks directly to this kind of question, given the polarized distribution in voters' judgments of Trump which were revealed by the ANES feeling thermometers in January 2016 (see Fig. 6.3). French voting experiments in particular have shown a persistent pattern across three presidential elections: Even when experimental multi-mark ballots did not change the overall winner of the contest, they always demoted the National Front candidate (Jean-Marie Le Pen in 2002 and 2007, his daughter Marine in 2012) to a lower place than 1MB voting had yielded in the real election. Researchers therefore concluded that "the two-round system favors 'exclusive' candidates, that is[,] candidates who elicit strong feelings, while evaluative [i.e. multi-mark] rules favor 'inclusive' candidates, that is[,] candidates who attract the support of a large span of the electorate."[7]

This conclusion about polarizing candidates, or those who mobilize a minority of hard-core loyalists against a plurality or majority of largely hostile opponents, might be open to further empirical testing. The RES method could be applied in a different national context to see whether 1MB ballots have the same effect of favoring polarizing candidates, while comparing it with a different sort of multi-mark ballot, a *ranking* rather than a *grading* ballot.

Theoretically, the distortive feature of the 1MB structure which appears to benefit polarizing candidates is the inflexibility of expressions of judgment which is imposed on voters. A voter's most favored (or least despised) candidate can never receive less than 100% support, a voter's second- and third-choice candidates can never receive more than zero support, and the difference between a mediocre candidate and a detestable candidate can never be registered at all (if the mediocre candidate is not also the first-choice candidate). To put the point about inflexibility another way, supporters of a polarizing candidate may be largely satisfied with these means of expression, but supporters of any other candidate

---

[7] Quotation at Baujard et al. (2014, 133–34).

have no way of expressing the judgment that a polarizing candidate is considerably worse than even their second- or third-choice candidates. Moreover, unless the opponents of a polarizing candidate can unite behind a single alternative, they may well find that the exclusive ballot bestows a plurality victory on their bete noire. With multiple marks, however, varying intensities of preference have a greater chance of being counted in the final result. There is no reason in principle why grading types of ballot (as in the French experiments) should be regarded as the only means of expressing variable intensities of preference across multiple candidates; indeed, ranking ballots are much more common in real elections. The ranking type of ballot structure should therefore show some capacity for diminishing 1MB's beneficent effects for polarizing candidates.

Making the Trump candidacy subject to RCV is an apt test. Trump looks like a polarizing figure of the Le Pen type. In January 2016, the ANES feeling thermometer showed that Trump's supporters rated him at 91 on average, while other Republican candidates' supporters gave him an average score of only 50—a massive discrepancy in an intra-party comparison. Gary Jacobson seemed justified in saying that Trump "excited a substantial and enthusiastic portion of the Republican base" but "had little crossover appeal."[8]

The RCV system is ripe for RES applications. It has the potential to change outcomes when preference rankings are incorporated after the first count and a leap-frog winner emerges. Polarizing figures and parties seem to understand the threat posed to them by RCV. When experiments in France exposed voters to multi-mark ballot types, including RCV, Le Pen supporters named the status quo (2RS) as their favorite system in greater numbers than any other category of voter. When the UK was considering a change to the Alternative Vote (virtually the same as RCV), the Conservative Party emerged as the most intense opponents of reform because they saw little chance of gaining from second or lower preferences: Voters for Labour and the Liberal Democrats would gang up to oust them in competitive districts.[9]

---

[8]On feeling thermometers: Abramowitz and McCoy (2019, 148). Quotation at Jacobson (2016, 235).

[9]On Le Pen supporters: Blais et al. (2015, 433). On the British Tories: Renwick (2017, 343).

RCV has been implemented in some American elections and is continuously under consideration for adoption in various local and state jurisdictions around the USA (see Chapter 7). It is a viable reform there. In the specific area of ballot structure—alongside the reforms of contest structure known as jungle primaries, which mainly affect ballot options— RCV is the prime election-reform proposal in the USA in the early twenty-first century.

Case Selection: Eleven Republican Primaries from 2016

For better or worse, issuing a counter-factual prediction about how the Republican nomination struggle would have unfolded under different ballot rules is not possible. The state-level data on voters' judgments which would be required to rerun every state-level election with a high level of confidence are not publicly available. Moreover, many states witnessed a landslide result for one candidate, rendering it less likely that a different ballot structure could construct a different result. An achievable goal, however, is to explore the conditions under which distributive inputs could have changed results that were relatively close under 1MB. Since Trump was the most polarizing candidate in the Republican field, a focus on his narrower victories could test questions parallel to those raised in the French simulations about the National Front.

The state-by-state Republican primary process was also theoretically interesting for research on smarter ballots because they were unusually multi-competitive beyond two viable candidates, and therefore unlike most American elections at the state and national levels. Many local elections and some statewide elections, however, are also multi-competitive and will likely continue to be affected by similar dynamics in the future. With more than two options on the ballot, the issue of vote-splitting arises. Vote-splitting is a fundamental problem in the broader ecology of electoral democracy around the world (see Chapter 3), and multi-mark ballots offer a potential solution.

I selected 11 of the Republican primaries for simulation. As of April 2016, prior to the election in his home state of New York, Trump had never secured majority support in any state, despite having won 17 primaries out of 22 and three caucuses out of eight. I decided to focus only on primaries rather than caucuses, since voters in caucuses are notoriously activist and unrepresentative; in any case, Trump was already losing the caucuses. I also excluded primaries that Trump actually lost. Of the 17 primary elections prior to New York that Trump won, five of these were excluded because of apparently insurmountable leads of around 20% or more; a sixth, in Mississippi, was excluded because Trump took over 47% of the first-choice votes and therefore needed relatively few transfers to obtain a majority. The remaining 11 primary states, then, are the cases of interest: primary elections that Trump won with fewer than 45% of votes and a margin of victory smaller than 20%. These cases are (in chronological order on the 2016 primary calendar) South Carolina, Arkansas, Georgia, Tennessee, Vermont, Virginia, Louisiana, Michigan, Illinois, Missouri, and North Carolina.

Presidential primaries are unusual elections in certain respects. Despite being regarded, reported, and campaigned for as a single-winner contest, a state's primary does not produce one occupant for one office but rather a slate of multiple delegates. The party's nominee is then produced indirectly from the aggregation of delegates at a national convention. In turn, various states have various rules for allocating delegates to candidates. The winner-take-all allocation rule, by which the plurality winner of a state primary obtains all the state's delegates, was not universally used in the 2016 primaries. Instead, most states mingled a semi-proportional allocation of delegates with delegate bonuses for plurality winners and minimum thresholds for other winners of delegates. In the early Republican contests, 10 out of 29 primaries (South Carolina, Arkansas, Vermont, Florida, Ohio, Arizona, Connecticut, Delaware, Maryland, and Indiana) used the winner-take-all system, which mimics a traditional single-seat plurality (SSP) election for the House of Representatives or the Senate. Most of the other 19, however, did at least use a plurality-winner bonus. Only Massachusetts, Virginia, North Carolina, and Rhode Island ended up allocating delegates in a way that was nearly proportional, with little or no over representation in the plurality winner's share.

These details matter because the multi-mark system being simulated here, RCV, uses rankings, eliminations, and transfers to identify a single winner. Any state can choose a strictly proportional allocation of delegates and thereby lessen the anti-majoritarian dilemma that the 2016 Republican primaries suffered through. For those with a winner's bonus, whether that bonus is 100% of delegates or some smaller portion, the comparison of the RCV and SSP ballot structures retains real-world relevance. But the inclusion of the strictly proportional states of North Carolina and Virginia means that our counter-factual assumption, for the purpose of this simulation, must be that each of the eleven contests had aimed to identify a single winner. Given how media coverage and campaign narratives actually exploit first-place status for all states, even the most proportional ones, the heuristic intentions here are not entirely divorced from counter-factual implications, in any case.

Caroline Tolbert and Kellen Gracey conducted several simulations of American presidential contests in 2016, including a hypothetical national primary to select the Republican nominee with RCV. Their results showed that Trump won 55% to Cruz's 25% and Marco Rubio's 19% after the seventh count, compared to an initial count of 41% for Trump, 20% for Cruz, and 11% for Rubio. They used the feeling thermometers from the January ANES study, with its national sample, to construct each respondent's rankings of Republican candidates. (They then had to devise an algorithm for which respondents would have voted in a Republican primary, since the January study did not include that information among the survey items reported.)[10]

Two difficulties surround this simulation which have to be accounted for in similar efforts. First, and as noted above, the January data preceded the first actual primaries, and a lot changed after the voting started. Second, one of the things that changed was the field of candidates. The January survey only asked respondents to grade six Republican candidates, not including Kasich, who became more prominent after the voting started and others dropped out. This partiality in the January data makes it impossible to conduct RCV simulations that include Kasich as a candidate, since there is no way of knowing how many supporters of candidates who dropped out early (like Jeb Bush, Chris Christie, and Fiorina) would have gravitated to Kasich, or where supporters of the other main candidates would have placed Kasich in their rankings. But excluding Kasich altogether is out of the question, since he actually won the simulated grading ballots in March which were reported above.

---

[10]Tolbert and Gracey (2018, 81–82). The assessment of methodological challenges in the simulation is my own, not the authors'.

SIMULATION PROCEDURE

I have therefore adopted a different method, in between SimVote 1.0 and 2.0. Taking the official vote tallies as first-preference votes, the key mechanism that RCV simulations require is a battery of "next-preference rules": the proportion of voters who voted for Candidate X and would have given their second ranking to Candidate Y, the proportion of voters who ranked Candidate Y second and would have ranked Candidate Z third, and so on. Estimating next-preference rules, with some thought for voters who would have stopped marking any preferences after a certain ranking, enables the conduct of a full RCV count after starting with the official 1MB results.

One aspect of this procedure does threaten, theoretically, to introduce imprecision into the simulation: assuming that first preferences as expressed on a hypothetical ranking ballot would mirror first preferences as expressed on the real exclusive ballot. An analysis of single-winner elections in legislative districts using plurality rules in the Canadian province of Ontario, for example, found that around 10% of survey respondents indicated that they would have given their top ranking in an RCV election to a different candidate or party from the one they actually voted for. Since this range of numbers exceeds the typical margin of error in voter surveys, it is generally advisable not to simulate an RCV election by assuming that first preferences would play out identically.[11]

Certain features of American presidential primaries, however, diminish the danger for this RES analysis. American voters are accustomed to thinking of the nominating season as a lengthy process, in which their state's primary offers one moment at which to contribute their voices. Their primary vote is not do-or-die. The incentives to vote tactically, or to choose the lesser evil, are not strong compared to more definitive general-election contests for president, senator, or governor. Conceivably, then, the proportion of voters who would have indicated a different first choice with a ranking ballot before them may have been closer to the typical figure for spoiled and invalid ballots, viz. 1% or 2%.

I have structured the RCV simulations by first dividing Republican primary voters into six categories, including first-choice supporters of the top five candidates who lasted beyond the first few contests, plus a sixth bloc covering all others. We then must develop rules for determining

---

[11] Blais et al. (2012, 831).

each of the six voting blocs' second preferences. Finally, we must develop rules for third preferences for each bloc that ranked one particular candidate first and another particular candidate second. Here is where the crucial choices in the conduct of the simulation had to be made.

NEXT-PREFERENCE RULES

The nominating processes of 2016 ruthlessly exposed factional divides in both major parties, and Henry Olsen and Dante Scala's "four faces" conceptualization of the Republican Party can help in developing protocols for estimating next-preference rules for our simulations. On this analysis, four stable factions have been apparent within Republican primary electorates in the twenty-first century: centrists, "main street" conservatives, religious conservatives, and secular ideologues.[12]

The four faces of the Republican Party are revealed in a different light by survey data than by mainstream media commentary. Main-street conservatives are the largest faction nationally (35–40% of Republican primary voters) and are evenly distributed across the country. Centrists are, contrary to media portrayals, the second-largest group (25–30%), though also concentrated in the northeastern and midwestern portions of the country. Religious conservatives are the third-largest faction (around 20%), heavily concentrated in the southern states. Secular ideologues typically make up only 5–10% of the Republican primary electorate, in idiosyncratic proportions state-by-state.[13]

Certain preference patterns among the four factions are noteworthy. Centrists look more favorably on main-street conservatives' preferred candidates than on either religious conservatives' or secular ideologues'. Main-streeters are suspicious of ideological as opposed to pragmatic candidates and are therefore reticent around both religious and secular "movement" figures. Religious conservatives and secular ideologues are both intensely suspicious of centrists and more likely to feel comfortable with a main-streeter. Religious conservatives' favored candidates have generally struggled to appeal to the other three factions.

---

[12] Olsen and Scala (2016, 3–7); I have modified the authors' original labels for the four factions, which were (respectively) "moderate and liberal," "somewhat conservative," "very conservative and religious," and "very conservative and secular".

[13] Olsen and Scala (2016, 33–121).

Among the five leading candidates of 2016 who feature in our simulations, only Trump was polling as either the first- or second-choice candidate of all four factions in late 2015. Still, Trump also had the highest negative ratings across all factions, particularly among main-streeters and centrists. Among Trump's rivals, Cruz and Ben Carson most closely fit the preference profile of religious conservatives, while Kasich and Rubio were best positioned to pursue centrists and main-streeters.[14]

Clear affinities existed between Kasich and Rubio, on the one hand, and between Carson and Cruz, on the other. But Rubio more than Kasich, and Carson more than Cruz, showed some appeal in early surveys beyond one or two factions: For example, Rubio was favored by some secular ideologues and Carson by some main-street conservatives. The wild card for next-preference rules is Trump: How many voters for his rivals considered him an acceptable second or third choice, and how many judged him utterly unacceptable? To account for this uncertainty, I run the simulations below with two different models of Republicans' next-preference rules: a "Never Trump" model in which very few second or third preferences go to Trump and a "Maybe Trump" model in which a higher proportion do so.

The "Never Trump" movement held that all other candidates' supporters would be very reluctant to move to Trump if their candidate dropped out, while the vast majority of them would move instead to one of his rivals. For the sake of simplicity, I operationalized the next-preference rules in intervals of 10% of each candidate's voters, starting with transfer rules for second preferences (see Fig. 6.4). Since Trump himself is never eliminated in any of the 11 cases, rules about Trump voters' second or third preferences are never called into play.

RCV transfers always leave some "exhausted" ballots, those of voters who either truncate their rankings (thereby leaving blanks for unfamiliar or disliked candidates) or indicate a final preference for a candidate already eliminated. I assumed that supporters of Kasich and Rubio, as party "regulars" who are likely familiar with more than one candidate in the field, would have relatively low truncation rates; that supporters of Carson and Trump, the most unorthodox and inexperienced candidates,

[14]Olsen and Scala (2016, 134–37, 142).

BC voters: 30% to TC, 20% to MR, 10% to JK, 10% to DT, 30% exhausted.
JK voters: 50% to MR, 20% to TC, 10% to BC, 10% to DT, 10% exhausted.
MR voters: 40% to JK, 30% to TC, 10% to BC, 10% to DT, 10% exhausted.
TC voters: 30% to BC, 20% to MR, 10% to JK, 10% to DT, 30% exhausted.
Others voters: 70% to JK + MR + TC,* 10% to BC, 10% to DT, 10% exhausted.

BC = Ben Carson, **DT** = Donald Trump, **JK** = John Kasich, **MR** = Marco Rubio, **TC** = Ted Cruz

In states with less than a 10-percent gap between second and third, each of those candidates gets 30 percent of Others' second preferences while the fourth-placed candidate gets 10 percent; with more than a 10-percent gap between second and third, the second-placed gets 40 percent of Others' second preferences, the third-placed gets 20 percent, and the fourth-placed gets 10 percent.

Fig. 6.4 "Never Trump" transfer rules (first to second)

would have relatively high truncation rates; and that supporters of Cruz and Others would fall somewhere in between.

These next-preference rules are assumed, for the purposes of these simulations, to apply nationally. Place matters in American politics, and some variation in any bloc's second preferences from one state to another likely existed. But a complex and cumbersome simulation process would have been required, and without the benefit of publicly available state-level opinion data, to model them precisely across all 11 cases. State-by-state variation within our simulations therefore originates in the varying starting-points of all candidates, based on official vote tallies, before the RCV process of eliminations and transfers begins.

With transfer rules for moving from second to third preferences (see Fig. 6.5), I assumed that all supporters of Others, once their votes were transferred to one of the five majors, would afterward behave as if their second choice had been a first choice, so no separate second-to-third rules would be required for this relatively small group.

Fourth preferences are never counted in these simulations. In five out of the 11 cases, only four candidates were on the ballot, meaning that counting always stopped after third preferences. In the other six cases, fourth preferences could have been counted. I checked the tabulations of count stages and found that the percentage of ballots exhausted by not having an assigned fourth preference was rarely large enough to change the outcome. Both Georgia and Tennessee could mathematically have changed from victories to defeats for Trump in the "Never Trump" model if tiny proportions of fourth preferences

BC > JK voters: 40% to TC, 30% to MR, 20% to DT.
BC > MR voters: 50% to TC, 20% to JK, 20% to DT.
BC > TC voters: 60% to MR, 20% to DT, 10% to JK.
JK > BC voters: 30% to MR, 30% to TC, 30% to DT.
JK > MR voters: 50% to TC, 20% to BC, 20% to DT.
JK > TC voters: 40% to MR, 30% to DT, 20% to BC.
MR > BC voters: 50% to TC, 30% to JK, 10% to DT.
MR > JK voters: 50% to TC, 20% to BC, 20% to DT.
MR > TC voters: 40% to JK, 30% to BC, 20% to DT.
TC > BC voters: 60% to MR, 20% to DT, 10% to JK.
TC > JK voters: 40% to MR, 30% to DT, 20% to BC.
TC > MR voters: 40% to BC, 30% to JK, 20% to DT.

N.B. The notaton "BC > JK" indicates the bloc of voters who ranked BC frst and JK second.

Fig. 6.5 "Never Trump" transfer rules (second to third)

(1.4% and 3.4%, respectively) had gone overwhelmingly against him. The decision not to assign fourth preferences thus made the first set of simulations slightly conservative in their estimate of Trump's vulnerability to losing elections to leap-frog winners under RCV.

RESULTS FROM THE "NEVER TRUMP" MODEL

The counting procedure under RCV is to eliminate candidates in order, according to the lowest vote totals, and to redistribute the eliminated ballots to their next available preferences (i.e., only to candidates not yet eliminated). When a lower-placed candidate is eliminated, each of the higher-placed candidates receives a boost in percentage of votes received. The count stops whenever it becomes mathematically impossible for the leader to be overtaken by further eliminations and transfers: when either one candidate crosses the threshold of 50% of all votes or the third-place candidate is eliminated, leaving the top two with their final vote totals.

The 11 simulations under "Never Trump" assumptions produced eight changes in the winning candidate: eight new losses for Trump (see Fig. 6.6). The margins of victory for Trump's rivals, after transfers, are considerable in some cases. Only Georgia, Tennessee, and Michigan prove resistant to the ability of the RCV ballot structure to construct a leap-frog winner by taking account of variable levels of support across multiple candidates.

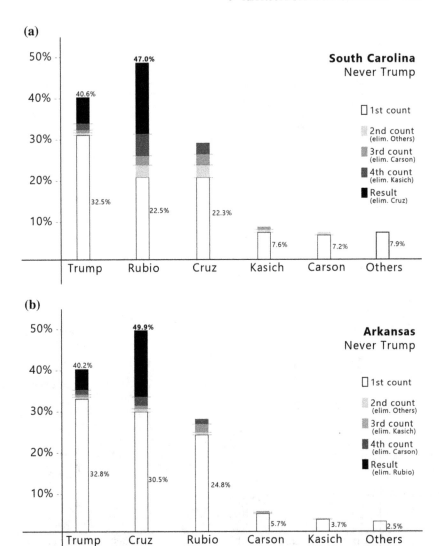

Fig. 6.6 "Never Trump" simulation results with RCV

(c)

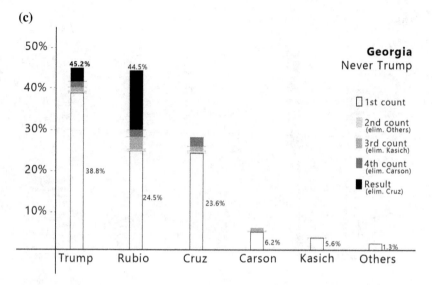

(d)

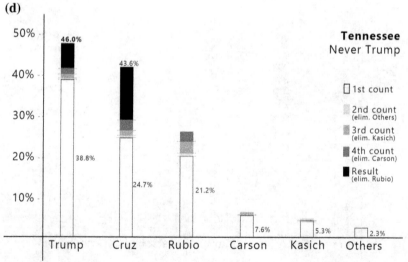

Fig. 6.6 (continued)

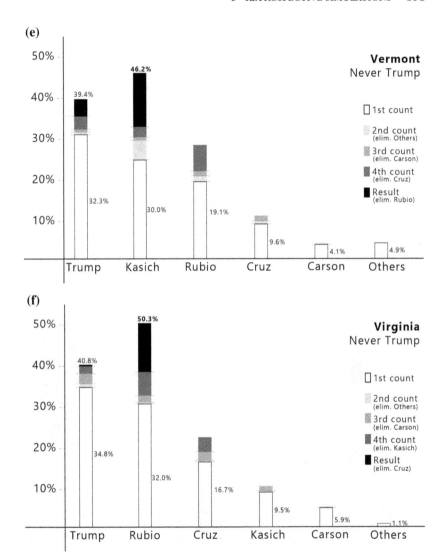

Fig. 6.6 (continued)

(g)

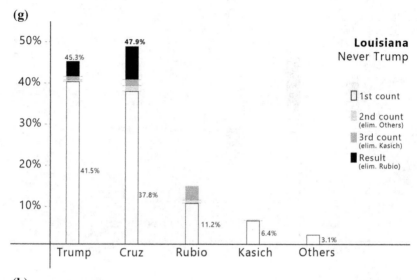

(h)

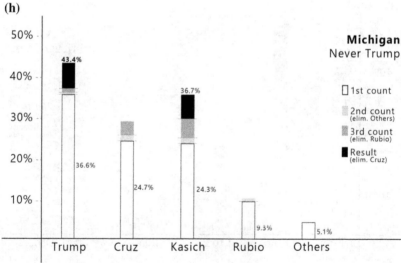

Fig. 6.6   (continued)

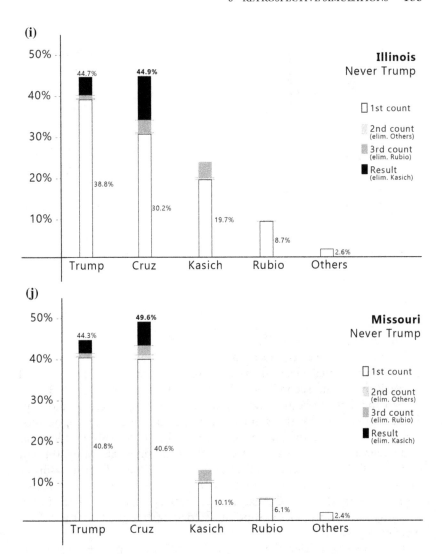

Fig. 6.6 (continued)

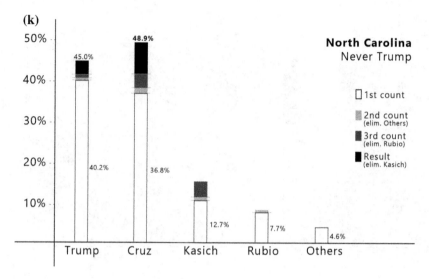

Fig. 6.6 (continued)

The example of South Carolina, one of the winner-take-all states in 2016, can serve to illustrate how the "Never Trump" simulations proceed. In the actual election, Trump won the state with 32.5% of all votes; Rubio came second with 22.5% and Cruz third with 22.3%; all other candidates were in single digits. After Carson, Kasich, and others are eliminated by the simulation procedure, and their supporters' votes transferred according to next-preference rules, Rubio widens his lead over Cruz from 0.2% to 1.8%. At the same time, Trump's 10-point lead over Rubio shrinks to 4.2%, thanks to low levels of enthusiasm for Trump among all other candidates' supporters (especially Kasich's). With Cruz in third, and next to be eliminated, the rush to Rubio is enough to hand him a 6-point victory with only two candidates remaining.

These results reflect the "Never Trump" assumptions, accentuating the front-runner's polarizing nature and exclusive base of support. But can we tell how empirically sound were those assumptions, much trumpeted in the mainstream media throughout the 2016 primary season?

EMPIRICAL PROBES OF "NEVER TRUMP" ASSUMPTIONS

A few data sources allow us to probe "Never Trump" assumptions indirectly. The key question is whether anti-Trump feeling within the Republican Party was strong enough to give him significantly fewer second- and third-choice votes than his rivals would have received when weaker candidates were eliminated. If the answer is mixed or negative, the hypothesis about Trump's RCV losses from leap-frog results may or may not still hold up, depending on the results of rerunning the simulation with a second, revised set of next-preference rules.

Four sources can help this probe and guide any necessary revisions to transfer rules. The ANES January study took feeling thermometer scores for some, but not all, Republican candidates; a Pew Research Center survey in January 2016 asked for ratings on a five-point scale of some, but not all, Republican candidates; a Pew survey in March repeated that item for the last three candidates standing (Cruz, Kasich, and Trump); and Pew matched its April survey with comparable data from December 2015 to track the paths by which supporters of some Republican candidates migrated to others over time.

The two sources of January data defy "Never Trump" assumptions, showing broad support for Trump even among other candidates' supporters. Comparing January data with March data, however, shows significant change in a short time. For example, Trump and Cruz both declined in "good" and "great" ratings while rising in "poor" and "terrible" ratings (even among self-described Republican voters), whereas Kasich's trends went in the opposite direction on both counts. Among those who gave high marks in January to Cruz and Kasich, respectively, 64% and 59% said that Trump would make a "good" or "great" president; in the March survey of Cruz voters and Kasich voters, respectively, that figure was only 25% and 21%. In January, 31% of all respondents said they had never heard of Kasich, and 13% said that he would make a "good" or "great" president; in March, only 9% had not heard of him while 33% said that he would make a "good" or "great" president. These considerations add fuel to the "Never Trump" fire: Trump lost support as voters gained familiarity with him, while at least one of the going alternatives gained support.[15]

---

[15] On support for Trump in January: Pew (2016d, 7). For March data: Pew (2016a, 47, 50, 72; 2016d, 13).

BC voters: 30% to TC, 30% to DT, 10% to MR, 10% to JK, 20% exhausted.
JK voters: 50% to MR, 20% to DT, 10% to TC, 10% to BC, 10% exhausted.
MR voters: 40% to JK, 30% to TC, 20% to DT, 10% to BC, none exhausted.
TC voters: 30% to MR, 30% to DT, 10% to BC, 10% to JK, 20% exhausted.
Others voters: 30% to DT, 20% to TC, 10% to JK, 10% to MR, 10% to BC, 20% exhausted.

Fig. 6.7 "Maybe Trump" transfer rules (first to second)

A limitation of the March data is that Carson and Rubio were excluded because they had dropped out of the race. We can at least see where Carson and Rubio supporters are likely to have migrated over time. From December 2015 to April 2016, Carson supporters went 35% to Trump, 34% to Cruz, 11% to Kasich, and 9% to "undecided"; in the same period, Rubio supporters went 21% to Trump, 26% to Cruz, 29% to Kasich, and 4% to "undecided"; those who started as "undecided" went 31% to Trump, 14% to Cruz, and 6% to Kasich, while 41% remained "undecided" as of April. Though these numbers do not allow us to see the full picture, they suggest the weakness of "Never Trump" assumptions in more compelling fashion, albeit to a lesser degree, than the January data. Carson supporters went roughly equally for Trump and Cruz despite the latter's pronounced evangelical outlook, and Rubio saw his supporters drift to Kasich and Cruz over Trump by margins of less than 10%.[16]

We can now make adjustments to the "Never Trump" assumptions to arrive at a more realistic set of "Maybe Trump" assumptions (see Figs. 6.7 and 6.8), keeping with percentages divisible by 10 for convenience. Trump's share of second-preference votes shifts from 10% among all other candidates' voters to 20% among Kasich's and Rubio's supporters and 30% among Carson's, Cruz's, and others' less pro-establishment voters. In the process, Cruz, Kasich, and Rubio each lose 10% transfer support among various blocs of other candidates' voters. For moving from second to third preferences, I used the "Never Trump" rules above as a template but made two modifications: First, Trump's share of second-to-third transfers always rises by 10%; second, every other candidate's share drops by 10%, except when that candidate's share was already at only 10%.

[16]Pew Research Center (2016c).

BC > JK voters: 30% to TC, 30% to DT, 20% to MR.
BC > MR voters: 40% to TC, 30% to DT, 10% to JK.
BC > TC voters: 50% to MR, 30% to DT, 10% to JK.
JK > BC voters: 40% to DT, 20% to MR, 20% to TC.
JK > MR voters: 40% to TC, 30% to DT, 10% to BC.
JK > TC voters: 40% to DT, 30% to MR, 10% to BC.
MR > BC voters: 40% to TC, 20% to JK, 20% to DT.
MR > JK voters: 40% to TC, 30% to DT, 10% to BC.
MR > TC voters: 30% to JK, 30% to DT, 20% to BC.
TC > BC voters: 50% to MR, 30% to DT, 10% to JK.
TC > JK voters: 40% to DT, 30% to MR, 10% to BC.
TC > MR voters: 30% to BC, 30% to DT, 20% to JK.

N.B. The notaton "BC > JK" indicates the bloc of voters who ranked BC frst and JK second.

Fig. 6.8 "Maybe Trump" transfer rules (second to third)

RESULTS FROM THE "MAYBE TRUMP" MODEL

The results of the revised model show significantly less difference between the outcomes produced by RCV and the actual ballot structures used (see Fig. 6.9). Only in Arkansas does the RCV process change the outcome. In most of the other ten cases, Trump's margin of victory after the full RCV count of voters' second and third preferences remains about the same or even increases.

The example of South Carolina is again illustrative. Recall that Trump finished the actual contest in first with 32.5% of all votes, Rubio came second with 22.5%, and Cruz was third with 22.3%; all other candidates were in single digits. After Carson, Kasich, and all other candidates are eliminated in the RCV simulation, and their supporters' votes transferred according to the revised, "Maybe Trump" next-preference rules, Rubio widens his lead over Cruz but without gaining ground on Trump. In this second model, supporters of Others and of Carson are significantly more sanguine toward Trump than Rubio, though Kasich supporters remain heavily pro-Rubio at this stage of the count. As a result, Trump's lead over Rubio increases by 0.8%, whereas under "Never Trump" assumptions it drops by 5.8%. With Cruz now in third and next

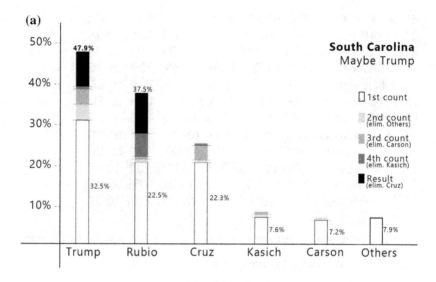

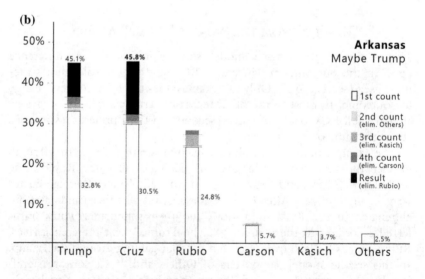

Fig. 6.9   "Maybe Trump" simulation results with RCV

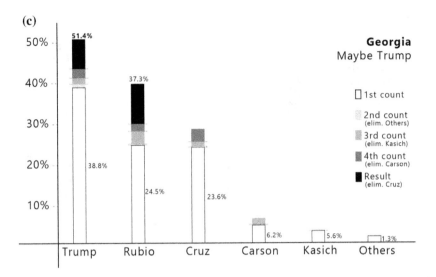

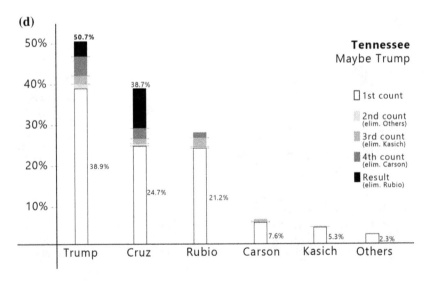

Fig. 6.9 (continued)

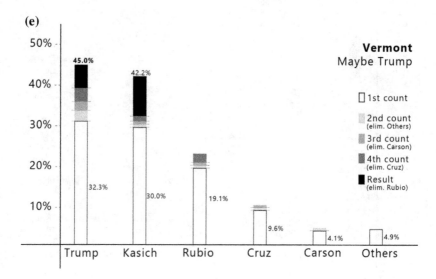

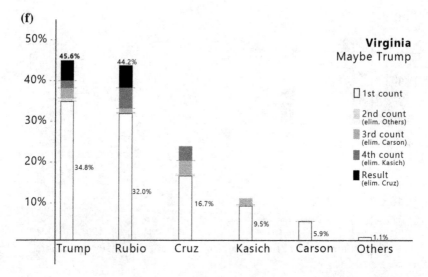

Fig. 6.9 (continued)

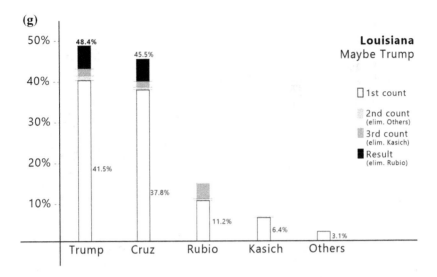

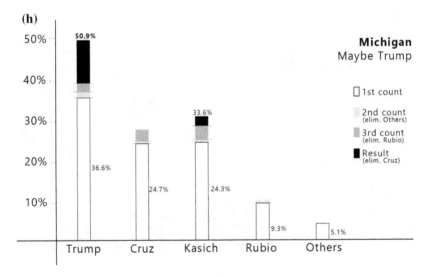

Fig. 6.9 (continued)

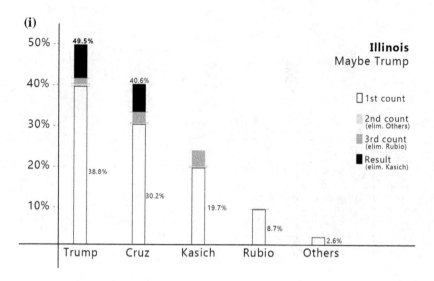

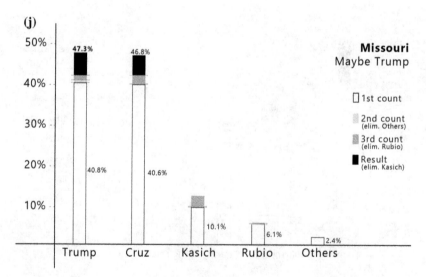

Fig. 6.9   (continued)

(k)

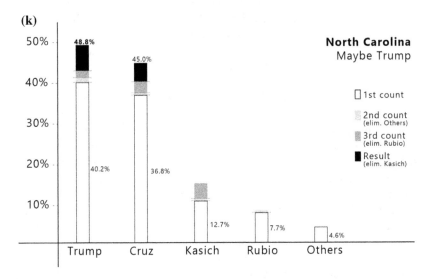

Fig. 6.9 (continued)

to be eliminated, his supporters' next preferences barely favor Rubio over Trump under the new, more realistic assumptions. As a result, the RCV process of eliminations and transfers ultimately enables Trump to increase his margin of victory slightly, from 10% to 10.4%.

The discrepancies between "Never Trump" and "Maybe Trump" assumptions may have seemed modest, in percentage terms. But the differences in RCV contest results were not: from eight out of 11 Trump losses, in the first model, to 10 out of 11 Trump wins, in the second.

THE VISE ON THE PEOPLE

The conclusion from these simulations is conditional: If the "Never Trump" movement's assumptions about the polarizing nature and exclusive appeal of their nemesis were correct, the RCV ballot structure could indeed have changed significant numbers of outcomes in the 2016 Republican primaries. The use of the 1MB structure—aided by the fact that American polling does not consistently ask voters about variable levels of support across multiple candidates in a single contest—is what prevents us from knowing whether the premise of this conclusion was in fact true. "Never Trump" partisans will never know how right or wrong they were. Voters in similar predicaments in countries that use RCV are not so unlucky, nor are scholars who decide to insert multi-mark ballot forms directly into their survey instruments.

It is also notable that the rate of leap-frog results is not particularly high in countries that use RCV or its STV cousin. In Australia, Ireland, and parts of the UK, a figure of 10% of leap-frog winners for all contests in any given year would be considered high. My RES analysis of the Republican primaries suggests that, on the "Never Trump" model, as many as 36% (eight out of 22, giving Trump his victories in the other 11 not simulated here) of the primary elections that occurred prior to Trump's first majority win, in New York, could have seen leap-frog results go against him. That would have been a truly remarkable outcome, not just in American politics but in the larger world of democratic elections.[17]

What such results indicate, among other things, is the power of electoral constructivism as an adjunct of democratic theory and a guide to institutional reform. Whereas election returns tend to cause an idealist to hail "the voice of the people," but a naturalist might rather lament "the vice of the people," a constructivist is more likely to pinpoint structures like 1MB voting as "the vise on the people." American presidential elections, effectively a two-round system when primaries are taken into consideration, were squeezing voters in 2016 from both sides of the dilemma of disempowerment: Vote-splitting in the Republican primaries produced Trump, leading to a lesser-evil choice in the final round of voting.

The constructivist approach to electoral studies assumes, to put it another way, that bad rules and procedures can blunt sharp voters just as surely as bad voters can blunt sharp rules and procedures. The attempt to test propositions of this sort runs into difficulty when voters' variable intensities of preference across more than two candidates or parties per contest have not been measured. Voting-behavior surveys in the USA are lagging behind those of other countries in this respect. With forecasting privileged over "back-casting," Americans are left with little but the official ballots themselves. The 1MB structure may be the bluntest measure yet devised for registering voters' judgments, and it offers inadequate leverage for determining, for example, whether or not "Never Trump" assumptions were more mythical than real.

---

[17] On the frequency of leapfrog results in ranking-ballot (RCV and STV) elections: Baldini and Pappalardo (2009, 55).

A new research agenda on ballot structures and their potential impacts will not be serviceable without integrating bodies of knowledge from both voting theory and comparative electoral studies. What that integration might look like, and how it might feed into practical political reform efforts, is the final question to be pursued.

REFERENCES

Abramowitz, A.I., & J. McCoy. 2019. "United States: Racial Resentment, Negative Partisanship, and Polarization in Trump's America." *Annals of the American Academy of Political and Social Science* 681: 137–56.

Abramson, P.R., J.H. Aldrich, A. Diskin, A.M. Houck, R. Levine, & T.J. Scotto. 2013. "The British General Election of 2010 under Different Voting Rules." *Electoral Studies* 32: 134–39.

Alos-Ferrer, C., & D.-G. Granic. 2012. "Two Field Experiments on Approval Voting in Germany." *Social Choice and Welfare* 39: 171–205.

Baldini, G., & A. Pappalardo. 2009. *Elections, Electoral Systems, and Volatile Voters.* Basingstoke, UK: Palgrave Macmillan.

Balinski, M., & R. Laraki. 2010. *Majority Judgment: Measuring, Ranking, and Electing.* Cambridge, MA: MIT Press.

Balinski, M., & R. Laraki. 2016. "Trump and Clinton Victorious: Proof that U.S. Voting System Doesn't Work." *The Conversation*, May 9 (Accessed on August 16, 2017 at theconversation.com/trump-and-clinton-victorious-proof-that-us-voting-system-doesnt-work-58752).

Bassi, A. 2015. "Voting Systems and Strategic Manipulation: An Experimental Study." *Journal of Theoretical Politics* 27: 58–85.

Baujard, A., & H. Igersheim. 2010. "Framed Field Experiments on Approval Voting: Lessons from the 2002 and 2007 French Presidential Elections." *Handbook on Approval Voting*, eds. J.-F. Laslier & M.R. Sanver. Berlin: Springer.

Baujard, A., & H. Igersheim. 2011. "Framed-Field Experiment on Approval Voting and Evaluative Voting: Some Teachings to Reform the French Presidential Election System." *In Situ and Laboratory Experiments on Electoral Law Reform*, eds. B. Dolez, B. Grofman, & A. Laurent. New York: Springer.

Baujard, A., H. Igersheim, I. Lebon, F. Favrel, & J.-F. Laslier. 2014. "Who's Favored by Evaluative Voting? An Experiment Conducted during the 2012 French Presidential Election." *Electoral Studies* 34: 131–45.

Berg-Andersson, R.E. 2017. "The Green Papers" (Accessed on August 13, 2017 at www.thegreenpapers.com).

Blais, A., M. Heroux-Legault, L.B. Stephenson, W. Cross, & E. Gidengil. 2012. "Assessing the Psychological and Mechanical Impact of Electoral Rules: A Quasi-Experiment." *Electoral Studies* 30: 829–37.

Blais, A., J.-F. Laslier, F. Poinas, & K. Van der Straeten. 2015. "Citizens' Preferences about Voting Rules: Self-Interest, Ideology, and Sincerity." *Public Choice* 164: 423–42.

Farvaque, E., H. Jayet, & L. Ragot. 2011. "French Presidential Election: A Field Experiment on the Single Transferable Vote." *In Situ and Laboratory Experiments on Electoral Law Reform*, eds. B. Dolez, B. Grofman, & A. Laurent. New York: Springer.

Granic, D.-G. 2017. "The Problem of the Divided Majority: Preference Aggregation under Uncertainty." *Journal of Economic Behavior and Organization* 133: 21–38.

Igersheim, H., A. Baujard, F. Gavrel, J.-F. Laslier, & I. Lebon. 2016. "Individual Behavior under Evaluative Voting: A Comparison between Laboratory and *In Situ* Experiments." *Voting Experiments*, eds. A. Blais, J.-F. Laslier, & K. Van der Straeten. Heidelberg: Springer.

Jacobson, G.C. 2016. "Polarization, Gridlock, and Presidential Campaign Politics in 2016." *Annals of the American Academy of Political and Social Science* 667: 226–46.

Olsen, H., & D.J. Scala. 2016. *The Four Faces of the Republican Party: The Fight for the 2016 Presidential Nomination*. New York: Palgrave Macmillan.

Pew Research Center. 2016a. "Campaign Exposes Fissures over Issues, Values, and How Life Has Changed in the U.S." March Report.

Pew Research Center. 2016c. "Republican Voters' Path to Backing Donald Trump" (Accessed on December 13, 2017 at www.people-press.org/interactives/gop-candidate-switching).

Pew Research Center. 2016d. "Voters Skeptical that 2016 Candidates Would Make Good Presidents." January Report.

Renwick, A. 2017. "What Do Political Scientists Know that Practitioners Do Not? Lessons from the UK Referendum of 2011." *Election Law Journal* 16: 341–48.

Steed, M. 1974. "The Results Analysed." *The British General Election of February 1974*, eds. D. Butler & D. Kavanagh. London: Macmillan.

Tolbert, C.J., & K. Gracey. 2018. "Changing How America Votes for President." *Changing How America Votes*, ed. T. Donovan. Lanham, MD: Rowman & Littlefield.

CHAPTER 7

Conclusion:
A Realist's Agenda for Research and Reform

A single-winner election that offered voters a lesser-evil choice between
a crook and a fascist would be regarded in many quarters as a sign of
fundamental institutional failure. In most societies, a majority of voters
would feel utterly disempowered by such a contest. Any community
possessing a dynamic, innovative, and public-spirited culture would
undoubtedly respond with multiple competing projects of electoral
re-engineering to undertake urgent structural repairs.

Even allowing for inevitable shades of interpretation, this type of
election is what large numbers of voters saw in Louisiana's gubernatorial
election of 1991, France's presidential election of 2002, and America's
presidential election of 2016. If we include cases where extreme epithets
like "crook" and "fascist" are not quite justified—for example, a party har-
boring too much zealotry against another with too little competence—
it is possible that many more elections in various jurisdictions around the
world could be cited as examples of the dilemma of disempowerment. In
Louisiana after 1991, nothing was done in the way of reform. In France
after 2002, several academics launched multiple voting experiments to test
alternative ballot structures, hoping to build up relevant knowledge that
might indicate new ways of voting. It is still too early to tell if 2016 will
spawn anything similar in the various places affected by that year's electoral upheavals.

Reform can be a perilous business, and most academics keep their
distance from it. Anti-reform realists are usually on hand to warn

© The Author(s) 2019
J. S. Maloy, *Smarter Ballots*, Elections, Voting, Technology,
https://doi.org/10.1007/978-3-030-13031-2_7

that professional politicians and their financial sponsors never willingly change the rules of the game in ways that harm their interests. But some anti-reform notions stray from both logic and evidence. Elites are generally clever enough to realize that more precious things than political careers or bank balances can get lost amid the discontents of highly unequal societies. People with power therefore have some interest in making deals with "people power" for peaceful, legal, and institutionalized change. Indeed, studies of historical movements for election reform confirm not only that politicians can and do promote changes diminishing their own power, but also that ideas, as against interests, can open windows of opportunity for doing so. It does not even take civil strife or uncivil politics, in some places, to make reform happen.[1]

This concluding chapter is about the future role of academic research in supplying answers to reform-relevant questions. Reform-relevant research is not the same as pro-reform research. Much of this book, nonetheless, elaborates a perspective that I would call both realist and reformist, going against the grain of anti-reform realism in academia. Sober assessments of ground-level realities are vitally important and not to be dismissed out of hand. But anti-reform realists have said little about ballot structure, as I have defined it (the input and output rules that structure electoral judgments), perhaps because that type of reform has been less commonly enacted than others. Constructivism teaches us that what we observe happening within one structural framework cannot show us all that would transpire inside different structures. For this reason, political research has to supplement ground-level activity with tower-view activity, such as experiments and simulations with rare or speculative ballot structures. Neither reformers nor anti-reformers are ever certain, but they should at least be thoughtful; researchers can supply better materials and tools for being more thoughtful about reform.[2]

[1]On windows of opportunity for electoral reform in New Zealand in the 1990s and in British Columbia, Canada, in the 2000s: Nagel (2004) and Carty et al. (2008). On the capacity of reform projects to use ideologies and values to overpower calculations of partisan advantage: Renwick (2018, 121–22).

[2]For important challenges from anti-reform realism (with much attention on failures in California, where ballot inputs have gone untouched at the state level but contest structures are often modified): Bowler and Donovan (2013) and Cain (2015).

EXPERIMENTAL BALLOT PROPOSALS

The common-sense democratic objectives behind my version of realistic reform are embodied in the triad of voter empowerment: selection, accountability, and expression (see Fig. 1.2). As tools of political judgment with expressive potential, ranking and grading types of ballot are more or less equally worth pursuing further in reform experiments and reform-relevant research. Four major families of ballot structure, as defined by their distinctive ways of combining input and output rules, stand out (see Fig. 5.2). Two of these, Grade-Point Average (GPA) and Ranked-Choice Voting (RCV), are here made the basis of two new templates for ballot structure (see Fig. 7.1).

First is a modified version of GPA. The standard critique of grading inputs is that they allow unconstrained over- and under-stating, in which voters exaggerate their support for options on the ballot with the highest and lowest allowed levels. This possibility is structurally inherent in grading inputs and is potentially a problem for voter empowerment. A realist would not be concerned about questions of insincerity. More to the point, if real voters could be persuaded by public narratives of the scarcity of electoral viability (i.e., only two "real" candidates) to over- and under-state tactically, the syndrome of incentives associated with "wasted" votes and "spoiler" candidates would persist. In a culture of polarization and negative partisanship, deliberate under-stating that dragged down the mean scores of the major-party candidates might lead to the election of an obscure non-entity whom no one thought important enough to give a failing grade.

B-GPA

votes	A +3	B +2	C +1	D 0	F -1
Blue					
Green					
Orange					
Red					
Yellow					

Place no more than one mark in each candidate's row. Rows with no marks or more than one count for zero. No more than one mark is allowed in each gray column.

RCV-A

ranks	1st	2nd	3rd	4th	5th
Blue					
Green					
Orange					
Red					
Yellow					

Rank only candidates that you approve, leaving those that you disapprove blank. Place no more than one mark in each row and column.

Fig. 7.1 Two templates for smarter (single-winner) ballots

If further experimental study suggested that many voters would perceive and act on such incentives, one way to combat the danger of exaggerated grades would be to limit the availability of the highest and lowest levels of support. On a ballot with a five-point scale ranging from -1 to $+3$, for example, the highest and lowest levels of support might be confined by rule to one candidate each. After each voter singled out one favorite and one least favorite, all candidates in the middle ranges of merit would then be graded on a narrower scale of 0, $+1$, and $+2$. Boundaries would thereby be set to the voters' ability to give extreme grades, and the grading scales themselves would be bounded for all candidates beyond the highest- and lowest-graded—hence "Bounded GPA," or B-GPA.

My second proposal responds to two worries about RCV. First, the order of eliminating candidates can seem both arbitrary and consequential. The traditional Hare rule, eliminating candidates with low numbers of first-choice votes, could penalize candidates with large numbers of second or third preferences in favor of polarizing candidates with more first-choice votes but widespread hostility beyond core supporters. It is also possible for a small swing of votes to produce a different order of elimination, such that an entirely different outcome may arise. But solving this problem about the order of elimination goes hand-in-hand with addressing a second problem. With RCV (and STV, its multi-seat cousin), there is no clean way to differentiate indifference from disapproval. Does a blank vote represent active hostility or mere ignorance? In a world of partisan decomposition and populist rage, disapproval on the ballot has its uses. An alternative rule, the Coombs rule, re-orders the candidates to be eliminated by starting with the most last-place votes rather than the fewest first preferences. But this rule only makes sense if we institute compelled ranking, invalidating any ballot with more than one blank. The Coombs rule, in the real world, would probably lead to higher rates of rejected ballots—and eventually of party-list voting of the Australian variety.[3]

For an alternative way to build disapproval into RCV's elimination rule, imagine that a blank vote counts as a specific form of disapproval. The order of elimination could be determined by an initial count of any ranking as equivalent to a single approval for each candidate.

---

[3] On the Coombs version of RCV: Grofman and Feld (2004).

In other words, the candidates that receive fewer blanks overall show a higher level of approval across the electorate. This rule would eliminate candidates with the lowest number of approvals, regardless of their first-preference totals, before transferring their votes to second preferences. How many candidates are to survive the first cut, based on counting blanks, would have to be specified in advance: say, three or four. This tweak to the process of ranking, eliminating, and transferring would ensure that the most widely disliked candidates are eliminated earliest, even if they have relatively high numbers of first-choice votes. (Where intuitions about legitimacy require it, an exemption from early elimination could be provided for any candidate who is the leading vote-getter but also the leading blank-getter after the first count.) We can call this system "RCV-Approval," or RCV-A.

The label for either of these new ballot types could easily take a more elegant form in case some jurisdiction were to try one and find it satisfactory: "the [your town's name here] Ballot." The Utah legislature in 2018 specifically authorized the state's municipalities to undertake RCV-type pilot elections, and relatively small-scale local contests would be ideal testing grounds for these two new templates for smarter ballots.[4]

SMARTER REFERENDUMS

Referendums have been on the rise in democracies around the world in the early twenty-first century. The Brexit referendum of 2016, in which 52% of British voters opted to "leave the European Union," is only the most celebrated recent example. Putting policy options to a direct vote of all eligible citizens is one response to democratic deficits, a way of narrowing the representational gap. As everyone knows who has investigated referendums, they face serious theoretical and empirical obstacles to their ability to empower ordinary citizens. Smarter ballots, though, could overcome some of those obstacles.[5]

The classic referendum offers voters only two, predetermined options, such as "yes" and "no" to a proposition. This is not the only possible or advisable contest structure for all referendums, but academic researchers and political practitioners often pretend that it is. A ranking ballot has no use in two-option contests, since aggregating hierarchic orderings of first and second logically produces the same result as aggregating one-mark

---

[4]On Utah: Potyondy (2018).

[5]On the geographic (and thematic) expansion of referendums in recent decades: Beramendi et al. (2008, 20). On the vulnerability of referendums to elite manipulation: Tierney (2013, 510, 515).

ballots (1MB). Grading ballots, however, are another matter. If voters assign degrees of support to two options, either mean outputs (i.e., GPA) or median outputs (Median Grade) might construct a different result from an exclusive-input ballot. The expressive advantage of a grading referendum lies in taking account of uncertainty about the proposition offered. Whereas some voters will deem one option 100% desirable and the other not at all, others will feel less strongly about the desirability (or even the meaning) of the question posed. A 1MB referendum forces such voters either to falsify their judgments or to exclude themselves from the count (by abstaining). Experimental research could test how many voters take advantage of grading referendum ballots and how many plump for one option while zeroing out the other.

For referendums with more than two options on the ballot, either ranking or grading could apply. Multi-option referendums are a generally neglected political possibility. The vast majority of actual referendums are two-option affairs, as in the hundreds of ballot propositions put to voters across American states each year. Typically, these referendums formulate specific legal text for statutory or constitutional amendments for the state in question; there are no national referendums for changing American federal law. When voting on a proposed legal text, "yes" and "no" are appropriate options. But it is a mistake to believe that all referendum contests should be two-option affairs.

The people of Newfoundland voted on their country's constitutional status in 1948, with three options on the ballot. New Zealanders were presented with no fewer than five different electoral systems on a referendum ballot in 1992. Among other examples from around the world, these two relate to significant constitutional changes, as a result of which Newfoundland left the British Empire to join independent Canada and New Zealand changed its parliamentary elections from single-seat plurality (SSP) to "mixed member" proportional (MMP). In each case, a two-round contest structure was used.[6]

The Newfoundland and New Zealand examples are not, however, models of voter empowerment. Combining a two-round contest structure with 1MB voting, as in France's presidential and Louisiana's

[6]On Newfoundland: Webb (1998, 179–80, 187) and Blake (1994, 22). On New Zealand: Vowles (1995, 104).

gubernatorial elections (see Chapter 3), can exacerbate the dilemma of disempowerment. It will fairly routinely happen that vote-splitting in the first round induces a lesser-evil choice in the second.

A better model was used in another Canadian province, Prince Edward Island, in 2016. A referendum on the system of legislative elections there presented five options, as in New Zealand. This time, however, the RCV ballot constructed a winner from a single round of voting. Eliminations and transfers proceeded after none of the options won a majority of first preferences; ultimately, a version of MMP prevailed. This was an advisory, non-binding referendum, like the Brexit vote. But voter turnout was only 36.5% in PEI, and political leaders cited this figure when declaring that there was no mandate for making a formal change.[7]

The points of comparison and contrast with Brexit are striking. In PEI, a referendum result with an unmistakable meaning (because no fewer than five distinct options were being judged) was followed by elite inaction. In the UK, a referendum result subject to multiple interpretations (with two vague options that each meant different things to different people) was followed by a massive and protracted reorganization of elite political energies. Was it more the fault of dull voters or dull ballots that political parties subsequently spent years bickering internally and externally over what the vote meant? In the PEI case, by contrast, ballot structure and contest structure were well matched. The only obstacle to people power was the room for maneuver that elites had carved out by consenting to an advisory rather than obligatory vote in the first place.[8]

Partly from recognition of the structural problem in the 2016 Brexit vote, advocates subsequently emerged for a multi-option version of a second referendum on UK-EU relations. There was precedent for such a debate, since the Scottish independence referendum of 2014 had initially been contemplated by some politicians as including a third option of Scotland's gaining more legal autonomy inside the UK. An academic study group on the topic of a second Brexit referendum specifically ruled out using 1MB with a plurality winner, while noticing strengths and weaknesses of multi-mark ballot structures. In a similar vein, the International IDEA (Institute for Democracy and Election Assistance)

[7] Milner (2017, 352).
[8] On the conflicted meanings of Brexit votes in 2016: Jenkins (2017).

<table>
<tr><td colspan="2">

Referendum on the United Kingdom's membership of the European Union

</td></tr>
<tr><td colspan="2">

Vote only once by putting a cross ⊠ in the box next to your choice

</td></tr>
<tr><td colspan="2">

Should the United Kingdom remain a member of the European Union or leave the European Union?

</td></tr>
<tr><td>

Remain a member of the European Union

</td><td>☐</td></tr>
<tr><td>

Leave the European Union

</td><td>☐</td></tr>
</table>

Fig. 7.2 Brexit ballot, 2016 (*Source* UK Electoral Commission)

recommended in 2008 that ranking ballots be used for multi-option referendums, without specifying any output rules.[9]

The primary, political decision in referendum design is about contest structure: How many relevant options would give voters clarity for the subject on which their judgments are required? Once contest structure is settled, ballot structure can be selected to match. If more than two options are needed to present the relevant alternatives, the ballot structure may be GPA or RCV; for only two options, grading is the multi-mark alternative. In theory, two perfectly clear options can be decided by 1MB with no lesser-evil residue. In practice, democratic realists know that many politicians live in mortal fear of clarity. A GPA ballot for two options, particularly if a minimum threshold for victory is set at the midpoint of the grading scale (e.g., two out of four), would present political elites with the prospect of public humiliation in case voters showed their disgust with (or incomprehension of) the options offered by grading

---

[9]On the Scottish independence referendum of 2014: Tierney (2013, 521). On a hypothetical second Brexit ballot: Sargeant et al. (2018, 29–32, 36–39). For the International IDEA recommendations: Beramendi et al. (2008, 54, 196).

What action should Parliament take with respect to the United Kingdom's relationship to the European Union?

	Option A	Option B	Option C
Which, if any, is best? (+2) (mark one or none)	◯	◯	◯
Which, if any, is worst? (-1) (mark one or none)	◯	◯	◯
Which are acceptable? (+1) (you may choose any or none)	◯	◯	◯

First Referendum (ca. 2016)
    A. Preserve the existing relationship.
    B. Negotiate the U.K.'s withdrawal from the E.U. within two years, making a clean break at that time if no terms are agreed.
    C. Negotiate a new relationship for the U.K. inside the E.U. within two years, initiating withdrawal at that time if no terms are agreed.

Second Referendum (ca. 2019)
    A. Remain in the E.U.
    B. Leave under the terms recently negotiated by the Government.
    C. Leave without negotiated terms.

Fig. 7.3 Template for a smarter Brexit ballot

both of them too low to pass. These are the guidelines that designers of referendums should be following in a post-Brexit world.

The real Brexit ballot of 2016 took the worst possible form for voter empowerment (a two-option contest, a 1MB vote; see Fig. 7.2), but I am offering here a hypothetical ballot template to illustrate how the same issue could have been handled with a smarter referendum (see Fig. 7.3). Since a ranking ballot for three options is easily imagined, my proposed template visualizes instead a simplified version of B-GPA. One set text for three options is given for a pre-negotiation vote, as in 2016, and a second set for a post-negotiation vote. Similar hypothetical ballots could serve as templates for use in experimental research to accumulate more experience with multi-mark referendums.

MULTI-WINNER BALLOT REFORMS

A referendum is a single-winner contest, as are elections for president, mayor, Best Supporting Actress, Man of the Match, and so on. But there is a long tradition in democratic theory which holds that, when selecting members of a collective agency such as a 500-person legislature, basic values of fairness and equality are better served by a smaller number of multi-winner contests than a larger number of single-winner contests. The system of proportional representation (PR) for legislative elections is defined, in part, by the use of multi- rather than single-seat districts, with as few as three seats in some districts in Ireland or as many as 150 in Netherlands' single national district. Though most of this book has focussed on single-winner contests, smarter ballots have a role to play in multi-seat elections as well.[10]

The debate between PR and SSP for electing legislatures proceeds on several fronts, but the fact that most countries of both types use 1MB input rules is important. One of this book's central claims is that one mark per voter per contest spawns the same dilemma of disempowerment wherever it is used, for however many seats to be filled, whether parties' or candidates' names are on the ballot. This dilemma, trapping voters between their fear of vote-splitting and disgust with lesser-evil choices, may not arise for voters in PR systems who build stable political identities within multi-party systems. But that is a vanishing breed, and the dilemma remains a live possibility for everyone else. In case no single party wins a majority and building a cross-party coalition becomes necessary, the largest party usually becomes *formateur*, or coalition-leader. Voters therefore consider the jockeying for the position of *formateur* by the two or three largest parties—where lesser-evil votes are likeliest to originate under PR.

Multi-mark ballots offer a way to break the dilemma of disempowerment with either single- or multi-seat contest structures. Indeed, the combination of multi-seat districts with ranking ballots is used to elect the primary assemblies of Ireland and Malta as well as lesser legislative bodies in various other places. This Single Transferable Vote (STV) system uses a counting system of eliminations and transfers which escapes the dilemma of disempowerment. There is no vote-splitting because a

---

[10]For a defense of closed-list PR in a single national district as the most democratic (on several criteria) method of electing a legislature: McGann (2006).

vote for a candidate that proves non-viable can be transferred through lower rankings to another, more viable candidate. Because there is no danger of vote-splitting, plentiful alternatives on the ballot can safely be sought to avoid lesser-evil choices. Despite a relatively personalistic political culture and relatively weak parties, electoral accountability appears relatively robust under STV. For instance, Ireland did not re-elect the incumbent government after its policy failures were exposed by the financial crisis of 2008—unlike roughly two out of five European countries that held elections within four years.[11]

Empirical researchers occasionally speak of "dual-vote" and "multiple-vote" systems of PR in several countries, but most of these have multi-tiered contest structures with one mark on the ballot in each one, rather than multiple marks in any one contest; Germany is one example. "Free list" PR in Ecuador, Switzerland, and elsewhere does actually allow multiple marks for multiple candidates within one contest. These countries tend to allow binary (pass-fail) grading or cumulative input rules—two schemes with only modest potential for advancing voter empowerment (see Chapters 4 and 5). On the other hand, since they are actually operating in public elections, they deserve more attention from researchers interested in the lessons of experience. Also crucial to notice are historical cases of smarter ballots under PR which eventually changed voters' options to 1MB, such as Finland and Italy, sounding cautionary notes for the idea of multi-mark PR. Voting theorists have also proposed several schemes for applying ranking ballots to multi-seat elections which remain at the hypothetical or experimental stage.[12]

My own proposed template for a smarter ballot structure for PR systems attacks the dilemma of disempowerment through the role of *formateur*. By informal custom or legal right, it usually falls to the largest party to take the lead in forming a coalition with a legislative majority. This lead role constitutes a single-winner prize within an otherwise multi-seat contest structure: Only one party can go first in organizing potential partner parties. If voters were allowed to rank all parties in order of

[11] On post-2008 elections around Europe: LeDuc and Pammett (2013, 496).

[12] On Ecuador: Mustillo and Polga-Hecimovich (2018, 125–26). On Switzerland: Lakeman (1974, 105, 154). On Finland: Von Schoultz (2018, 602). On Italy: Passarelli (2018, 855). On experimental "multiple-vote" proposals for PR elections: McGann (2006, 44–47).

preference, first-choice votes could be counted toward the proportional allocation of seats in the usual way. In the event that no majority party emerged, a second, *formateur* contest would commence, using the RCV method of eliminations and transfers to produce a decisive winner. Supporters of smaller parties (around 40% of the electorate in Spain in 2016, around 20% in the UK in 2017) could continue to support their favorites while also delivering their judgments about larger parties' suitability to lead the next government. The dilemma between vote-splitting and lesser-evil choices would be dissolved. In some cases, the plurality party on first preferences would lose the *formateur* role because small-party voters wanted someone else in charge. The constructive possibilities for electoral accountability would be strengthened.

This proposal, which I call "PR with *Formateur* Ranking" or PR-FR, would be most practical in PR systems with national lists, such as Israel and Netherlands. In countries with several multi-seat districts, by contrast, the RCV count for national *formateur* might prove difficult to administer. The reason is that the counting process of eliminations and transfers requires that all ballots be collected and sorted in one place (either physically or virtually). Where the technical and logistical challenges of this system are unpalatable, the Borda system of simple aggregation and mean counts could be used instead, since local counting centers need only report their totals to the central authority without having individual ballots examined. Grading inputs could also be used for the *formateur* contest, and as readily administered as the Borda Count.

PR elections are one potential ingredient in efforts to remedy the malaise of established democracies. There is reason to believe, from both theory and evidence, that they can increase "institutionalized popular inclusion," in tandem with other institutions such as unicameral legislatures and compulsory-voting rules. By itself, however, altering the contest structure of electoral systems seems unlikely to close democratic deficits, particularly if ballot-structure reform is not part of the bargain. Further investigation is well warranted of how distributive input rules can best be combined with output rules appropriate to multi-seat contests.[13]

---

[13] On PR as part of a structural ensemble of "institutionalized popular inclusion": Joshi et al. (2015, 2019).

Is Resistance Futile?

Actual adoption of reforms for public elections is out of the hands of scholars, but reform-relevant scholarship should not proceed in ignorance of the priorities and concerns of practical politics. The USA is fabled for having "laboratories of democracy" in its myriad local and state jurisdictions. Currently, the most viable, in-motion idea for ballot reform is RCV, the single-winner version of the STV family of ballot structure. RCV is far from a perfect reform, but ignoring it would be a serious mistake.

The reform movement to replace 1MB with ranking ballots has been slowly gathering steam in the USA ever since the 2000 presidential election. Both Al Gore and George Bush the younger carried several states that could have gone the other way if vote-splitting had not occurred. Because there happened to be a recount in one of the states that Bush won but Gore could have won (viz. Florida), and not in any of the states that Gore won but Bush could have won (viz. Iowa, New Mexico, Oregon, or Wisconsin), Ralph Nader was the unlucky winner of the "spoiler" label for 2000. It could have been Pat Buchanan instead.

Ranking inputs, when combined with the counting method of eliminations and transfers, offer a solution to the vote-splitting problem, in turn diminishing the force of the lesser-evil problem. Noting this fact, about a dozen American cities subsequently adopted RCV—sometimes also called Instant Runoff Voting (IRV)—in their local elections. Other cities and dozens of American states have at least entertained this reform option in legislative and other public debates. Though the reform effort has been successful in some places, it has always faced the opposition of established powers. Everywhere that ranking ballots are proposed, the proverbial empire stands poised to strike back. After Jean Quan's famous victory in Oakland in 2010 (see Chapter 5), the local chamber of commerce launched a campaign to repeal RCV. In tandem, the area's newspapers presented the new mayor to their readers as the beneficiary of an illegitimate electoral system. 1MB is not just an archaic voting method; it is also an entrenched mind-set.[14]

While ranking ballots have survived the onslaught in Oakland and neighboring cities, including San Francisco and Berkeley, the reform was indeed rolled back in Burlington, Vermont, after mayoral elections in

[14] Cote (2011) and Tervalon-Daumont and Garza (2011).

2006 and 2009. Both contests were won by the same left-wing candidate, Bob Kiss, running under the Progressive label against Democratic and Republican candidates. The 2009 election was particularly controversial because Kiss was a leap-frog winner, and the Republican who had polled more first-choice votes led the ensuing effort to repeal RCV by referendum. Even some Democratic voters appear to have helped repeal the system that allowed them to avoid vote-splitting on the left and keep a Republican out of the mayor's seat. In a stridently left-wing city like Burlington, Democrats won back the mayor's seat in 2012 for the first time in over three decades. But the center-left must now cater to far-left voters for fear of losing them to a vote-splitting insurgent in the future.[15]

Elsewhere campaigners for RCV have lost even after thinking they had won. In Santa Fe, New Mexico, voters approved ranking ballots for local elections in an advisory referendum in 2008. The mayor simply refused to take the voters' advice, as was his legal right. Memphis, Tennessee, witnessed a similar pattern of events in the same year when the election commission decided that the voters' preferred system was too much trouble to implement, though other jurisdictions had already done so with similar infrastructure. Ten years later, a formal repeal of RCV (called IRV in Memphis) was put to a referendum and failed, with only 37% of voters wanting to abandon a system that had never been implemented. Other cities where RCV has received voter approval without permanent, official implementation include Davis, California; Ferndale, Michigan; and Hendersonville, North Carolina.[16]

The recurring pattern is that the opposition to ranking ballots comes first and foremost from established political interests that are jealous of their privileges. In British jurisdictions that use STV in multi-seat districts, partisan elites dislike the system for its enabling effects on independent candidacies. The backlash includes not only major parties but also professional consultants, whose jobs are made simpler when the winning strategy is mobilizing your base and demobilizing everyone else's. In the American state of Maine, some activists wondered what would happen with a different approach. Reformers elsewhere had tried

[15] For Burlington as a *cause celebre* of voting theorists, who criticized RCV for not having selected the Condorcet winner: Ornstein and Norman (2014).

[16] I am indebted to Steven Mulroy for information about RCV in Memphis; see also Munks (2018). The progress of RCV in American cities and states is monitored by Fair Vote, an advocacy group, on its Web site, www.fairvote.org.

advisory referendums at the municipal level, where the vast majority of voters pay little or no attention to local issues such as the voting system. Perhaps the introduction of ranking ballots would go more smoothly if they could earn the support of a legally binding vote at the state level, placing the full force of state government subsequently behind the reform.[17]

A MAINE SAGA

No American state is geographically closer to the British Isles than Maine, and none has proved more fertile ground for the use of ranking ballots. In 2016, the year of Trump and Brexit, Maine voters approved RCV by a margin of 52% to 48%—about the same as the Brexit vote. Unlike the UK's exit from the EU, however, Maine's ballot reform involved a vote with direct legal effect. This was not an advisory referendum, as Brexit was, but a statutory initiative.[18]

The referendum victory was the culmination of over a decade of reform effort, and along the way the city of Portland adopted RCV for its mayoral elections. With a robust tradition of independent and third-party politics, Maine is used to having more than two viable candidates on the ballot. Governor's races in particular have tended to yield plurality winners, and vote-splitting is an ever-present concern—the price of having plentiful ballot options and thereby reducing the chances of a "lesser of two evils" choice. From 1974 to 2014, only two out of eleven gubernatorial elections produced a majority winner. The victor in the 2010 and 2014 races, Paul LePage, was an especially controversial and divisive governor who was widely believed to have benefitted from vote-splitting. The Republican LePage first entered office with 37.6% of votes, compared to 35.9% for independent Eliot Cutler and 18.8% for Democrat Libby Mitchell. LePage was re-elected in 2014 with a healthier vote-share, 48.2%, but with Cutler taking third place with 8.4% and now looking like the spoiler rather than the spoiled. With ranking ballots, LePage's loyal but exclusive support might not have been enough to secure his initial victory. Maine voters' approval of RCV in 2016

[17] On partisan elites' dislike for STV: Lundberg (2018, 629–30, 637).

[18] I am indebted to Kenneth Palmer and Scott Thistle for valuable points of information about the role of RCV in Maine politics. Except where otherwise noted, points of interpretation and attributions of motive are strictly my own.

therefore drew its strength in part from anti-incumbent sentiment and in part from a desire to escape the dilemma of disempowerment—the zero-sum game that traps voters between the lesser-evil and vote-splitting problems.

The rebels thought they had prevailed, until the empire struck back. The backlash against RCV came as surely in Maine as elsewhere. It began when the Republican-controlled Senate, possibly encouraged by LePage himself, requested an advisory opinion from the state's highest court. The Maine constitution allows the Senate to declare a "solemn occasion" in which the judges' non-binding legal opinion is sought in an emergency situation, even though no actual lawsuit is underway. In this instance, the judges responded that the Maine constitution would be violated by the use of RCV in certain elections: those that the constitution explicitly awards to the candidate with "a plurality of all votes returned." For these offices (including the state's governor and legislature), but not for others (including US senators and representatives), the court suggested that a fully fledged constitutional amendment would be required to inoculate RCV against a legal challenge. But the voters who approved RCV were making a statutory initiative rather than a constitutional amendment. The successful RCV referendum must give way, therefore, to superior constitutional norms.[19]

With the issuance of the "solemn occasion" opinion, the opposition to ranking ballots in Maine was confirmed as a bipartisan movement, at least at the elite level. Whereas Democratic and Libertarian voters had been generally in favor of RCV in the 2016 vote, with Republican voters mostly against, elites were less predictably aligned on the issue by party. Both Democrats and Republicans signed the unanimous court's opinion, and both Democrats and Republicans in the state legislature now cited the legally non-binding pronouncement of the judges as more compelling than the legally binding pronouncement of the voters. Full implementation of the voters' will would have required majority support in the legislature; so would implementing the law in some races but not others, according to the judges' suggestions about constitutionality; so would repealing the law altogether, mere months after the referendum. The only legislative option that was concretely pursued in 2017 was repeal. Though this effort narrowly failed, a successor bill passed the following

---

[19]Thistle (2017a).

year when the legislature suspended the new voting system pending judicial challenges, setting a time limit after which formal legal repeal would take effect.[20]

In 2018, an elaborate dance of citizen petitioning and elite maneuvering, at both legislative and judicial levels, resulted in the odd spectacle of a second referendum on RCV to repeal the legislature's repeal of the first referendum on RCV. Tangling matters further, RCV elections were actually conducted under court order for primary elections to select nominees for certain offices—on the same ballot where citizens were also voting on whether to repeal the new system that they were already using. Disappointing the hopes of the reform backlash's orchestrators, voters in Maine (as in Memphis in the same year) gave the same answer to the RCV question the second time.[21]

With the process of implementing RCV elections having begun in earnest in 2018, the national midterm elections of that year thrust the state of Maine unexpectedly into the spotlight. Because of the state courts' peculiar interpretation of the Maine constitution's wording about "plurality" elections, only federal races were subject to the new RCV law. One Senate seat and two House of Representatives seats thereby became the first elections to the US Congress ever to be contested via ranking ballots. The odds were against any leap-frog victory in these three contests: Under 10% of all ranking-ballot elections worldwide have yielded a winning candidate who was not the plurality leader after the first count. Remarkably, the second House district, in upper Maine, witnessed such a result. In a four-candidate field, the Republican incumbent led by 46.4% to 45.5% over his Democratic challenger after first preferences were tallied, but the challenger turned the initial deficit into a 1% margin of victory after the 8.1% of independent voters had their second and third preferences incorporated in the count. An electoral sanction was thereby delivered to an incumbent representative unable to secure majority support for continuation in office.[22]

The fact that RCV survived the 2018 efforts to repeal it by referendum in Maine and Memphis, after previously succumbing in Burlington

---

[20]On the legislative tussle: Thistle (2017b). On partisanship in the 2016 vote: Santucci (2018, 301–2).

[21]Russell (2018).

[22]Miller and Thistle (2018). On the frequency of leap-frog results: Baldini and Pappalardo (2009, 55).

in 2010, suggests that American voters' interest in smarter ballots is growing as loyal partisans in America become more rabid but less numerous. Similarly, when French experiments gave people several different voting systems to work with and asked them about their favorite one afterward, RCV prevailed (with 41% approval) over binary grading (Approval), the traditional 2RS, and 1MB with plurality winners. This result from France is particularly striking because political scientists tend to believe that the RCV/STV family enjoys a narrow cultural appeal in former British colonies (e.g., Australia, Ireland, USA).[23]

GAPS TO CLOSE

"Democratic deficits" has become the definitive phrase that captures the experience of the world's older constitutional republics since the end of the Cold War. A lot of academic commentary says so, and a lot of murmuring in the halls of power seconds the motion. Democratic deficits occur when democracies betray themselves, opening gaps between the governors and the governed and between civic expectations and political realities. The aftermath of the global financial crisis of 2008 might have been an opportunity to close some of the gaps, but the opposite occurred.

This book has tackled the role within this process of electoral institutions, especially ballot structures, assisted by concepts and evidence from academic research. Using the logic of electoral realism and voter empowerment, I have made the case for replacing 1MB voting with multi-mark or distributive ballots as a potential remedy for the electoral dysfunction of our times. There appears to be no other solution to the dilemma of disempowerment, which traps voters between the vote-splitting problem and the lesser-evil problem. Which particular ballot type is called for may vary from one political context to another. But the general criterion for identifying a smarter ballot is the same across parliamentary and presidential systems and across PR and SSP systems: per voter per contest, many marks are better than one.

A change in ballot structure may even catalyze changes in other institutional features. In the American context, "top two" and "jungle" primaries have had mixed results in the last few decades. But the operation of jungle primaries when smarter ballots are used is bound to be different from their effects under 1MB. In a rigid two-party system such as the USA's, there may be little point in adopting distributive inputs without plentiful ballot options; jungle primaries are one way to expand the options available per contest. In some countries, other cultural and institutional factors address the adequacy of ballot options already. Under American conditions, at least, jungle primaries and smarter ballots may need one another to fulfill their potential.

Ranking and grading ballots are the two most viable reform options. My new proposals for the B-GPA and RCV-A ballot structures could provide plausible weapons for voters against the dilemma of disempowerment. Crucially, they do not require reconstructing a bygone world of robust partisan organizations and ironclad partisan loyalties in order to re-empower voters in an era of democratic deficits. In fact, they fit neatly into a world in which teams of professional politicians can no longer expect their followers to declare "no god but God" at every election—where political polytheism is the order of the day for growing numbers of citizens.

Democratic societies are justified in expecting a spirit of experimentation and innovation from their professional researchers, whether for the designing of buildings, the healing of bodies, or the reforming of institutions. But another gap would have to be closed for the social purpose of the ivory tower to be met in this respect. In the study of elections, voting theorists and empirical scholars would have to do more to remedy one another's weaknesses and compound one another's strengths.

In virtually any field of research, theorists tend to be hyper-active conceptually and complacent observationally; empiricists tend to be hyper-active observationally and complacent conceptually. But realism demands fairly intense, co-ordinated activity in both conceptual and observational spheres. Specialists in conceptual and observational analysis must engage and collaborate. But this is merely operational; there is also something prior, culturally. Specialists have to be willing to learn from non-specialists. Otherwise, societies may find themselves supporting professional researchers who spend their careers muddling around the edges of elite doctrine while missing significant chunks of reality.

The buildings that currently house such muddling should by no means come down. To tweak the ivory-tower metaphor, what societies need in their towers of academia are well-functioning elevators (or, to save energy and improve health, broad spiral staircases!): some means of carrying people from ground level to tower view, and back again.

Many societies also support full-time elected officers, and the demanding task of realism might be part of their job description too. Given what we know about democratic deficits and electoral accountability in the twenty-first century, it appears that dealing with realities collaboratively is not the outcome that existing schemes of electoral incentives do best. Some institutional changes will have to occur before governments are likely to become better realists, and the structure of the ballot itself is a place to start.

References

Baldini, G., & A. Pappalardo. 2009. *Elections, Electoral Systems, and Volatile Voters.* Basingstoke, UK: Palgrave Macmillan.

Beramendi, V., A. Ellis, B. Kaufman, M. Kornblith, L. LeDuc, P. McGuire, T. Schiller, & P. Svensson. 2008. *Direct Democracy: The International IDEA Handbook.* Stockholm: Institute for Democracy and Election Assistance.

Blais, A., J.-F. Laslier, F. Poinas, & K. Van der Straeten. 2015. "Citizens' Preferences about Voting Rules: Self-Interest, Ideology, and Sincerity." *Public Choice* 164: 423–42.

Blake, R.B. 1994. *Canadians at Last: Canada Integrates Newfoundland as a Province.* Toronto: University Press of Toronto.

Bowler, S., & T. Donovan. 2013. *The Limits of Electoral Reform.* New York: Oxford University Press.

Cain, B.E. 2015. *Democracy, More or Less: America's Political Reform Quandary.* New York: Cambridge University Press.

Carty, R.K., A. Blais, & P. Fournier. 2008. "When Citizens Choose to Reform SMP: The British Columbia Citizens' Assembly on Electoral Reform." *To Keep or to Change First Past the Post? The Politics of Electoral Reform,* ed. A. Blais. Oxford: Oxford University Press.

Cote, J. 2011. "S.F. Ranked-Choice Voting Confusing, Poll Says." *San Francisco Chronicle,* March 10 (Accessed on August 16, 2017 at www.sfgate.com/politics/article/S-F-ranked-choice-voting-confusing-poll-says-2389425.php).

Grofman, B., & S.L. Feld. 2004. "If You Like the Alternative Vote (a.k.a. the Instant Run-Off), then You Ought to Know about the Coombs Rule." *Electoral Studies* 23: 641–59.

Jenkins, S. 2017. "Hardliners Won't Like this Soft Brexit Plan." *Guardian* (London), July 27 (Accessed on July 27, 2017 at www.theguardian.com/commentisfree/2017/jul/27/hardliners-soft-brexit-tough-negotiate-properly).

Joshi, D.K., J.S. Maloy, & T.M. Peterson. 2015. "Popular vs. Elite Democratic Structures and International Peace." *Journal of Peace Research* 52: 463–77.

Joshi, D.K., J.S. Maloy, & T.M. Peterson. 2019. "Popular vs. Elite Democracies and Human Rights: Inclusion Makes a Difference." *International Studies Quarterly* 63: 111–26.

Lakeman, E. 1974. *How Democracies Vote: A Study of Electoral Systems.* 4th edn. London: Faber.

LeDuc, L., & J.H. Pammett. 2013. "The Fate of Governing Parties in Times of Economic Crisis." *Electoral Studies* 32: 494–99.

Lundberg, T.C. 2018. "Electoral Systems in Context: United Kingdom." *The Oxford Handbook of Electoral Systems*, eds. E.S. Herron, R.J. Pekkanen, & M.S. Shugart. Oxford: Oxford University Press.

McGann, A. 2006. *The Logic of Democracy: Reconciling Equality, Deliberation, and Minority Protection.* Ann Arbor: University of Michigan Press.

Miller, K., & S. Thistle. 2018. "Jared Golden Declared Winner of First Ranked-Choice Congressional Election, but Challenge Looms." *Portland* (Maine) *Press-Herald*, November 15 (Accessed on December 31, 2018 at www.press-herald.com/2018/11/15/final-ranked-choice-vote-count-slated-for-noon).

Milner, H. 2017. "Electoral System Reform: The Canadian Experience." *Election Law Journal* 16: 349–56.

Munks, J. 2018. "Instant Runoff Voting Survives at the Polls, but Will It Be Implemented in Memphis?" (Memphis) *Commercial Appeal*, November 7 (Accessed on January 5, 2018 at www.commercialappeal.com/story/news/2018/11/07/instant-runoff-voting-memphis-shelby-county-midterm-election/1858041002).

Mustillo, T.M., & J. Polga-Hecimovich. 2018. "Measures and Votes: Party Performance under Free-List Proportional Representation, with Evidence from Ecuador." *Electoral Studies* 56: 124–35.

Nagel, J.H. 2004. "New Zealand: Reform by (Nearly) Immaculate Design." *Handbook of Electoral System Choice*, ed. J.M. Colomer. New York: Palgrave Macmillan.

Ornstein, J.T., & R.Z. Norman. 2014. "Frequency of Monotonicity Failure under Instant Runoff Voting: Estimates Based on a Spatial Model of Elections." *Public Choice* 161: 1–9.

Passarelli, G. 2018. "Electoral Systems in Context: Italy." *The Oxford Handbook of Electoral Systems*, eds. E.S. Herron, R.J. Pekkanen, & M.S. Shugart. Oxford: Oxford University Press.

Potyondy, P.R. 2018. "Maine Becomes the First State to Use Ranked-Choice Voting." National Conference of State Legislatures, June 14 (Accessed on October 21, 2018 at www.ncsl.org/blog/2018/06/14/maine-becomes-the-first-state-to-use-ranked-choice-voting.aspx).

Renwick, A. 2018. "Electoral System Change." *The Oxford Handbook of Electoral Systems*, eds. E.S. Herron & M.S. Shugart. Oxford: Oxford University Press.

Russell, E. 2018. "Mainers Vote to Keep Ranked-Choice Voting." *Portland* (Maine) *Press-Herald*, June 13 (Accessed on October 21, 2018 at www.pressherald.com/2018/06/12/ranked-choice-voting-takes-lead-in-early-balloting).

Santucci, J. 2018. "Maine Ranked-Choice Voting as a Case of Electoral-System Change." *Representation* 54: 297–311.

Sargeant, J., A. Renwick, & M. Russell. 2018. "The Mechanics of a Further Referendum on Brexit." University College, London.

Tervalon-Daumont, E., & A. Garza. 2011. "Reforms that Helped Elect Candidates of Color in SF, Oakland under Attack." *New American Media*, April 29 (Accessed on August 16, 2017 at newamericamedia.org/2011/04/reforms-that-helped-elect-candidates-of-color-in-sf-oakland-under-attack.php).

Thistle, S. 2017a. "Maine's Highest Court Rules Ranked-Choice Voting Is Unconstitutional." *Portland* (Maine) *Press-Herald*, May 23 (Accessed on August 23, 2017 at www.pressherald.com/2017/05/23/maine-high-court-says-ranked-choice-voting-is-unconstitutional).

Thistle, S. 2017b. "Voter-Approved Ranked-Choice Voting Stays in Effect as Repeal Bills Fail." *Portland* (Maine) *Press-Herald*, June 28 (Accessed on August 23, 2017 at www.pressherald.com/2017/06/28/legislature-fails-to-repeal-voter-passed-ranked-choice-voting-law).

Tierney, S. 2013. "Using Electoral Law to Construct a Deliberative Referendum: Moving beyond the Democratic Paradox." *Election Law Journal* 12: 508.

Von Schoultz, A. 2018. "Electoral Systems in Context: Finland." *The Oxford Handbook of Electoral Systems*, eds. E.S. Herron, R.J. Pekkanen, & M.S. Shugart. Oxford: Oxford University Press.

Vowles, J. 1995. "The Politics of Electoral Reform in New Zealand." *International Political Science Review* 16: 95–115.

Webb, J.A. 1998. "Confederation, Conspiracy, and Choice: A Discussion." *Newfoundland Studies* 14: 169–87.

Appendix:
Methodological and Theoretical Issues
in Electoral Studies

This appendix discusses several themes in the fields of comparative electoral studies and voting theory in greater detail than was possible, or seemed advisable, in the body of the text. The topics covered below include measurement choices for electoral sanction, interpretations of statistical results in empirical studies of accountability, and fuller details on my new taxonomy of ballot structure.

Measurement Strategies for Electoral Sanction

Part of the difficulty in evaluating direct empirical tests of electoral accountability lies in the variety of operational schemes used to measure the dependent variable. It is essential to distinguish the stronger from the weaker measurement choices and to ensure that how we interpret quantitative results bears a reasonable relation to the conceptual rationales behind the variables used. I will now explain the main alternatives for measuring accountability, beginning with the weakest and moving toward the strongest.[1]

The least plausible option for operationalizing electoral accountability is to use *approval ratings* of parties or politicians as the dependent variable. Despite the fact that this methodological problem has long been recognized (Lewis-Beck and Stegmaier 2000, 188; Powell 2004, 103), some studies essentially ignore it. The same caution applies to other types of data from opinion surveys, such as self-reported *vote-choice* at the individual level. The well-known perils of relying on voters' self-reported behavior, whether before (Lau 1994) or after (Burden 2000) the election, leave considerable room for error in such studies.

Moving from survey responses to actual electoral data is a step in the right direction, and change in *vote-share* has been a popular choice for operationalizing the dependent variable. The problem, simply, is that losing votes is not the same thing as losing elections. The fact that a college instructor's evaluation scores by students go down does not in itself amount to punishment, unless the instructor is extremely sensitive to criticism. Politicians generally are not. What matters for politicians is actual electoral victory or defeat, and the more deft and less risk-averse are the ones likeliest to stick around (Maravall 1999, 172–191). The next step, then, would be to use *electoral survival* as the dependent variable. This is related to the concept, in time-series analysis, of "hazard rate." Only a few studies have taken this methodological option, but they have also been the most comprehensive in their global scope and long-range chronological coverage (Cheibub and Przeworski 1999; Maravall 2010). These analyses are both pessimistic about electoral accountability. Among studies that have appeared to vindicate accountability, very few have actually made a direct challenge to this measurement strategy; three of the best are considered below.

The scholarly movement toward electoral skepticism has not been unanimous but has proceeded with regular relapses and reservations, and conceptual and measurement choices play a role here too. One strategy for upholding the conventional wisdom about electoral accountability is to interpret the evidence as though accountability were nothing more than answerability. The anodyne claim that "the general pattern is that we see political elites reacting to voters"—which

---

[1]This section gives an abridged version of the more thorough treatment previously published in Maloy (2014, 20–22).

well and truly fails the "grandmother test" (Shapiro 2005, 52)—is occasionally presented in defense of the success of electoral accountability, as if that's the same thing as being "reined in," "replaced," and "often changed" by elections (Eijk and Franklin 2009, 220–221). "Answerability" has even been explicitly used as the definition of accountability, with the obvious conclusion that electoral victories and defeats have no bearing on the incidence of the phenomenon (Franklin et al. 2014, 390–391). This approach to rescuing the ideal of electoral accountability is commendably frank in its definitional fiats, at least.

How (Not) to Interpret "Mixed" Results

The previous section leads to some firm recommendations about the best measurement strategy for the first link in the chain of electoral accountability. Electoral survival is the best thing to measure when studying the voter-election linkage. One of the indicators of political science's shift toward a skeptical position on electoral accountability is the growing recognition that vote-share is a less demanding measurement choice which tends to find more positive results for accountability, while electoral survival is a more demanding choice that finds less positive results (Healy and Malhotra 2013, 297n).

Whenever we hear about "mixed results," we should be mindful of the possibility that mixed measurement tools may be one of the causes. Even so, some survival-based studies have themselves announced mixed or even positive results. Do they therefore offer solid ground for challenging or reversing the skeptical trends? Three examples of high-quality political research that fits this description are worth considering.

First, a single-country study of economic voting in Poland has employed electoral survival as the dependent variable and announced positive but conditional results (Zielinski et al. 2005). The second example comes from Brazilian cities (Ferraz and Finan 2008), where incumbents who were incriminated by public audits were more likely to lose their re-election bids than clean incumbents were. The third example comes from Italy, where an analysis of corruption trials in the 1990s measured their effects on the actual success or failure of incumbents' re-election bids (Chang et al. 2010), finding that unusual circumstances of intense exposure seemed to have been necessary to activate the accountability function of elections.

All three of these studies took on the most challenging measurement approach to accountability, which also happens to be the most conceptually relevant, and found some significant effect of expected stimuli on electoral survival. Yet the Polish study was sober in its conclusions, while the Brazilian and Italian studies were actively positive and negative, respectively. The Brazilian study's conclusion sounds categorical, theoretical, and optimistic: "Our paper lends strong support to the value of information and the importance of local media in promoting political accountability" (Ferraz and Finan 2008, 706). The Italian study's conclusion is that, "if our interpretation is correct, it does not bode well for political accountability in established democracies" (Chang et al. 2010, 216).

Why the stark difference in interpretation? Numbers alone cannot explain it, at least not quite. Chang and colleagues' quantitative results are broadly similar to Ferraz and Finan's: Incumbents implicated in corruption are significantly but not overwhelmingly less likely (slightly under 10% in Italy, somewhat over 20% in Brazil) to win re-election. The difference appears to have another origin. Ferraz and Finan couched their positive results in terms of a specific theory that says that, given high-quality information, voters will punish bad incumbents at the polls. They claim to find *strong confirmation of the theory*, which is not the same thing as finding evidence of a *high incidence of the phenomenon*, of accountability. If the theory predicts that electoral accountability should be weak or rare in the real world because of the extreme difficulties associated with voter information (and it does; see Maloy 2015, 78–79), then good news for the theory is not necessarily good news for democracy. Chang and colleagues seem to be more concerned about the normative bearing of their evidence than the technical success of a theory, and that is why they sound more pessimistic.

It should also be noted that a second team of researchers came along, sliced and diced the Brazilian data differently, and came to the opposite conclusion: The corrupt incumbents were more likely than the clean ones both to take their chances in a re-election bid and to win new terms (Pereira et al. 2009). Apparently, not all politicians are so risk-averse that they would do anything to avoid provoking voters' wrath. Perhaps one reason is that politicians and other non-risk-averse people develop plans for managing risk—such as political manipulation and electoral campaigning. This possible explanation for the second Brazilian study's findings calls to mind the Polish legislators who switched parties and won re-election. Voters' difficulties in handling political information, media's poor track-record at delivering it, and politicians' fine track-record at controlling it are all connected to the trend in electoral skepticism over the last two decades.

The moral of the story is that mixed results are sometimes subjected to over-interpretation, and positive findings are not always what they seem.

Another consideration has to do with reasoning from the evidence. When it comes to electoral accountability, there is plenty of observational evidence of incumbents' losing and winning elections. The range of plausible mechanisms, however, is considerably greater than is the case with, say, global warming. Not everything that happens in an electoral democracy can or should be assumed to be caused by elections. A political system could be modestly representative, after all, because the governing elites in a particular country tend to be conscientious and well-informed; or, perhaps more realistically, the governing elites might be afraid of violent revolution rather than electoral defeat.

Imagine, for the sake of argument, that most members of the US Congress happen to sleep better at night when they're able to look their constituents in the eyes and tell them that they've done their best to give them the kind of government they want. They could always find a handful of wealthy donors, hire a team of expert consultants, baffle the media and the voters with political stunts and striking symbolism which have no relation to real policy, and make different promises to different groups of voters to win their support. And some of them do just that. But most of them simply can't and don't operate that way: We could say (in this purely hypothetical scenario) that they came to the office already accountable on the inside, regardless of how insistently elections could or would intervene to leave them no choice in the matter. The point is that elites act according to cultural norms to greater and lesser degrees at different times and in different places. Here is just one of a variety of plausible mechanisms that are different from the sanctioning properties of electoral institutions.

In constitutional democracies, institutions are supposed to be there to keep politicians from doing wrong whenever cultural norms decay to the point that they no longer constrain the naked pursuit of wealth and power. If we don't really know whether electoral sanctions work as Hamilton and Madison imagined, then we don't really know how bad things could get if and when our governing elites decide to start pushing the envelope of democratic traditions.

That's why the trend of electoral skepticism in academic political research matters for the public at large. And it's also why scholars should always insist on using the most demanding methods, and the least casual approaches to interpreting evidence, when studying electoral accountability.

BALLOT STRUCTURE AND VOTING THEORY

My new taxonomy of ballot structure leaves a lot of fertile ground for discussion and debate, most of which it seemed advisable to withhold from Chapter 4, in the interest of moving expeditiously from realist theory to realistic reform. Here some of the main issues that may merit further explanation or exploration can be covered more fully.

The scholarly touchstone for categorizing electoral systems is Douglas Rae's 1967 book, *The Political Consequences of Electoral Laws*. In terms of the general concept of electoral structure (see Fig. A.1), Rae focused only on three of our eight categories. He included only one feature of contest structure, "district magnitude," while calling input rules "ballot structure" and output rules "electoral formula." The popularity of Rae's choices of terminology, which have often been used by subsequent scholars despite their awareness of their shortcomings, should not distract us from the conceptual gaps in need of filling. When it comes to input rules, Rae saw a continuum of possible variation between two extremes, the "categorical" and the "ordinal" ballot (Rae 1967, 16–18). The first

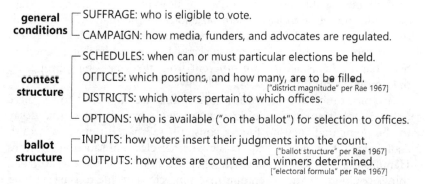

Fig. A.1   Elements of electoral structure (with Rae's terminology)

kind of ballot allows only a single, unconditional expression of support; the second allows the voter to rank multiple options in a hierarchic order (first, second, third choice, etc.).

The problem is, categorical and ordinal inputs are not the only possibilities; they weren't even the only input rules in use at the time he was writing. The Swiss *panachage* ("cocktail") system has nothing to do with ranking and was therefore wrongly called ordinal by Rae. The Swiss use instead a version of a cumulative ballot, with a per-candidate limit of two votes. Rae's scheme had no place for grading ballots, perhaps because no major political elections have used them, but arguably the Limited Vote (LV) system that was widely prevalent in nineteenth-century elections and is still used for the Spanish Senate is a kind of binary grading system—almost like the Pass–Fail (a.k.a. Approval Vote) ballot applied to a multi-seat district, but with a ceiling on voters' total number of votes to give. Scholarly criticisms of Rae's conceptual scheme abound (e.g., Blais 1988, 104; Gallagher and Mitchell 2005, 7, 9; Renwick and Pilet 2016, 22–23), but alternative classifications have usually been purpose-built for specific empirical agendas.

Some admirable, though perhaps only partial, exceptions to this trend include Gallagher and Mitchell's taxonomy (Gallagher and Mitchell 2005, 7–10), which certainly improves on Rae's. But it also calls the German parliamentary ballot "dividual" despite its restriction of the voter to a single vote for each of two contests: in other words, two votes for two tiers for two separate batches of seats, not two votes for a single contest. Colomer's scheme (Colomer 2011, 8–10) is also useful, but it similarly makes the (questionable and imprecise) claim that a two-tier contest structure with one vote per contest somehow places the ballot structure of 2RS, dual-vote systems, and open-list PR in an intermediate category. Mine is the first revisionist effort, I believe, which takes the distinction between ballot structure and contest structure seriously—thereby sticking to the analytic principle that a different ballot type from 1MB must have different input rules *per contest*, not per election day or per elected assembly. My taxonomy is also unique, as far as I know, in its intent to lay out a conceptual map that can accommodate experimental and reformist possibilities that are not yet actualities.

In our new, post-Rae taxonomy, "first past the post" is abandoned as a label for the more precise and descriptive "one-mark ballot" (1MB). Both the modal and the mean output rules necessarily give the same result when each voter is forced by exclusive input rules to support only a single candidate with only a 100% measure of support. If the modal winner is supported by a bloc containing 40% of all voters, the mean voter gives that candidate an average value of 0.4. That value being higher than the mean voter's of any other candidate, the mean winner is the same as the modal winner. Both combinations are essentially the same: 1MB. If we insisted on talking about horses and posts, it would obviously be more intuitive to say that the horse whose nose is "first past the post" can only be supported by the modal bloc of voters—thereby leading us astray from an important analytic detail.

Some combinations of input and output rules are left blank because their input-output combinations seem to me either implausible or vague and speculative. The reasons for these gaps may be worth specifying, but the gaps themselves could be viewed as an invitation for readers to fill them if they can be more imaginative than I.

The modal output rule is to award victory to the candidate favored by the largest single bloc of voters who submitted identical ballot inputs. Ranking inputs can be combined with modal outputs only after an unusual counting process of eliminations and transfers which manages to keep each vote whole, and that is what the Single Transferable Vote (STV) accomplishes. With cumulative and grading inputs, however, each vote cannot be kept whole in the possession of only one candidate, as a rule, because voters are allowed to split their support exactly evenly across two or more candidates. The only way to pick a winner modally would be to separate all voters into many blocs according to identical support profiles. With multi-mark ballots and more than two candidates, however, the largest bloc of voters submitting identical inputs is likely to be quite a small group. There could be many more blocs of voters than there are candidates, and a modal voter under such circumstances may represent only 10% or less of all voters. Either a cumulative or a grading input rule with a modal output rule therefore seems implausible.

The median output rule also gives rise to some odd combinations. It is implausible with exclusive inputs, at least for three or more candidates, because it may not select any winner. In case none of the candidates has a majority of votes, the median voters for each candidate will all represent a value of zero. The election would then have to be rerun with a different system.

The combinations of ranking and cumulative inputs with median outputs are speculative because they have not, to my knowledge, been

developed in sufficient detail to enable any sort of experimental testing, even in principle. The ranking-median combination has been proposed once in an academic journal, at least (Bassett and Persky 1999).
As far as I know, the cumulative-median combination has not even been
entertained in print. The difficulty for the latter would be normative
more than technical. All that is required to apply median output rules
is some sort of one-dimensional scale on which voters can locate their
support for candidates. Cumulative inputs are certainly consistent with
such a scale, ranging from zero to whatever number marks the per-voter
limit. But the distribution on that scale would seem to be rather sticky,
given that voters would be constrained by the rules of arithmetic in how
freely they could take positions on the scale for multiple candidates. If we
like median output rules, their logic seems to recommend the relatively
unconstrained grading scheme—within a given scale and over a particular
list of candidates, voters are absolutely unconstrained in indicating their
support.

It is certainly possible to come up with different counting rules than
the ones discussed above, such as the League Table (LT) method (gran-
diosely called "Majority Rule" by Dasgupta and Maskin 2004) in which
rankings are used to simulate a round-robin tournament among all pairs
of candidates. LT generates outputs by conducting a large number of
one-on-one contests—two-candidate races gone wild. After tallying up
results from every encounter, with each candidate's ranking determining the outcome of each match-up for each voter, all candidates are
arrayed from top to bottom according to wins and losses (or winning
percentage), as in a sports league. This method of selecting a single winner could be characterized as a mean output rule, since the winner has
the largest average likelihood of winning a head-to-head contest for any
voter, but the counting process would obviously be very different from
the Borda Count (BC). Its advocates might also want to claim that there
is a median output rule at work, in the sense that the median voter might
be proven to give head-to-head victory to the LT winner more often
than to any other candidate. Though quite popular among voting theorists, LT has not (to my knowledge) been tested on a large electorate in
any kind of field-like setting.

Another system with eccentric features, recently fashionable among
some economists and mathematicians, is the Quadratic Vote (QV)
(Posner and Weyl 2015; Posner and Stephanopoulos 2017). This is a
version of the Cumulative Vote but with unusual distribution rules and

incentives. Here each voter gets a fixed budget of vote-dollars which can be exchanged for a number of actual votes equal to the square-root of the number of vote-dollars. This quadratic function yields a per-voter bonus for spreading instead of plumping. Whereas a cumulative ballot may encourage a voter to send all votes to a lesser-evil candidate, the quadratic scheme offers slightly less stark incentives. For example, 25 vote-dollars buy a package of five votes (because five times five equals 25), 16 vote-dollars buy four, nine vote-dollars buy three, and so on. For the same amount of your vote budget, therefore, you could deliver a package of five votes to one candidate or four votes to that candidate plus three votes to a second candidate (because nine plus 16 equals 25). By effectively offering bonus votes to any voter who is willing to spread support across more than one candidate, the quadratic function sets up a structure of incentives in which tactical voting and the spoiler effect may be alleviated—at least in comparison with standard cumulative input rules, which may be little better than exclusive ballots in this regard. The arithmetic required of the voter obviously goes up, and accessibility goes down, when QV is assessed against the other multi-mark ballot structures. A practical issue with giving more votes to voters if they elect to spread them across more than one candidate is that constitutional courts (in the USA, at least) would almost certainly invalidate such a scheme as violating basic political equality. Why should voters who are intensely loyal to only a single option on the ballot get fewer votes?

A more complete picture of my new taxonomy of ballot structure would include some of these marginal types (see Fig. A.2). I hasten to add that the purpose of a taxonomy of ballot structure is not to itemize every good voting system, since elements from more than one ballot structure can be incorporated into a single system. Several combinatory schemes, not fully acknowledged here, are popular among voting theorists.

As a final word, this particular conceptual map has been deliberately concocted with a single-winner contest structure taken as given. Change that premise to a multi-winner contest structure, and the map gets busier. By my reckoning, two more kinds of output rule (making a total of five) would have to be added which have no application to a single-winner contest. Allocation formulas for proportional representation (PR) display many variations. In principle, though PR formulas are usually combined with exclusive input rules (a single mark bestowing 100%

	Mode	Mean	Median
Exclusive	1MB	1MB	
Ranking	STV	BC	LT, RV?
Cumulative		CV, QV	
Grading		GPA, PF	MG

1MB = One-Mark Ballot
BC = Borda Count
CV = Cumulative Vote
GPA = Grade-Point Average
LT = League Table

MG = Median Grade
PF = Pass-Fail
QV = Quadratic Vote
RV = Robust Vote
STV = Single Transferable Vote

N.B. Proportional formulas and quota-based rules belong to fourth and fifth output columns, applicable only to multi-winner contests.

Fig. A.2   Taxonomy of ballot structure (with minor ballot types)

support to only one ballot option), they could in principle work with any of the other input rules. In other words, there is no analytic reason why the relevant proportions for determining representation in a multi-member assembly should be predicated on people's all-or-nothing judgments as opposed to their more finely graded judgments. Normatively, as long as each voter has the same-sized package of support and the same opportunity to distribute it, basic political equality is sustained even where Borda-type counts, cumulative distributions, or grading averages are used in formulas of party proportionality.

The fifth type of output rule involves the quota- or threshold-based counting procedure. Typical of STV in multi-seat districts, this output process distinctively involves—in addition to the single-seat version's eliminations and transfers—redistributing surplus votes from candidates who pass the quota. This is decidedly not the same as applying a formula for proportionality to party-list or party-pooled votes, and it is basically unlike the modal output rule. The latter can be applied to a multi-winner contest, of course, but with no thresholds we are then left with the Single Non-Transferable Vote (SNTV)—rather different from STV's counting and winning rules. It seems that any of the multi-mark input rules could also be combined with quota output rules, in principle, provided that someone comes up with consistent and defensible parameters for determining what the quotas should be.

REFERENCES

Bassett, G.W., & J. Persky. 1999. "Robust Voting." *Public Choice* 99: 299–310.

Blais, A. 1988. "The Classification of Electoral Systems." *European Journal of Political Research* 16: 99–110.

Burden, B.C. 2000. "Voter Turnout and the National Election Study." *Political Analysis* 8: 389–98.

Chang, E.C.C., M.A. Golden, & S.J. Hill. 2010. "Legislative Malfeasance and Political Accountability." *World Politics* 62: 177–220.

Cheibub, J.A., & A. Przeworski. 1999. "Democracy, Elections, and Accountability for Outcomes." *Democracy, Accountability, and Representation*, eds. A. Przeworski, S.C. Stokes, & B. Manin. New York: Cambridge University Press.

Colomer, J.M. 2011. "Introduction: Personal and Party Representation." *Personal Representation: The Neglected Dimension of Electoral Systems*, ed. J.M. Colomer. Colchester, UK: ECPR.

Dasgupta, P., & E. Maskin. 2004. "The Fairest Vote of All." *Scientific American* 290: 92–97.

van der Eijk, C., & M.N. Franklin. 2009. *Elections and Voters*. Basingstoke, UK: Palgrave Macmillan.

Ferraz, C., & F. Finan. 2008. "Exposing Corrupt Politicians: The Effects of Brazil's Publicly Released Audits on Electoral Outcomes." *Quarterly Journal of Economics* 123: 704–45.

Franklin, M.N., S.N. Soroka, & C. Wlezien. 2014. "Elections." *The Oxford Handbook of Public Accountability*, eds. M. Bovens, R.E. Goodin, & T. Schillemans. Oxford: Oxford University Press.

Gallagher, M., & P. Mitchell. 2005. "Introduction." *The Politics of Electoral Systems*, eds. M. Gallagher & P. Mitchell. Oxford: Oxford University Press.

Healy, A., & N. Malhotra. 2013. "Retrospective Voting Reconsidered." *Annual Review of Political Science* 16: 285–306.

Lau, R.R. 1994. "An Analysis of the Accuracy of 'Trial Heat' Polls During the 1992 Presidential Election." *Public Opinion Quarterly* 58: 2–20.

Lewis-Beck, M.S., & M. Stegmaier. 2000. "Economic Determinants of Electoral Outcomes." *Annual Review of Political Science* 3: 183–219.

Maloy, J.S. 2014. "Linkages of Electoral Accountability: Empirical Results and Methodological Lessons." *Politics and Governance* 2.2: 13–27.

Maloy, J.S. 2015. "Intermediate Conditions of Democratic Accountability: A Response to Electoral Skepticism." *Politics and Governance* 3.2: 76–89.

Maravall, J.M. 1999. "Accountability and Manipulation." *Democracy, Accountability, and Representation*, eds. A. Przeworski, S.C. Stokes, & B. Manin. New York: Cambridge University Press.

Maravall, J.M. 2010. "Accountability in Coalition Governments." *Annual Review of Political Science* 13: 81–100.

Pereira, C., M.A. Melo, & C.M. Figueiredo. 2009. "The Corruption-Enhancing Role of Re-election Incentives? Counter-Intuitive Evidence from Brazil's Audit Reports." *Political Research Quarterly* 62: 731–44.

Posner, E.A., & N. Stephanopoulos. 2017. "Quadratic Electoral Law." *Public Choice* 172: 265–82.

Posner, E.A., & E.G. Weyl. 2015. "Voting Squared: Quadratic Voting in Democratic Politics." *Vanderbilt Law Review* 68: 441.

Powell, G.B. 2004. "The Chain of Responsiveness." *Journal of Democracy* 15: 91–105.

Rae, D.W. 1967. *The Political Consequences of Electoral Laws*. New Haven: Yale University Press.

Renwick, A., & J.-B. Pilet. 2016. *Faces on the Ballot: The Personalization of Electoral Systems in Europe*. Oxford: Oxford University Press.

Shapiro, I. 2005. *The Flight from Reality in the Human Sciences*. Princeton: Princeton University Press.

Zielinski, J., K.M. Slomczynski, & G. Shabad. 2005. "Electoral Control in New Democracies: The Perverse Incentives of Fluid Party Systems." *World Politics* 57: 365–95.

BIBLIOGRAPHY

Abramowitz, A.I., & J. McCoy. 2019. "United States: Racial Resentment, Negative Partisanship, and Polarization in Trump's America." *Annals of the American Academy of Political and Social Science* 681: 137–56.

Abramowitz, A.I., & S. Webster. 2016. "The Rise of Negative Partisanship and the Nationalization of U.S. Elections in the 21st Century." *Electoral Studies* 41: 12–22.

Abramson, P.R., J.H. Aldrich, A. Blais, M. Diamond, A. Diskin, I.H. Indridason, D.J. Lee, & R. Levine. 2010. "Comparing Strategic Voting under FPTP and PR." *Comparative Political Studies* 43: 61–90.

Abramson, P.R., J.H. Aldrich, A. Diskin, A.M. Houck, R. Levine, & T.J. Scotto. 2013. "The British General Election of 2010 under Different Voting Rules." *Electoral Studies* 32: 134–39.

Achen, C., & L.M. Bartels. 2016. *Democracy for Realists*. Princeton: Princeton University Press.

Alameda County. 2018. "County of Alameda, CA: Elections" (Accessed on December 31, 2018 at www.acgov.org/government/elections.htm).

Alcaniz, I., & T. Hellwig. 2011. "Who's to Blame? The Distribution of Responsibility in Developing Democracies." *British Journal of Political Science* 41: 389–411.

Alos-Ferrer, C., & D.-G. Granic. 2012. "Two Field Experiments on Approval Voting in Germany." *Social Choice and Welfare* 39: 171–205.

Amy, D.J. 2000. *Behind the Ballot Box: A Citizen's Guide to Electoral Systems*. Westport, CT: Praeger.

Anderson, C.J. 2007. "The End of Economic Voting? Contingency Dilemmas and the Limits of Accountability." *Annual Review of Political Science* 10: 271–96.

Argersinger, P.H. 1985. "New Perspectives on Election Fraud in the Gilded Age." *Political Science Quarterly* 100: 669–87.

Arnold, R.D. 2004. *Congress, the Press, and Political Accountability*. Princeton: Princeton University Press.

Bailey, T.A. 1937. "Was the Presidential Election of 1900 a Mandate on Imperialism?" *Mississippi Valley Historical Review* 24: 43–52.

Baldini, G., & A. Pappalardo. 2009. *Elections, Electoral Systems, and Volatile Voters*. Basingstoke, UK: Palgrave Macmillan.

Balinski, M., & R. Laraki. 2010. *Majority Judgment: Measuring, Ranking, and Electing*. Cambridge, MA: MIT Press.

Balinski, M., & R. Laraki. 2014. "What Should 'Majority Decision' Mean?" *Majority Decisions: Principles and Practices*, eds. S. Novak & J. Elster. New York: Cambridge University Press.

Balinski, M., & R. Laraki. 2016. "Trump and Clinton Victorious: Proof that U.S. Voting System Doesn't Work." *The Conversation*, May 9 (Accessed on August 16, 2017 at theconversation.com/trump-and-clinton-victorious-proof-that-us-voting-system-doesnt-work-58752).

Barkin, N. 2016. "Who Do You Hate the Least? The Dilemma for French Voters." *Reuters*, August 17 (Accessed on December 29, 2016 at www.reuters.com/article/us-france-politics-column-idUSKCN10P0FY).

Bartels, L.M. 2016. "Elections in America." *Annals of the American Academy of Political and Social Science* 667: 36–49.

Bassi, A. 2015. "Voting Systems and Strategic Manipulation: An Experimental Study." *Journal of Theoretical Politics* 27: 58–85.

Baujard, A., & H. Igersheim. 2010. "Framed Field Experiments on Approval Voting: Lessons from the 2002 and 2007 French Presidential Elections." *Handbook on Approval Voting*, eds. J.-F. Laslier & M.R. Sanver. Berlin: Springer.

Baujard, A., & H. Igersheim. 2011. "Framed-Field Experiment on Approval Voting and Evaluative Voting: Some Teachings to Reform the French Presidential Election System." *In Situ and Laboratory Experiments on Electoral Law Reform*, eds. B. Dolez, B. Grofman, & A. Laurent. New York: Springer.

Baujard, A., H. Igersheim, I. Lebon, F. Favrel, & J.-F. Laslier. 2014. "Who's Favored by Evaluative Voting? An Experiment Conducted during the 2012 French Presidential Election." *Electoral Studies* 34: 131–45.

Beramendi, V., A. Ellis, B. Kaufman, M. Kornblith, L. LeDuc, P. McGuire, T. Schiller, & P. Svensson. 2008. *Direct Democracy: The International IDEA Handbook*. Stockholm: Institute for Democracy and Election Assistance.

Berg-Andersson, R.E. 2017. "The Green Papers" (Accessed on August 13, 2017 at www.thegreenpapers.com).

Berman, S. 2017. "The Pipe Dream of Undemocratic Liberalism." *Journal of Democracy* 28: 29–38.

Bermeo, N. 2019. "Can American Democracy Still Be Saved?" *Annals of the American Academy of Political and Social Science* 681: 228–33.

Blais, A., & A. Degan. 2018. "The Study of Strategic Voting." *The Oxford Handbook of Public Choice*, eds. R.D. Congleton, B. Grofman, & S. Voigt. Oxford: Oxford University Press.

Blais, A., M. Heroux-Legault, L.B. Stephenson, W. Cross, & E. Gidengil. 2012. "Assessing the Psychological and Mechanical Impact of Electoral Rules: A Quasi-Experiment." *Electoral Studies* 30: 829–37.

Blais, A., J.-F. Laslier, F. Poinas, & K. Van der Straeten. 2015. "Citizens' Preferences about Voting Rules: Self-Interest, Ideology, and Sincerity." *Public Choice* 164: 423–42.

Blais, A., J.-F. Laslier, & K. Van der Straeten, eds. 2016. *Voting Experiments*. Heidelberg: Springer.

Blake, R.B. 1994. *Canadians at Last: Canada Integrates Newfoundland as a Province*. Toronto: University Press of Toronto.

Bovens, M. 2005. "Public Accountability." *The Oxford Handbook of Public Management*, eds. E. Ferlie, L.E. Lynn, & C. Pollitt. New York: Oxford University Press.

Bowler, S., & T. Donovan. 2013. *The Limits of Electoral Reform*. New York: Oxford University Press.

Bowler, S., & B. Grofman. 2000. "Conclusion: STV's Place in the Family of Electoral Systems." *Elections in Australia, Ireland, and Malta under the Single Transferable Vote: Reflections on an Embedded Institution*, eds. S. Bowler & B. Grofman. Ann Arbor: University of Michigan Press.

Bowler, S., T. Donovan, & D. Brockington. 2003. *Electoral Reform and Minority Representation: Local Experiments with Alternative Elections*. Columbus: Ohio State University Press.

Bowler, S., G. McElroy, & S. Muller. 2018. "Voter Preferences and Party Loyalty under Cumulative Voting: Political Behaviour after Electoral Reform in Bremen and Hamburg." *Electoral Studies* 51: 93–102.

Brams, S.J., & P.C. Fishburn. 2007. *Approval Voting*. 2nd edn. New York: Springer.

Brennan, J. 2016. *Against Democracy*. Princeton: Princeton University Press.

Brown, A.R. 2010. "Are Governors Responsible for the State Economy? Partisanship, Blame, and Divided Federalism." *Journal of Politics* 73: 605–15.

Burnett, C.M., & V. Kogan. 2015. "Ballot (and Voter) 'Exhaustion' under Instant Runoff Voting: An Examination of Four Ranked-Choice Elections." *Electoral Studies* 37: 41–49.

Cain, B.E. 2015. *Democracy, More or Less: America's Political Reform Quandary.* New York: Cambridge University Press.

Campbell, T. 2005. *Deliver the Vote: A History of Election Fraud, an American Political Tradition, 1742–2004.* New York: Avalon.

Canes-Wrone, B. 2015. "From Mass Preferences to Policy." *Annual Review of Political Science* 18: 147–65.

Carty, R.K. 2010. "Canadian Democracy: An Assessment and an Agenda." *Auditing Canadian Democracy,* ed. W. Cross. Vancouver: University of British Columbia Press.

Carty, R.K., A. Blais, & P. Fournier. 2008. "When Citizens Choose to Reform SMP: The British Columbia Citizens' Assembly on Electoral Reform." *To Keep or to Change First Past the Post? The Politics of Electoral Reform,* ed. A. Blais. Oxford: Oxford University Press.

Castillo-Manzano, J.I., L. Lopez-Valpuesta, & R. Pozo-Barajas. 2017. "Six Months and Two Parliamentary Elections in Spain." *Electoral Studies* 45: 157–60.

Chamberlin, J.R. 1985. "An Investigation into the Relative Manipulability of Four Voting Systems." *Behavioral Science* 30: 195–203.

Cheibub, J.A., & A. Przeworski. 1999. "Democracy, Elections, and Accountability for Outcomes." *Democracy, Accountability, and Representation,* eds. A. Przeworski, S.C. Stokes, & B. Manin. New York: Cambridge University Press.

Chwalisz, C. 2015. *The Populist Signal: Why Politics and Democracy Need to Change.* Lanham, MD: Rowman & Littlefield.

Claassen, R.L., & B. Highton. 2006. "Does Policy Debate Reduce Information Effects in Public Opinion? Analyzing the Evolution of Public Opinion on Health Care." *Journal of Politics* 68: 410–20.

Clark, A. 2013. "Second Time Lucky? The Continuing Adaptation of Voters and Parties to the Single Transferable Vote in Scotland." *Representation* 49: 55–68.

Colomer, J.M. 2005. "The General Election in Spain, March 2004." *Electoral Studies* 24: 149–56.

Colomer, J.M. 2011. "Introduction: Personal and Party Representation." *Personal Representation: The Neglected Dimension of Electoral Systems,* ed. J.M. Colomer. Colchester, UK: ECPR.

Conseil Constitutionnel. 2017a. "Declaration du 26 Avril 2017." Decision no. 2017-169, April 26 (Accessed on August 15, 2017 at presidentielle2017.conseil-constitutionnel.fr).

Conseil Constitutionnel. 2017b. "Proclamation des Resultats de l'Election du President de la Republique." Decision no. 2017-171, May 10 (Accessed on August 15, 2017 at presidentielle2017.conseil-constitutionnel.fr).

Cote, J. 2011. "S.F. Ranked-Choice Voting Confusing, Poll Says." *San Francisco Chronicle*, March 10 (Accessed on August 16, 2017 at www.sfgate.com/politics/article/S-F-ranked-choice-voting-confusing-poll-says-2389425.php).

Crisp, B.F., S. Olivella, J.D. Potter, & W. Mishler. 2014. "Elections as Instruments for Punishing Bad Representatives and Selecting Good Ones." *Electoral Studies* 34: 1–15.

Curtice, J. 2015. "A Return to Normality? How the Electoral System Operated." *Britain Votes, 2015*, eds. A. Geddes & J. Tonge. Oxford: Oxford University Press.

Curtice, J., & M. Marsh. 2014. "Confused or Competent? How Voters Use the STV Ballot Paper." *Electoral Studies* 34: 146–58.

Denver, D., A. Clark, & L. Bennie. 2009. "Voter Reactions to a Preferential Ballot: The 2007 Scottish Local Elections." *Journal of Elections, Public Opinion, and Parties* 19: 265–82.

De Vries, C.E., & H. Solaz. 2017. "The Electoral Consequences of Corruption." *Annual Review of Political Science* 20: 391–408.

Dolez, B., B. Grofman, & A. Laurent, eds. 2011. *In Situ and Laboratory Experiments on Electoral Law Reform*. New York: Springer.

Duch, R.M., & R.T. Stevenson. 2008. *The Economic Vote: How Political and Economic Institutions Condition Election Results*. New York: Cambridge University Press.

Dummett, M.A.E. 1997. *Principles of Electoral Reform*. Oxford: Oxford University Press.

Edelman. 2017. "Global Implosion of Trust." January 15 (Accessed on January 16, 2017 at www.edelman.com/news/2017-edelman-trust-barometer-reveals-global-implosion).

Emerson, P.J. 2007. "The Art or Science of Manipulation." *Designing an All-Inclusive Democracy: Consensual Voting Procedures for Use in Parliaments, Councils, and Committees*, ed. P.J. Emerson. Berlin: Springer.

Farrell, D.M. 2011. *Electoral Systems: A Comparative Introduction*. 2nd edn. Basingstoke, UK: Palgrave Macmillan.

Farrell, D.M., & I. McAllister. 2005. "Australia: The Alternative Vote in a Compliant Political Culture." *The Politics of Electoral Systems*, eds. M. Gallagher & P. Mitchell. Oxford: Oxford University Press.

Farvaque, E., H. Jayet, & L. Ragot. 2011. "French Presidential Election: A Field Experiment on the Single Transferable Vote." *In Situ and Laboratory Experiments on Electoral Law Reform*, eds. B. Dolez, B. Grofman, & A. Laurent. New York: Springer.

Fearon, J.D. 1999. "Electoral Accountability and the Control of Politicians." *Democracy, Accountability, and Representation*, eds. A. Przeworski, S.C. Stokes, & B. Manin. New York: Cambridge University Press.

Fellowes, M.C., & P.J. Wolf. 2004. "Funding Mechanisms and Policy Instruments: How Business Campaign Contributions Influence Congressional Votes." *Political Research Quarterly* 57: 315–24.

Ferguson, T. 1995. *The Golden Rule: The Investment Theory of Party Competition and the Logic of Money-Driven Political Systems.* Chicago: University of Chicago Press.

Ferguson, T., P. Jorgensen, & J. Chen. 2013. "Party Competition and Industrial Structure in the 2012 Elections: Who's Really Driving the Taxi to the Dark Side?" *International Journal of Political Economy* 42: 3–41.

Field, B.N. 2009. "The Parliamentary Election in Spain, March 2008." *Electoral Studies* 28: 155–58.

Fiorina, M.P. 1981. *Retrospective Voting in American National Elections.* New Haven: Yale University Press.

Franklin, M.N., S.N. Soroka, & C. Wlezien. 2014. "Elections." *The Oxford Handbook of Public Accountability*, eds. M. Bovens, R.E. Goodin, & T. Schillemans. Oxford: Oxford University Press.

Gallagher, M. 2018. "Election Indices Dataset" (Accessed on December 17, 2018 at www.tcd.ie/political_science/staff/michael_gallagher/elsystems/index.php).

Gallagher, M., & P. Mitchell. 2005a. "Introduction." *The Politics of Electoral Systems*, eds. M. Gallagher & P. Mitchell. Oxford: Oxford University Press.

Gallagher, M., & P. Mitchell. 2005b. "The Mechanics of Electoral Systems." *The Politics of Electoral Systems*, eds. M. Gallagher & P. Mitchell. Oxford: Oxford University Press.

Gallup. 2016. "Trump and Clinton Finish with Historically Poor Images" (Accessed on January 18, 2017 at www.gallup.com/poll/197231/trump-clinton-finish-historically-poor-images.aspx).

Galston, W.A. 2018. "The Populist Challenge to Liberal Democracy." *Journal of Democracy* 29: 5–19.

Gant, M.M., & L. Sigelman. 1985. "Anti-candidate Voting in Presidential Elections." *Polity* 18: 329–39.

Gelineau, F., & K.L. Remmer. 2005. "Political Decentralization and Electoral Accountability: The Argentine Experience, 1983–2001." *British Journal of Political Science* 36: 133–57.

Geuss, R. 2008. *Philosophy and Real Politics.* Princeton: Princeton University Press.

Golder, M., & B. Ferland. 2018. "Electoral Systems and Citizen-Elite Ideological Congruence." *The Oxford Handbook of Electoral Systems*, eds. E.S. Herron, R.J. Pekkanen, & M.S. Shugart. Oxford: Oxford University Press.

Granic, D.-G. 2017. "The Problem of the Divided Majority: Preference Aggregation under Uncertainty." *Journal of Economic Behavior and Organization* 133: 21–38.

Grofman, B., & S.L. Feld. 2004. "If You Like the Alternative Vote (a.k.a. the Instant Run-Off), Then You Ought to Know about the Coombs Rule." *Electoral Studies* 23: 641–59.

Gschwend, T., & M.F. Meffert. 2017. "Strategic Voting." *The SAGE Handbook of Electoral Behaviour*, eds. K. Arzheimer, J. Evans, & M.S. Lewis-Beck. London: SAGE Publications.

Hamilton, A., J. Madison, & J. Jay. 2005 (1788). *The Federalist*, ed. J.R. Pole. Indianapolis: Hackett.

Hamm, K.E., & R.E. Hogan. 2008. "Campaign-Finance Laws and Candidacy Decisions in State Legislative Elections." *Political Research Quarterly* 61: 458–67.

Hardin, R. 2000. "Democratic Epistemology and Accountability." *Social Philosophy and Policy* 17: 110–26.

Hartlyn, J., J. McCoy, & T.M. Mustillo. 2008. "Electoral Governance Matters: Explaining the Quality of Elections in Contemporary Latin America." *Comparative Political Studies* 41: 73–98.

Healy, A., & N. Malhotra. 2013. "Retrospective Voting Reconsidered." *Annual Review of Political Science* 16: 285–306.

Hellwig, T., E. Ringsmuth, & J.R. Freeman. 2008. "The American Public and the Room to Maneuver: Responsibility Attributions and Policy Efficacy in an Era of Globalization." *International Studies Quarterly* 52: 855–80.

Herrnson, P.S., R.G. Niemi, M.J. Hanmer, B.B. Bederson, F.C. Conrad, & M.W. Traugott. 2008. *Voting Technology: The Not So Simple Act of Casting a Ballot*. Washington, DC: Brookings Institution.

Hill, S. 2002. *Fixing Elections: The Failure of America's Winner-Take-All Politics*. New York: Routledge.

Hobbes, T. 1996 (1651). *Leviathan*, ed. R. Tuck. Cambridge, UK: Cambridge University Press.

Hogan, R.E. 2004. "Challenger Emergence, Incumbent Success, and Electoral Accountability in State Legislative Elections." *Journal of Politics* 66: 1283–303.

Hoyo, V. 2018. "Electoral Systems in Context: France." *The Oxford Handbook of Electoral Systems*, eds. E.S. Herron, R.J. Pekkanen, & M.S. Shugart. Oxford: Oxford University Press.

Huber, G.A., S.J. Hill, & G.S. Lenz. 2012. "Sources of Bias in Retrospective Decision-Making: Experimental Evidence on Voters' Limitations in Controlling Incumbents." *American Political Science Review* 106: 720–41.

Igersheim, H., A. Baujard, F. Gavrel, J.-F. Laslier, & I. Lebon. 2016. "Individual Behavior under Evaluative Voting: A Comparison between Laboratory and *In Situ* Experiments." *Voting Experiments*, eds. A. Blais, J.-F. Laslier, & K. Van der Straeten. Heidelberg: Springer.

Ingham, S. 2019. *Rule by Multiple Majorities: A New Theory of Popular Control.* New York: Cambridge University Press.

Irwin, G.A., & J.J.M. Van Holsteyn. 2012. "Strategic Electoral Considerations under Proportional Representation." *Electoral Studies* 31: 184–91.

Jacobs, L.R., & R.Y. Shapiro. 2000. *Politicians Don't Pander: Political Manipulation and the Loss of Democratic Responsiveness.* Chicago: University of Chicago Press.

Jacobson, G.C. 2016. "Polarization, Gridlock, and Presidential Campaign Politics in 2016." *Annals of the American Academy of Political and Social Science* 667: 226–46.

Jamieson, K.H., & J.N. Cappella. 2008. *The Echo Chamber: Rush Limbaugh and the Conservative Media Establishment.* New York: Oxford University Press.

Jansen, H.J. 2004. "The Political Consequences of the Alternative Vote: Lessons from Western Canada." *Canadian Journal of Political Science* 37: 647–69.

Jenkins, S. 2017. "Hardliners Won't Like this Soft Brexit Plan." *Guardian* (London), July 27 (Accessed on July 27, 2017 at www.theguardian.com/commentisfree/2017/jul/27/hardliners-soft-brexit-tough-negotiate-properly).

Jones, D.W., & B. Simons. 2012. *Broken Ballots: Will Your Vote Count?* Stanford: CSLI Publications.

Joshi, D.K., J.S. Maloy, & T.M. Peterson. 2015. "Popular vs. Elite Democratic Structures and International Peace." *Journal of Peace Research* 52: 463–77.

Joshi, D.K., J.S. Maloy, & T.M. Peterson. 2019. "Popular vs. Elite Democracies and Human Rights: Inclusion Makes a Difference." *International Studies Quarterly* 63: 111–26.

Katz, R.S., & P. Mair. 2009. "The Cartel Party Thesis: A Restatement." *Perspectives on Politics* 7: 753–66.

Kelley, S. 1983. *Interpreting Elections.* Princeton: Princeton University Press.

Key, V.O. 1961a. *Public Opinion and American Democracy.* New York: Knopf.

Key, V.O. 1961b. "Public Opinion and the Decay of Democracy." *Virginia Quarterly Review* 37: 481–94.

Key, V.O. 1964. *Politics, Parties, and Pressure Groups.* 5th edn. New York: T. Crowell.

Key, V.O. 1966. *The Responsible Electorate: Rationality in Presidential Voting, 1936–60,* ed. M.C. Cummings. Cambridge, MA: Harvard University Press.

Kimball, D.C., & M. Kropf. 2016. "Voter Competence with Cumulative Voting." *Social Science Quarterly* 97: 619–35.

Kropf, M., & D.C. Kimball. 2012. *Helping America Vote: The Limits of Election Reform.* New York: Routledge.

Lakeman, E. 1974. *How Democracies Vote: A Study of Electoral Systems.* 4th edn. London: Faber.

Lamis, A.P. 2008. "Key, V.O., Jr." *International Encyclopedia of the Social Sciences*, ed. W.A. Darity. Vol. 4. 2nd edn. Detroit: Macmillan Reference.

Lancaster, T.D. 2017. "The Spanish General Elections of 2015 and 2016: A New Stage of Democratic Politics?" *West European Politics* 40: 919–37.

Laslier, J.-F. 2011a. "And the Loser Is … Plurality Voting." Cahier no. 2011–13. Paris: Ecole Polytechnique.

Laslier, J.-F. 2011b. "*In Silico* Voting Experiments." *Handbook on Approval Voting*, eds. J.-F. Laslier & M.R. Sanver. Berlin: Springer.

Laslier, J.-F. 2016. "Heuristic Voting under the Alternative Vote: The Efficiency of 'Sour Grapes' Behavior." *Homo Oeconomicus* 33: 57–76.

Laslier, J.-F., & M.R. Sanver, eds. 2011. *Handbook on Approval Voting*. Berlin: Springer.

Laver, M. 2004. "Analysing Structures of Party Preference in Electronic Voting Data." *Party Politics* 10: 521–41.

LeDuc, L., & J.H. Pammett. 2013. "The Fate of Governing Parties in Times of Economic Crisis." *Electoral Studies* 32: 494–99.

Lee, D.S., E. Moretti, & M.J. Butler. 2004. "Do Voters Affect or Elect Policies? Evidence from the U.S. House." *Quarterly Journal of Economics* 119: 807–59.

Lehoucq, F. 2003. "Electoral Fraud: Cases, Types, and Consequences." *Annual Review of Political Science* 6: 233–56.

Lenz, G.S. 2018. "Time for a Change." *Critical Review* 30: 87–106.

Levinson, S. 2007. "How the United States Constitution Contributes to the Democratic Deficit in America." *Drake Law Review* 55: 859.

Levitsky, S., & D. Ziblatt. 2018. *How Democracies Die*. New York: Crown.

Lewis, C., & C. Lucas. 2017. "A True Progressive Alliance Would Have Made Jeremy Corbyn Prime Minister." *Guardian* (London), June 13 (Accessed on June 13, 2017 at www.theguardian.com/commentisfree/2017/jun/13/true-progressive-alliance-made-jeremy-corbyn-prime-minister).

Lundberg, T.C. 2018. "Electoral Systems in Context: United Kingdom." *The Oxford Handbook of Electoral Systems*, eds. E.S. Herron, R.J. Pekkanen, & M.S. Shugart. Oxford: Oxford University Press.

Machiavelli, N. 1994. *Selected Political Writings*, trans. D. Wootton. Indianapolis: Hackett.

Mair, P. 2013. *Ruling the Void: The Hollowing of Western Democracy*. London: Verso.

Majone, G. 1998. "Europe's 'Democratic Deficit': The Question of Standards." *European Law Journal* 4: 5–28.

Maloy, J.S. 2008. *The Colonial American Origins of Modern Democratic Thought*. New York: Cambridge University Press.

Maloy, J.S. 2013. *Democratic Statecraft: Political Realism and Popular Power*. New York: Cambridge University Press.

Maloy, J.S. 2014. "Linkages of Electoral Accountability: Empirical Results and Methodological Lessons." *Politics and Governance* 2.2: 13–27.

Maloy, J.S. 2015. "Intermediate Conditions of Democratic Accountability: A Response to Electoral Skepticism." *Politics and Governance* 3.2: 76–89.

Manin, B. 1997. *The Principles of Representative Government.* New York: Cambridge University Press.

Manin, B., A. Przeworski, & S.C. Stokes. 1999a. "Elections and Representation." *Democracy, Accountability, and Representation*, eds. A. Przeworski, S.C. Stokes, & B. Manin. New York: Cambridge University Press.

Manin, B., A. Przeworski, & S.C. Stokes. 1999b. "Introduction." *Democracy, Accountability, and Representation*, eds. A. Przeworski, S.C. Stokes, & B. Manin. New York: Cambridge University Press.

Mansbridge, J. 2009. "A Selection Model of Political Representation." *Journal of Political Philosophy* 17: 369–98.

Mansbridge, J. 2014. "A Contingency Theory of Accountability." *The Oxford Handbook of Public Accountability*, eds. M. Bovens, R.E. Goodin, & T. Schillemans. Oxford: Oxford University Press.

Maravall, J.M. 1999. "Accountability and Manipulation." *Democracy, Accountability, and Representation*, eds. A. Przeworski, S.C. Stokes, & B. Manin. New York: Cambridge University Press.

Maravall, J.M. 2010. "Accountability in Coalition Governments." *Annual Review of Political Science* 13: 81–100.

Marsh, M. 2018. "Electoral Systems in Context: Ireland." *The Oxford Handbook of Electoral Systems*, eds. E.S. Herron, R.J. Pekkanen, & M.S. Shugart. Oxford: Oxford University Press.

Masket, S.E., & H. Noel. 2012. "Serving Two Masters: Using Referenda to Assess Partisan versus Dyadic Legislative Representation." *Political Research Quarterly* 65: 104–23.

Mayhew, D.R. 1974. *Congress: The Electoral Connection.* New Haven: Yale University Press.

McAllister, I., & T. Makkai. 2018. "Electoral Systems in Context: Australia." *The Oxford Handbook of Electoral Systems*, eds. E.S. Herron, R.J. Pekkanen, & M.S. Shugart. Oxford: Oxford University Press.

McCormick, J.P. 2006. "Contain the Wealthy and Patrol the Magistrates: Restoring Elite Accountability to Popular Government." *American Political Science Review* 100: 147–63.

McGann, A. 2006. *The Logic of Democracy: Reconciling Equality, Deliberation, and Minority Protection.* Ann Arbor: University of Michigan Press.

McGann, A. 2013. "Fairness and Bias in Electoral Systems." *Representation: Elections and Beyond*, eds. J.H. Nagel & R.M. Smith. Philadelphia: University of Pennsylvania Press.

McGhee, E., & D. Krimm. 2012. "California's New Electoral Reforms: How Did They Work?" Public Policy Institute of California. June Report.

McGhee, E., S.E. Masket, B. Shor, S. Rogers, & N. McCarty. 2014. "A Primary Cause of Partisanship? Nomination Systems and Legislator Ideology." *American Journal of Political Science* 58: 337–51.

McLean, I. 1991. "Forms of Representation and Systems of Voting." *Political Theory Today*, ed. D. Held. Oxford: Oxford University Press.

McLean, I., A. McMillan, & B.L. Monroe. 1996. "Introduction." *A Mathematical Approach to Proportional Representation: Duncan Black on Lewis Carroll*, eds. I. McLean, A. McMillan, & B.L. Monroe. Boston: Kluwer.

McMillan, J., & P. Zoido. 2004. "How to Subvert Democracy: Montesinos in Peru." *Journal of Economic Perspectives* 18.4: 69–92.

Mead, L.M. 2010. "Scholasticism in Political Science." *Perspectives on Politics* 8: 453–64.

Miguet, A. 2002. "The French Elections of 2002: After the Earthquake, the Deluge." *West European Politics* 25: 207–20.

Miller, K., & S. Thistle. 2018. "Jared Golden Declared Winner of First Ranked-Choice Congressional Election, but Challenge Looms." *Portland* (Maine) *Press-Herald*, November 15 (Accessed on December 31, 2018 at www.press-herald.com/2018/11/15/final-ranked-choice-vote-count-slated-for-noon).

Milner, H. 2017. "Electoral System Reform: The Canadian Experience." *Election Law Journal* 16: 349–56.

Mitchell, P. 2000. "Voters and Their Representatives: Electoral Institutions and Delegation in Parliamentary Democracies." *European Journal of Political Research* 37: 335–51.

Monbiot, G. 2016. "The European Union Is the Worst Choice, Apart from the Alternative." *Guardian* (London), June 15 (Accessed on January 5, 2017 at www.theguardian.com/commentisfree/2016/jun/15/european-union-eu-britain-sovereignty).

Mounk, Y. 2018. "The Undemocratic Dilemma." *Journal of Democracy* 29: 98–112.

Munks, J. 2018. "Instant Runoff Voting Survives at the Polls, but Will It Be Implemented in Memphis?" (Memphis) *Commercial Appeal*, November 7 (Accessed on January 5, 2018 at www.commercialappeal.com/story/news/2018/11/07/instant-runoff-voting-memphis-shelby-county-mid-term-election/1858041002).

Mustillo, T.M., & J. Polga-Hecimovich. 2018. "Measures and Votes: Party Performance under Free-List Proportional Representation, with Evidence from Ecuador." *Electoral Studies* 56: 124–35.

Myagkov, M., P.C. Ordeshook, & D. Shakin. 2009. *The Forensics of Election Fraud: Russia and Ukraine*. Cambridge, UK: Cambridge University Press.

Nagel, J.H. 2004. "New Zealand: Reform by (Nearly) Immaculate Design." *Handbook of Electoral System Choice*, ed. J.M. Colomer. New York: Palgrave Macmillan.

Neely, F., & C. Cook. 2008. "Whose Votes Count? Undervotes, Overvotes, and Ranking in San Francisco's Instant-Runoff Elections." *American Politics Research* 36: 530–54.

Neely, F., & J. McDaniel. 2015. "Overvoting and the Equality of Voice under Instant Run-Off Voting in San Francisco." *California Journal of Politics and Policy* 7: 1–27.

Norpoth, H. 2001. "Divided Government and Economic Voting." *Journal of Politics* 63: 413–35.

Norris, P. 2017. *Why American Elections Are Flawed (and How to Fix Them)*. Ithaca, NY: Cornell University Press.

Nurmi, H. 1987. *Comparing Voting Systems*. Dordrecht: D. Reidel.

O'Donnell, G. 2003. "Horizontal Accountability: The Legal Institutionalization of Mistrust." *Democratic Accountability in Latin America*, eds. S. Mainwaring & C. Welna. New York: Oxford University Press.

Olsen, H., & D.J. Scala. 2016. *The Four Faces of the Republican Party: The Fight for the 2016 Presidential Nomination*. New York: Palgrave Macmillan.

Ornstein, J.T., & R.Z. Norman. 2014. "Frequency of Monotonicity Failure under Instant Runoff Voting: Estimates Based on a Spatial Model of Elections." *Public Choice* 161: 1–9.

Paine, T. 2003. *Common Sense, Rights of Man, and Other Essential Writings*. New York: Signet Classics.

Passarelli, G. 2018. "Electoral Systems in Context: Italy." *The Oxford Handbook of Electoral Systems*, eds. E.S. Herron, R.J. Pekkanen, & M.S. Shugart. Oxford: Oxford University Press.

Pereira, C., M.A. Melo, & C.M. Figueiredo. 2009. "The Corruption-Enhancing Role of Re-election Incentives? Counter-Intuitive Evidence from Brazil's Audit Reports." *Political Research Quarterly* 62: 731–44.

Pereira, P.T., & J. Andrade e Silva. 2009. "Citizens' Freedom to Choose Representatives: Ballot Structure, Proportionality, and 'Fragmented' Parliaments." *Electoral Studies* 28: 101–10.

Pew Research Center. 2016a. "Campaign Exposes Fissures over Issues, Values, and How Life Has Changed in the U.S." March Report.

Pew Research Center. 2016b. "Clinton, Trump Supporters Have Starkly Different Views of a Changing Nation." August Report.

Pew Research Center. 2016c. "Republican Voters' Path to Backing Donald Trump" (Accessed on December 13, 2017 at www.people-press.org/interactives/gop-candidate-switching).

Pew Research Center. 2016d. "Voters Skeptical that 2016 Candidates Would Make Good Presidents." January Report.

Piketty, T. 2016. "We Must Rethink Globalization, or Trumpism Will Prevail." *Guardian* (London), November 16 (Accessed on January 15, 2017 at www.

BIBLIOGRAPHY 215

theguardian.com/commentisfree/2016/nov/16/globalization-trump-inequality-thomas-piketty).

Plescia, C. 2016. *Split-Ticket Voting in Mixed-Member Electoral Systems: A Theoretical and Methodological Investigation.* Colchester, UK: ECPR Press.

Potyondy, P.R. 2018. "Maine Becomes the First State to Use Ranked-Choice Voting." National Conference of State Legislatures, June 14 (Accessed on October 21, 2018 at www.ncsl.org/blog/2018/06/14/maine-becomes-the-first-state-to-use-ranked-choice-voting.aspx).

Poundstone, W. 2008. *Gaming the Vote: Why Elections Aren't Fair (and What We Can Do about It).* New York: Hill & Wang.

Powell, G.B. 2000. *Elections as Instruments of Democracy: Majoritarian and Proportional Visions.* New Haven: Yale University Press.

Powell, G.B., & G.D. Whitten. 1993. "A Cross-National Analysis of Economic Voting." *American Journal of Political Science* 37: 391–414.

Prior, M. 2007. *Post-broadcast Democracy: How Media Choice Increases Inequality in Political Involvement and Polarizes Elections.* New York: Cambridge University Press.

Przeworski, A. 2018. *Why Bother with Elections?* Cambridge, UK: Polity.

Rae, D.W. 1967. *The Political Consequences of Electoral Laws.* New Haven: Yale University Press.

Reilly, B. 2002. "Social Choice in the South Seas: Electoral Innovation and the Borda Count in the Pacific Island Countries." *International Political Science Review* 23: 355–72.

Reilly, B., & M. Malley. 2000. "The Single Transferable Vote and the Alternative Vote Compared." *Elections in Australia, Ireland, and Malta under the Single Transferable Vote: Reflections on an Embedded Institution*, eds. S. Bowler & B. Grofman. Ann Arbor: University Press of Michigan.

Renwick, A. 2017. "What Do Political Scientists Know that Practitioners Do Not? Lessons from the UK Referendum of 2011." *Election Law Journal* 16: 341–48.

Renwick, A. 2018. "Electoral System Change." *The Oxford Handbook of Electoral Systems*, eds. E.S. Herron, R.J. Pekkanen, & M.S. Shugart. Oxford: Oxford University Press.

Renwick, A., & J.-B. Pilet. 2016. *Faces on the Ballot: The Personalization of Electoral Systems in Europe.* Oxford: Oxford University Press.

Reynolds, A., B. Reilly, & C. Ellis. 2005. *Electoral System Design: The New International IDEA Handbook.* Stockholm: Institute for Democracy and Election Assistance.

Riera, P., & J.R. Montero. 2017. "Attempts to Reform the Electoral System in Spain: The Role of Experts." *Election Law Journal* 16: 367–76.

Riker, W.H. 1982. "The Two-Party System and Duverger's Law: An Essay on the History of Political Science." *American Political Science Review* 76: 753–66.

Romney, L. 2010. "Bay Area Races Increase Scrutiny of Ranked-Choice Voting." *Los Angeles Times*, November 20 (Accessed on August 24, 2017 at articles. latimes.com/2010/nov/20/local/la-me-ranked-choice-20101120).

Rousseau, J.-J. 1987. *The Basic Political Writings*, trans. D.A. Cress. Indianapolis: Hackett.

Russell, E. 2018. "Mainers Vote to Keep Ranked-Choice Voting." *Portland* (Maine) *Press-Herald*, June 13 (Accessed on October 21, 2018 at www.pressherald.com/2018/06/12/ranked-choice-voting-takes-lead-in-early-balloting).

Saltman, R.G. 2006. *The History and Politics of Voting Technology*. New York: Palgrave Macmillan.

Santucci, J. 2018. "Maine Ranked-Choice Voting as a Case of Electoral-System Change." *Representation* 54: 297–311.

Sargeant, J., A. Renwick, & M. Russell. 2018. "The Mechanics of a Further Referendum on Brexit." University College, London.

Sartori, G. 1997. *Comparative Constitutional Engineering: An Inquiry into Structures, Incentives, and Outcomes*. 2nd edn. New York: New York University Press.

Sawer, M. 2004. "Australia: Replacing Plurality Rule with Majority-Preferential Voting." *Handbook of Electoral System Choice*, ed. J.M. Colomer. New York: Palgrave Macmillan.

Schmitter, P.C. 2012. "A Way Forward?" *Journal of Democracy* 23: 39–46.

Schrodt, P.A. 2014. "Seven Deadly Sins of Contemporary Quantitative Political Analysis." *Journal of Peace Research* 51: 287–300.

Shapiro, I. 2005. *The Flight from Reality in the Human Sciences*. Princeton: Princeton University Press.

Sigelman, L., & M.M. Gant. 1989. "Anti-candidate Voting in the 1984 Presidential Election." *Political Behavior* 11: 81–92.

Sil, R., & P.J. Katzenstein. 2010. *Beyond Paradigms: Analytic Eclecticism in the Study of World Politics*. Basingstoke, UK: Palgrave Macmillan.

Singer, M.M. 2013. "Was Duverger Correct? Single-Member District Election Outcomes in Fifty-Three Countries." *British Journal of Political Science* 43: 201–20.

Singh, S.P. 2014. "Not All Election Winners Are Equal: Satisfaction with Democracy and the Nature of the Vote." *European Journal of Political Research* 53: 308–27.

Sinnott, R. 2010. "The Electoral System." *Politics in the Republic of Ireland*, eds. J. Coakley & M. Gallagher. 5th edn. London: Routledge.

Sleat, M. 2013. *Liberal Realism: A Realist Theory of Liberal Politics*. Manchester, UK: Manchester University Press.

Snyder, J.M., & D. Stromberg. 2010. "Press Coverage and Political Accountability." *Journal of Political Economy* 118: 355–408.

Starmer, K. 2017. "Labour Can Tackle the Challenges of Brexit in a Way Theresa May Simply Cannot." *Guardian* (London), January 3 (Accessed on January 9, 2017 at www.theguardian.com/commentisfree/2017/jan/03/labour-challenges-brexit-theresa-may-ivan-rogers-values).

Steed, M. 1974. "The Results Analysed." *The British General Election of February 1974*, eds. D. Butler & D. Kavanagh. London: Macmillan.

Stewart, C. 2010. "Voting Technologies." *Annual Review of Political Science* 14: 353–78.

Stimson, J.A. 1999. "Party Government and Responsiveness." *Democracy, Accountability, and Representation*, eds. A. Przeworski, S.C. Stokes, & B. Manin. New York: Cambridge University Press.

Stokes, S.C. 1999. "What Do Policy Switches Tell Us about Democracy?" *Democracy, Accountability, and Representation*, eds. A. Przeworski, S.C. Stokes, & B. Manin. New York: Cambridge University Press.

Sumner, W.G. 1934. *Essays of William Graham Sumner*, ed. A.G. Keller. 2 vols. New Haven: Yale University Press.

Tervalon-Daumont, E., & A. Garza. 2011. "Reforms that Helped Elect Candidates of Color in SF, Oakland under Attack." *New American Media*, April 29 (Accessed on August 16, 2017 at newamericamedia.org/2011/04/reforms-that-helped-elect-candidates-of-color-in-sf-oakland-under-attack.php).

Thistle, S. 2017a. "Maine's Highest Court Rules Ranked-Choice Voting Is Unconstitutional." *Portland* (Maine) *Press-Herald*, May 23 (Accessed on August 23, 2017 at www.pressherald.com/2017/05/23/maine-high-court-says-ranked-choice-voting-is-unconstitutional).

Thistle, S. 2017b. "Voter-Approved Ranked-Choice Voting Stays in Effect as Repeal Bills Fail." *Portland* (Maine) *Press-Herald*, June 28 (Accessed on August 23, 2017 at www.pressherald.com/2017/06/28/legislature-fails-to-repeal-voter-passed-ranked-choice-voting-law).

Thompson, D.F. 2002. *Just Elections: Creating a Fair Electoral Process in the United States*. Chicago: University of Chicago Press.

Thompson, D.F. 2004. *Restoring Responsibility*. New York: Cambridge University Press.

Tierney, S. 2013. "Using Electoral Law to Construct a Deliberative Referendum: Moving beyond the Democratic Paradox." *Election Law Journal* 12: 508.

Tolbert, C.J., & K. Gracey. 2018. "Changing How America Votes for President." *Changing How America Votes*, ed. T. Donovan. Lanham, MD: Rowman & Littlefield.

Took, C., & S. Donnelly. 2018. "Electionsireland.org" (Accessed on December 31, 2018 at www.electionsireland.org).

Tsai, L.L. 2007. *Accountability without Democracy: Solidary Groups and Public Goods Provision in Rural China*. New York: Cambridge University Press.

VandeHei, J., & M.A. Fletcher. 2005. "Bush Says Election Ratified Iraq Policy." *Washington Post*, January 16.

Van der Straeten, K., J.-F. Laslier, & A. Blais. 2016. "Patterns of Strategic Voting in Run-Off Elections." *Voting Experiments*, eds. A. Blais, J.-F. Laslier, & K. Van der Straeten. Heidelberg: Springer.

Von Schoultz, A. 2018. "Electoral Systems in Context: Finland." *The Oxford Handbook of Electoral Systems*, eds. E.S. Herron, R.J. Pekkanen, & M.S. Shugart. Oxford: Oxford University Press.

Vowles, J. 1995. "The Politics of Electoral Reform in New Zealand." *International Political Science Review* 16: 95–115.

Wattenberg, M.P. 1991. *The Rise of Candidate-Centered Politics: Presidential Elections of the 1980s*. Cambridge, MA: Harvard University Press.

Wattenberg, M.P. 1998. *The Decline of American Political Parties, 1952–96*. 2nd edn. Cambridge, MA: Harvard University Press.

Webb, J.A. 1998. "Confederation, Conspiracy, and Choice: A Discussion." *Newfoundland Studies* 14: 169–87.

Willsher, K. 2017a. "Fear of Neofascism Keeps Emmanuel Macron ahead of Marine Le Pen." *Guardian* (London), April 29 (Accessed on May 2, 2017 at www.theguardian.com/world/2017/apr/29/france-election-neofascism-le-pen-macron).

Willsher, K. 2017b. "Macron Is En Route to the Elysée, but May Find It Hard to Govern." *Guardian* (London), May 6 (Accessed on May 6, 2017 at www.theguardian.com/world/2017/may/06/macron-french-presidential-election-2017-future-govern-effective).

INDEX

voting rights, 8, 16
voting systems. *See* Approval Vote;
    Borda Count; Cumulative Vote;
    Grade-Point Average (GPA);
    League Table voting; Limited
    Vote; Median Grade; Plurality
    Vote; Quadratic Vote; Ranked-
    Choice Voting (RCV); Single
    Non-Transferable Vote (SNTV);
    Single Transferable Vote (STV);
    Two-Round System (2RS); voting
    theory
voting theory, 2, 12, 13, 80–83, 88,
    98, 99, 111, 165, 177, 185, 197,
    198. *See also* academia

W
Washington (state), 63
wasted votes, 11, 62, 70, 102, 110,
    115, 169
Whitten, Guy, 38
Wilson, Woodrow, 31, 64
Wisconsin, 64, 66, 179
World Wide Web, 37, 125

CPSIA information can be obtained
at www.ICGtesting.com
Printed in the USA
LVHW021611300619
622778LV00005B/9/P

9 783030 130305